POVERTY AND SUSTAINABLE DEVELOPMENT

Concepts and Measures

Poverty and Sustainable Development

Concepts and Measures

Edited by

DR. N.S. IYENGAR

Published on behalf of the
INDIAN ECONOMIC ASSOCIATION

DEEP & DEEP PUBLICATIONS PVT. LTD.
F-159, Rajouri Garden, New Delhi - 110027

POVERTY AND SUSTAINABLE DEVELOPMENT
Concepts and Measures

ISBN 978-81-8450-269-5

Typeset by THE LASER PRINTERS
8/15, 3rd Floor, Subhash Nagar, New Delhi-110027

Printed in India at MAYUR ENTERPRISES
WZ Plot No. 3, Gujjar Market, Tihar Village, New Delhi - 110 018

Published by DEEP & DEEP PUBLICATIONS PVT. LTD.,
F-159, Rajouri Garden, New Delhi-110027. Phones: 25435369, 25440916.
E-mail: ddpbooks@yahoo.co.in • ddpubs@gmail.com
Sales Showroom: 2/13, Ansari Road, Daryaganj, New Delhi-110002
Phone/Fax: 23245122

This Volume is dedicated
to the memory of
DR. N. SREENIVASA IYENGAR

DR. NARASIMHA SREENIVASA IYENGAR

CONTENTS

FOREWORD

Since 1994, when the undersigned was elected as the Hony. Secretary and Treasurer of the IEA, efforts were made to publish theme-wise edited volumes of IEA Conference/Seminar papers as due to space constraint, it is not possible to include many good papers in the Annual Conference Volumes. Ultimately in 1997, during 80 years of the IEA, a plan was formulated to publish such volumes since 1994 Conference which, with active co-operation of IEA Presidents Dr. G.S. Monga and Prof. Ajit Kumar Sinha, could materialise in 1999. This is continuing till now with cooperation from successive IEA Presidents and Secretaries. The present volume is an outcome of such papers contributed to the IEA 86th Conference held at the Shivaji University, Kolhapur.

Poverty and Sustainable Development: Concepts and Measures is an edited volume consisting of 17 contributed papers to one of the technical sessions of this Conference and 3 other articles by the editor. The articles are divided in the following sections:

I. Contributions from Dr. N.S. Iyengar, II. Poverty: Conceptual and Analytical Issues, III. Poverty and its Measurement, IV. Poverty Alleviation and Sustainable Development, and V. Poverty and Economic Reforms. Section I consists of three articles suggested by Prof. Iyengar himself. One can obtain an idea of the growing literature in this emerging and important area of economics from this volume. We are thankful to the contributors of these articles without whose co-operation the publication of this volume could not be possible.

The first of the three articles, (*Poverty: Concepts and Measurement—A Review*) was first published in *Artha Beekshan*, Vol. 6, No. 1, June 1997, which was actually the key note address by the author at the National Seminar on Budget and Poverty, University of Mysore, held on April 20, 1996. This has reference to the debate on the decline or rise of poverty in India during the initial years of economic reforms about which Iyengar has given his views in this article.

The second article is *'On Nutrition and Poverty'* based on the First Sukhatme Memorial Lecture delivered on 3rd December, 1999 and published in the *Journal of Social and Economic Development*, Vol. II, No. 2, July-Dec. 2000.

Here Iyengar has discussed in details the contributions of Sukhatme to problems of food and nutrition in developing countries. He has also raised a number of questions at the end of this article for examination by social scientists and statisticians.

The last article in this section is on '*Poverty, Income Inequality and Growth: An Analysis with Illustrations from Indian Data*'. It has dealt with the efforts to achieve growth with equity in India and a major purpose of this paper was to point out how new innovations in methodology can help to reduce margins of uncertainties in future analysis with updated data. The author adopted a parametric approach and considered the regional dimensions of poverty and inequality in India including an inter-state analysis. The findings are quite revealing and the author has included various suggestions for further work.

During the tenure as President, IEA, I came in close touch with Professor Iyengar and was deeply impressed by his modest behaviour and sincere approach to his work inspite of his falling health. He carefully read all the full papers submitted to him as Chairman of one of the technical sessions of the Kolhapur Conference and categorised them according to their merit. For this edited volume he suggested the inclusion of three of his earlier papers on poverty concepts, definitions, measurement, data and policy implementation problems in controlling poverty in India for the benefit of young researchers.

The publication of this volume has been delayed due to the falling health of Prof. Iyengar and his sad demise in 2005. Unfortunately, the conference papers awaiting publication could not be traced and the authors had to send them again. I sincerely thank them for the trouble they have undertaken. Prof. Iyengar actually enjoyed participating in the Kolhapur Conference which according to him was a good Conference. He also appreciated the publication work of the IEA and the presidential dynamism behind it.

I am thankful to the family members of Prof. Iyengar for encouraging me to complete his unfinished work and I am happy that ultimately the work could see the light of the day. Special thanks are due to Sri Srinivasa V. Giri, son of Prof. Iyengar for sending his photo and dates of his birth and death. Major part of bio-data of Prof. Iyengar was prepared by Prof. Iyengar while writing the Introduction of this volume and it has been supplemented from his obituary published in the *Journal of Quantitative Economics* in 2005. I am also thankful to Sri Samrat Roy of St Xavier's College (autonomous), Kolkata for his valuable assistance in the preparation of this volume. No thanks is sufficient for our good old friend Sri G.S. Bhatia, who undertook this publication in a meticulous manner. I sincerely hope that this volume will open up new frontiers in the economic literature on poverty and sustainable development for the benefit of all readers from all sections of the society.

Kolhapur

PROFESSOR RAJ KUMAR SEN
President (2003-04),
Indian Economic Association

About Narasimha Sreenivasa Iyengar

Dr. N. Sreenivasa Iyengar (b. Mysore, 19 April 1933) was Hon. Visiting Fellow and Member, Board of Governors, Institute for Social and Economic Change, Bangalore and Member, Editorial Board, Indian Economic Journal and served as Chairman, Expert Group on State Domestic Product, Government of Karnataka. Formerly, he was Dr. Sarvepalli Radhakrishnan Visiting Professor of Economics, Central University of Hyderabad, First (1967) UGC Professor of Econometrics, Osmania University, Retired Professor, Indian Statistical Institute, Rockefeller Foundation Fellow, Harvard University, where he worked with eminent economists like Professor H.S. Houthakker and Nobel Laureate Professor Wassily Leontieff, Indo-US Fellow, Columbia University (USA), Visiting Professor, University of Warwick (UK), Rhine-Ruhr University (Germany). Also, he visited France, Germany, Sweden, Norway, Canada, Italy, Singapore and Australia to present papers at some of the international conferences.

He was author of over 60 independent and joint research papers in reputed Indian and foreign journals like Econometrica, Sankhya, Journal of Royal Statistical Society, Indian Economic Review, Indian Economic Journal, Economic and Political Weekly, Journal of Quantitative Economics, Artha Beekshan, etc., author of three edited works, published respectively by the Indian Council of Social Science Research, the Indian Econometric Society, and the Springer-Verlog Company of New York. He was Life Member, Indian Statistical Institute, Indian Economic Association, Indian Society of Agricultural Economics, and held memberships in the World Econometric Society and the International Statistical Institute. He served the Indian Econometric Society as its Founder-Secretary (1960-76), Vice-president (1982-87), President (1988) and Member of Council, Indian Statistical Institute. He was a founder member of the Institute for Social and Economic Change (ISEC).

His original works include the development of techniques of measuring income and expenditure elasticities of households from grouped Sample Survey data available in published official statistics by using concentration curves and early attempts to estimate poverty and income distributions in different States of India. His theoretical contributions to econometrics are widely recognised and quoted in learned journals and books. His work on inflation made quite an impact in India and led to a flood of investigations by other noted economists. His later works were focussed on estimation of the standard errors and decomposition of consumption inequality, LIML estimates and multicollinearity and applications of Bayesian methods in the estimation of poverty lines.

Dr. Iyengar had a first class honors degree in Statistics from Mysore University in 1955 (with first rank and Gold Medal) and M. Stat. and Ph.D. (1964) degrees from the Indian Statistical Institute. He wrote his Ph.D. Thesis entitled, 'Contributions to Analysis of Consumer Expenditures', under the guidance of Professor P.C. Mahalanobis, FRS and Professor M. Mukherjee. At the age of 32, he became Professor at ISI Delhi and worked in the distinguished company of Professor B.S. Minhas and Professor T.N. Srinivasan. He won in 1978 the prestigious P.C. Mahalanobis Gold Medal for outstanding contribution to quantitative economics (awarded once in two years to an Indian national), following Professor Jagdish Bhagwati (Columbia University) and Professor Sukhamoy Chakraborty (University of Delhi), and Professor Amartya Kumar Sen (Nobel Laureate).

He was the Chairman in one of the technical sessions on Poverty and Sustainable Development in the IEA Kolhapur Conference (2003) and nearly completed this edited volume before he passed away in Bangalore on 8th March, 2005 at the age of 71. This ended a glorious professional career of a great statistician, econometrician and applied quantitative economist of international repute. Inspite of his outstanding achievements, Professor Iyengar was a modest person, easily accessible to students and colleagues and ever willing to share his valuable ideas with them. His life time vision was that India should develop its own statistical standards suited to her conditions even if they appear somewhat inefficient from western standards. This should remain a source of inspiration for the present and future generation of students, teachers and policy-makers of India.

List of Contributors

1. **Dr. N.S. Iyengar,** Formerly S.R. Professor of Economics, University of Hyderabad.
2. **Ms. Sunipa Das Gupta,** M.Phil. Student, Calcutta University.
3. **Sri Ranesh Kumar Ray,** Kidderpore College (Retd.), Kolkata.
4. **Dr. Tapan Kumar Shandilya,** College of Commerce, Patna.
5. **Dr. Ram Naresh Thakur,** Samastipur College, Samastipur.
6. **Prof. K.S.S. Uduman Mohideen,** University of Madras, Chennai.
7. **Dr. K. Ramchandran,** NGM College, Pollachi.
8. **Dr. Vimal Shankar Singh,** DAV Degree College.
9. **Ms. Subhra Singh,** CHGS, Kamacha.
10. **Ms. Shweta Singh,** MBA Student, BHU, Varanasi.
11. **Dr. Arvind Awasthi,** University of Lucknow, Lucknow.
12. **Dr. S. Borbora,** IIT, Guwahati.
13. **Sri R. Mahanta,** North Gauhati College, Guwahati.
14. **Dr. P.K. Pal,** Rabindra Bharati University, Kolkata.
15. **Dr. P. Jegadish Gandhi,** Vellore Institute of Development Studies, Vellore.
16. **Dr. S.K. Dhage,** Waghire College, Pune.
17. **Sri Rahul S. Mhopare,** Research Scholar, Shivaji University, Kolhapur.
18. **Dr. Swami Prakash Srivastava,** Dayalbag Educational Institute, Agra.
19. **Dr. Asim K. Karmakar,** Economics Department, Jadavpur University, Kolkata.
20. **Dr. Arun Prabha Chowdhury,** M.L. Sukhadia University, Udaipur.
21. **Prof. R. Arunachalam,** University of Madras, Chennai.
22. **Dr. Puspa Tarafdar,** Sarojini Naidu College (Retd.), Kolkata.
23. **Dr. Basudev Sahoo,** N.K.C. Institute (Retd.), Bhubaneswar.
24. **Prof. Raj Kumar Sen,** President, IEA (2003-04) (*for Foreword*).

Poverty and Sustainable Development: Concepts and Measures—An Overview

N. Sreenivasa Iyengar

As is well known, poverty anywhere in the world, is a multidimensional concept. Various attempts have been made by social scientists and statisticians to quantify this concept. Poverty is variously described; it is a curse on humanity and its eradication is the greatest challenge for any country infected by mass poverty. Considerable effort has been made all over the world to design and implement public policies to combat it. Despite all this effort, almost 400 million people live in conditions of abject poverty, unable to receive even one US dollar a day. They constitute a third of the world population, according to a World Bank report.

Public policies to eradicate poverty emphasize the need to evolve an optimal mix of strategies like acceleration of growth and through the initiation of direct anti-poverty intervention through employment generation and building safety nets. Rapid growth by itself could contribute to generation of black money, but it is important that the poor also should be empowered to have enough opportunities to reap benefits from growth. It is in this context that one has to examine the relevance of the 'trickle-down" hypothesis as applicable to the developing countries like India, that have adopted the World Bank—IMF-sponsored 'economic reforms' in recent years.

Generally speaking, inequality refers to an uneven distribution of income and wealth as well as status, power, and access to employment opportunities. It is a common feature of all economies, irrespective of their stage of economic development, political system, social and cultural values. Inequality (absolute or relative) and poverty are closely linked, and their inter-relationship can be analytically demonstrated by choosing an appropriate model of size distribution. Examination shows that policies designed to reduce poverty are precisely those, which will also serve as instruments to reduce poverty. Exploiting this basic idea, it should be possible to evolve an alternative definition of poverty that is almost price-invariant.

Please let me thank you and the Indian Economic Association President,

Professor Raj Kumar Sen and his distinguished colleagues on the Executive Committee, for asking me to chair this important session. Needless to say, I consider it a great honor and recognition of my theoretical works on poverty measurement and analysis in India. I am also thankful to the IEA to edit the present volume consisting of 17 contributed papers and three of my previous papers method to this subject. The following are my comments on each of these 17 articles, which have enriched not only this present volume but also the economic literature on Poverty and Sustainable Development.

The Economy of Dependency and Sustained Poverty: Sunipa Das Gupta and Ranesh Kumar Ray.

The purpose of the paper is to show that growth eradicates absolute poverty, but in a country with direct/indirect foreign intervention. This kind of absolute poverty persists in countries like India, where perpetual dependence on foreign finance capital is dominant. Foreign capital not only uses India as a potential market to reap its profits, but also utilizes the country as a seaboard to penetrate into other dependent Afro-Asian nations. Dependency perpetuates even in modern independent India, as a legacy of its colonial past, where modernization has been imposed on the country to convert it into a mere appendage of capitalism. Subservience on monopoly capital has created a class alignment in India, predominantly feudal in nature. These semi-feudal class relations work as a device of appropriation of primitive surplus to cater to the expansionist policy of capitalism. There occurs huge repatriation, which represents a substantial leakage from the circular flow of income. Such repatriation exhausts foreign exchange and soon the country is compelled to contract external assistance at high interest rates and amortization costs with its imperial conqueror. On the other hand, heterogeneous class alignment gives rise to a dominant coalition of rent seeking proprietary classes that work as agents of monopoly capitalism. Power dealings are carried out with such agents who convert the public money into an intricate network of subsidies and patronage that swell up their pockets. The public money gets exposed. But to substantiate its vote bank, the government never forgets to pay lip services to poverty alleviation. The funds allocated for this purpose are proliferated towards maintaining the vested interest of the proprietary classes. Such proliferation adds to the destabilization of the government's fiscal house. It remains difficult to remain aloof from foreign aids and grants, which usually come with high price tags. The country is caught in a debt trap. Independent economic growth under such circumstances is a mirage and so is poverty alleviation.

Poverty: A Danger to Prosperity: Tapan Kumar Shandilya.

Poverty is a universal and multifaceted concept. It does not only affect the individuals but also poses a danger to the nation. Poverty is a relative term and is understood in relation to prosperity. Hence from time immemorial, the poor have coexisted with the rich, not only in India but also in the rest of the world. India has launched several programs, which aim at reduction of rural poverty. These programs are designed to provide productive employment and assets to the targeted poor households. The author describes some of the state-sponsored projects and comments on their working.

Poverty—Progeny of Progress: Ram Naresh Thakur.

Poverty is the greatest enemy of human development. However, economic growth reduces the intensity of poverty and provides relief to the poor, via creation of jobs, improving the revenue and creation of infrastructure to enable the poor to have easy access to information and opportunities.

Poverty in India: K.S.S. Uduman Mohideen and K. Ramchandran.

Poverty is a curse on humanity. It is cursed not only because of the misery it inflicts but also for the moral degradation it brings to people. Indians, by and large, are fatalists; they believe in *kismet*. The man in poverty reconciles himself to his poverty. His rich neighbour may show all sympathy he can but feels that nothing can be done lo relieve him of his poverty, because he believes that he is condemned to poverty by his previous *karma*. In the past, therefore, the Indian society had learnt to live with poverty and there, the matter ended. But times have changed. Philanthropists like Dadabhai Naoroji took up the case of the poor. The socialistic preaching awakened the Indian masses that no longer sweat by the thesis that the poor must remain poor. Indira Gandhi's election slogan "Garibi Hatao" caught the imagination of the masses, though they are at present dejected and disillusioned and may think that this slogan was a cruel joke. It is however, gratifying that the Planning Commission in its *Approach Document* to the Fifth Plan has focused the attention of the government and the people to the serious problem of poverty. In India, the poverty estimates are made at national and state levels by the Planning Commission periodically, using the national Sample Survey data on household monthly expenditure. The 1993-94 estimates show a secular decline in the poverty ratio, though the number of poor remained almost stable for a fairly long period of two decades (1973-93) mainly because of population growth.

Poverty Re-examined: Vimal Shankar Singh, Subhra Singh and Shweta Singh.

In this essay, the authors recall a statement from the Vedas: "there is no greater sorrow than the sorrow of being poor". The world community is compelled to acknowledge the ancient truth that only equitable distribution of wealth and reduction of mass poverty could lead to all round development. The paper re-examines whether the idea of redistribution has any relevance in the present Indian context.

India adopted a planned economic development approach and democratic socialism model for the removal of poverty in the country. Under central planning, many older institutions and objectives lost their relevance; Kings, Landlords, Green and Industrial Revolution, Infrastructure Development, Savings, Investment, etc. have disappeared. In spite of a marked increase in national income and increase in the allocation of funds for social development, one still finds acute forms of poverty, unemployment, and misery. Statistics show that about 260 million people are still below the poverty line. A nation howsoever rich cannot cater to the Herculean task of feeding its hungry population. Thus population control can be the only solution for a poverty-stricken country with slow pace of development. The author asks: "Why breed poor and then cure their poverty? Instead, let not the poor be born." This may sound rather revolutionary: "So, let us change our policy from 'Reduce poverty and reduce poor' to 'Reduce poor and reduce poverty'. Let us do everything to achieve this policy."

Absolute and Relative Poverty in India: A New Way to Re-examine Old Issues: Arvind Awasthi.

There is no single source from which one can directly get consistent data for India regarding income distribution over a period of time, so that one can draw inferences about relative poverty or income disparities. In spite of this handicap, it is possible to track the pattern of changes in relative poverty and compare it with the movements in per capita income and absolute poverty. The author draws attention to various efforts to apply Kuznets hypothesis to Indian development.

Measurement and Indicators of Poverty in India: S. Borbora and Rathul Mahanta.

Poverty is a social phenomenon, which universally affects many a country, especially the developing countries. There are two concepts of poverty—absolute and relative poverty. The 'relative' concept is more suitable for developed countries, while the 'absolute' concept is perhaps more relevant to the developing economies. In India, for example, poverty line is defined on the basis of calorie norms only. However, for poverty measurement, the appropriate approach would be to estimate the minimal requirement of food, clothing, and shelter, as reflected in the purchasing power. The author quotes different sources of official and non-official statistics, to portray poverty in different states of India over the years, and finds that the three indicators mentioned above are really prominent. In the light of his findings, the author discusses some of the government programs to alleviate poverty and concludes that those programs have succeeded lo certain extent, though there is a long way to go.

Dimensions of Poverty in India: Measurement and Determinants: P.K. Pal.

According to *World Development Report (2000/2001)*, poverty implies lack of adequate food and shelter, deprivations that keep them away from a decent standard of living, i.e. better housing, sanitation, access to safe drinking water, and so on. It is a multidimensional concept. Its main dimensions are: (1) lack of income to attain basic necessities—food, shelter, clothing, and acceptable levels of health and education, (2) sense of voiceless and powerlessness in the institutions of state and society, and (3) vulnerability to adverse shocks, linked to an inability to cope with them. In this paper, an attempt has been made to examine the different dimensions of poverty in India during the decade, 1973-74 to 1999-2000, particularly the international and interregional aspects of poverty and its measurement in India. The author also looks at the causes of poverty in India and prescribes a few interesting solutions.

Poverty Measurement Studies in India: P. Jegadish Gandhi.

Poverty is a universal phenomenon but its peculiarity and permeability differ from country to country. "Who are the poor? What is their number and proportion in the total population? Where are the poor located? What do they do for a living and how do they survive? These are questions asked in all types of society today. The pathology of poverty shows the inherent deficiency of the socioeconomic system. Economists have tended to concentrate on absolute poverty. A minimum level of consumption expenditure is determined on the basis of calorie requirement. This minimum expenditure level is the "poverty line", drawn in relation to what is considered the minimum nutritional requirement for physical subsistence. The Indian Planning Commission has defined the poverty line on the basis of recommended nutritional requirements of 2435 rounded as 2400 calories per person per day for rural areas and 2095 rounded as 2100 calories for urban areas. The proportion of people below the poverty line (PBPL) in India is not a stable entity. Its geometry is always changing. According to official statistics, the PBPL was 54.9 per cent in 1973-74 and it came down to 36.0 per cent in 1993-94. It declined further to 26.1 per cent in 1999-2000, which meant nearly 10 per cent of the PBPL were enabled to rise above poverty thanks to various anti-poverty programs. When there is a substantial concentration of population around the poverty line, as in India, small changes in the level of consumption can shift a large number of people above or below it. This snake-and-ladder game points to the need to identify a new group, i.e. people on the poverty line (POPL). In the present case, it is debatable whether this 10 per cent actually crossed the poverty line or is beginning to live on the borderline. More objectively, it is assumed that these people are still on the poverty line due to the strong inflationary forces. Poverty reduction in India is not a number game; its dynamics lies in the redress of the deprived basic needs of the poor. The strategic step in the onslaught on poverty is to see it no longer self-perpetuating. Unless a comprehensive protective coverage of the socioeconomic content is evolved, may be in terms of better income-incremental opportunities or increasing the employability of the people on the poverty line, all the efforts taken in this sector will prove to be *Sisyphean.*

Causes, Trends and Alleviation of Poverty in India: S.K. Dhage.

Poverty is a social phenomenon in which a section of the society is unable to fulfil even its basic necessities of life. If we look at the poverty ratios in different states of India, we notice a decline in poverty from 1973-74 to 1999-2000. The combined poverty ratio in 1999-2000 was the lowest in Jammu and Kashmir (3.48 per cent). On the other extreme, it was 47.15 per cent in Orissa. It is well known that the main causes of poverty in India are rapid growth of population, low rate of economic development, price rise, and inequality. To control poverty, the government of India has taken some important measures like Minimum Needs Program, Rural Land-less Employment Guarantee Program, Training of Rural Youth for Self-employment, Crash Scheme for Rural Development, Village Development Program, *Antyodaya Yojana,* Development of Tribal Areas, and Prime Minister's *Rozgar Yojana.* These programs may have achieved some reduction in poverty ratios, but the problem of poverty still exists in a visible form.

Poverty, Old Age and Lack of Family Support: Rahul S. Mhopare.

In this paper, an attempt is made to present some interesting results from a few case studies of individuals who are senior citizens without family support. Admittedly, this is a very preliminary collection of information regarding the nature and causes of poverty verging on destitution. A specific objective of the investigation was to ascertain the reality of poverty of those who either have no family or some family members who do not consider necessary to support such senior citizens. The case study is, however, restricted to one village only from each taluka of one district, namely, Sangli (Maharashtra State of India). A process involving actual visit to each village, meeting the village officials as also local people present at the time of interview, selected one senior female member of family. No senior isolated male citizen was identified. Thus, the number of units in the sample included nine males and ten females. The paper portrays some of the scenarios studied.

Poverty, Inequality and Sustainable Development in India: Swami Prakash Srivastava.

According to Adam Smith, "*No society can surely be flourishing and happy, of which by far the greater part of the number are poor and miserable* ". Poverty is a multidimensional concept and depends upon several social and economic factors. It can be defined as a social phenomenon in which a section of the society is unable to fulfil even its basic necessities of life. When a substantial segment of a society is deprived of the minimum level of living and continues at a bare subsistence level, the society is said to be plagued with mass poverty. The subject of sustainable development and poverty has engaged the attention of scholars for centuries. In September 1994, the program of action at the Cairo International Conference on Population and Development asserted: "Despite decades of development efforts both the gap between rich and poor nations and inequalities within nations have widened. Widespread poverty remains the major challenge to development efforts." This view was echoed again and again at the United Nations World Summit for Social Development held in Copenhagen in March 1995 and attended by more than 134 heads of states. Despite significant improvements over the past half-century, extreme poverty remains widespread in the developing world. More than 1.2 billion people, almost half the world's population, live on less than US $2 a day. These impoverished people often suffer from under-nutrition and poor health, have little or no literacy, live in environmentally degraded areas, have little political voice, and attempt to earn a meager living on small and marginal farms or in dilapidated urban slums. The World Bank has recommended certain new suggestions for poverty reduction along with enhanced rates of growth, and several developing countries like India are experimenting with the Bank-IMF prescriptions for poverty eradication. This paper offers some comments on the working of these reforms in India.

Poverty Alleviation in India for a Sustainable Future: Asim K. Karmakar.

Poverty is commonly seen as the antithesis of growth and development. They are not exact opposites, since poverty is a condition while growth/development is a process or a set of processes, but there is an inter-relationship between the two: growth has been associated with substantial reduction in poverty. The recent empirical studies, however, show a 2 per cent annual rate of growth in consumption per person accompanied by a poverty gap index of 3 to 8 per cent. Further, it is also noticed that in India with high and persisting high inequality, the trickle-down effects of even high rates of growth have been so slow that without remedial pro-poor policy actions it will take an unnecessary long time before a sizable dent is made in the backlog of poverty. In this backdrop, the present paper, after noting some crucial conceptual and measurement aspects of poverty, tries to focus on the role of recent reforms in India's anti-poverty programs and concludes that a rapid growth and accompanying rigorous anti-poverty programme both necessary for India's sustainable future.

Plan Strategy, Economic Reforms and Eradication of Poverty: Arun Prabha Chowdhury.

In India, poverty has been defined on the basis of a minimum standard of living, as measured by monthly per capita household expenditure duly adjusted for prices. According to this definition, Indian population below the poverty line continues to suffer in spite of the state efforts under the various Five-Year Plans and the economic reforms launched in 1991. The author argues that the trickle-down effects of economic growth as envisaged in the reforms has not materially benefited the poor. The conclusion is obvious: the trickle-down approach may be dropped, and Indian planners might adopt a more effective employment-generating approach instead.

Poverty, Unemployment and Economic Reforms: R. Arunachalam.

The paradigm shift in economic policy seems to be biased towards capitalistic Brettonwoods system in the name of Liberalization, Privatization and Globalization (LPG). This paper attempts to throw light on the impact of LPG on poverty and unemployment in India and discusses the issues therein. The author points out the variations in the definition and measurement of poverty and carefully examines the poverty profile of India and its relationship with economic growth. The New Economic Policy (NEP) aims at reduction of poverty by accelerating growth. However, as per the 55th Round of National Sample Survey data on household consumer expenditure and employment (2000-01), the direction of change in poverty is mixed. The same official statistics also reveal that employment in rural India suffered during the reform period. The study, finally, describes the challenges ahead.

Impact of Globalization on Poverty: Puspa Tarafdar.

Globalization generally reduces poverty because more integrated economics tend to grow faster. In this paper, the author reviews various anti-poverty programs under the Ninth Five Year Plan, particularly the Integrated Rural Development Plan (IRDP), and concludes that sustained high rates of growth may not be sustainable if they are not accompanied by a wide dispersion of purchasing power with higher employment. In other words, growth is necessary to make a dent on poverty, but by no means a sufficient condition.

Changing International Scenario and the Poor in India: Basudeb Sahoo.

The international scenario has undergone a perceptible change since the collapse of the Soviet Union in early 80s. In this context, the International Monetary Fund (IMF), the World Bank (WB), and the World Trade

Organization (WTO), mainly at the instance of the United States, are increasingly influencing the working of economic policies and conditions in the developing countries. The policy of globalization, liberalization and privatization imposed on the member countries by these world organizations has affected, rather adversely, the economic conditions of the poor. Plans to protect the marginal farmers and unorganized labour are seriously undermined. In this paper, the author examines reasons for the observed decline in the rate of poverty reduction in India during the 90s, attributed to the new economic policy and openness of the Indian economy. The author pleads caution against unchecked growth of capitalism and argues for strengthening the base of domestic economies and bringing prosperity to the poor.

SECTION I

CONTRIBUTIONS FROM DR. N.S. IYENGAR

1

Poverty: Concepts and Measurement—A Review

N. Sreenivasa Iyengar

1. CURRENT DEBATE

Experience of developing countries which adopted the IMF-guided reforms to globalize their economies indicates that poverty had increased since July 1991 when India also joined the race. Globalization of prices without significant expansion in employment and globalization of incomes and a cut-back in public spending on various welfare programmes in order to reduce fiscal deficits, are common features of all present reforms. Public spending is a powerful instrument for fighting poverty, and certain categories of government expenditure which affect inequalities and poverty have been identified for decades: education and health, food subsidies, cash transfers, housing and public employment schemes. Any significant reduction in public spending on social welfare brings down the levels of consumption of the people who cannot afford to pay inflated prices without a commensurate rise in their capabilities, at least in the immediate short-run.

Recent studies in India based on Planning Commission's definition and National Sample Survey (NSS) data on household expenditures point to an increase in poverty levels since 1991, the year in which the current economic reforms were launched. Huppi's (1995) well-documented study on the impact of reform on the poor clearly supports such view. However, according to Suryanarayana (1996), who relies on the same source of data, the all-India poverty ratio declined from 29.9 per cent in 1987 to 18.9 per cent in 1993-94, but in the absence of fully published data for 1993-94 it may not be easy to validate such comparisons. Interestingly, other poverty experts like Tendulkar *et.al.* (1993) have argued, using NSS data for the years 1990-91 and 1992, that poverty in rural India has actually increased from 36.65 per cent to 48.07 per cent between 1990-91 and 1992. During the same period, urban poverty increased marginally from 32.85 to 33.87 in percentage terms. Senior government officials and economic advisers, whose estimates are much lower, recognize and even admit that NSS results for 1990-91 and 1992 are not adequately reliable since they are based on what they regard as "thin" samples. Acharya (1995), for example, vehemently differs from Gupta. In his own words, ". . . Some analysts have been quick to rush to adverse (and incorrect) judgments on the basis of inappropriate periodization and misinterpreted data. A recent example is Gupta (1995), whose negative assessment of the impact of reforms, is based on serious analytical errors. The most glaring of these is the inclusion of the crisis-hit year of 1991-92 as part of the post-reform period (Indeed, in his deeply flawed analysis of rural wage trends in agriculture, Gupta even includes the year 1990-91 as part of the post-reform period). Second, and associated, is the uncritical use of the NSS 48th round data for 1992 to draw conclusions about the impact of economic reforms on poverty and unemployment based on "thin" sample. A much better, though by no means wholly satisfactory, basis for analysis and assessment will be provided by the large quinquennial NSS survey for 1993-94 which is presently being processed".

On March 1, 1996, the Prime Minister of India formally informed the nation's Upper House, the Rajya Sabha, that the number of people below poverty line in the country had decreased by 8 or 9 per cent since his government assumed office in 1991. He assured members that the country would continue with a mixed economy, as visualized by Jawaharlal Nehru, with government's full resolve to uplift the downtrodden (*The Times of India*, Bangalore, March 2, 1996, p. 1). The message is dear: the State will continue with its anti-poverty programmes and policies. However, in a poor country, there is always a basic conflict between budgetary notions of fiscal discipline and social reforms deeply rooted in its cultural values. In any case, the truth about the state of poverty is confounded, while debate after debate will continue to engage attention of some of our renowned economists and statisticians, absorbing a good deal of our precious resources.

2. POVERTY CONCEPTS

Poverty is a multidimensional concept involving economic, social, political and cultural dimensions. If one confines to economic aspects only, say income *or* wealth, then two types of definitions are available in the literature. Rowntree's (1901) work in Great Britain was perhaps the first systematic attempt to define poverty in absolute terms. According to this definition, a *family* is in poverty if its total earnings are inadequate even to obtain the minimum necessities for the maintenance of normal physical efficiency. The minimum necessities are food, clothing, housing, heating,

* A Keynote address at the National Seminar on Budget and Poverty, University of Mysore, April 20, 1996. Reprinted from *Artha Beekshan*, Vol. 6, No. 1, June 1997.

lighting and utensils for cooking and washing—all purchased at the lowest prices and in quantities necessary for physical subsistence only. Once the subsistence standard is scientifically defined, all that is needed is to update it to take into account the rise in prices of the basic necessities. As this concept of income inadequacy is itself dynamic, as is the case in industrially advanced countries, Rowntree's definition of poverty may not be so useful for long-term comparisons. If such definition can be applied to India, for example, its current poverty line would be many times smaller than the one based on Rowntree's methodology.

However, if standard of living is the main concern, then the most straightforward way to determine the poverty line is to specify a basket of commodities by commodity vector q $(q_1, q_2 \ldots q_n)$ purchasable at market prices p $(p_1, p_2 \ldots p_n)$ and to set the poverty standard as a subsistence standard $(1 + h)\, pq$, where h is a provision for items not included in the list q. This was in effect the method followed in the United States in the derivation of the official poverty line, where q represents food items and h stands for allowance for spending on other items of consumption. The list q is based on the U.S. Department of Agriculture's "economy food plan" for households of different compositions, and the multiplier allowed for other commodities is 3. This method differs from, but has some relation to, the definition of poverty line as the income at which households spend as specified proportion of their total budget on necessities. The Canadian low-income cut-off is based on the income level at which more than 70 per cent of average is spent on food, clothing, and shelter (*Puduluk*, 1967). When the U.S official poverty line was introduced, there was considerable disagreement about the subsistence standard, but political judgment played a considerable role in determining the "$3,000 for a family of four" that featured prominently in the speeches launching the war on poverty. Similarly, political considerations guided the European Commission in arriving at a bench mark of 50 per cent of average national income in measuring poverty in Europe. The above analyses serve to illustrate the poverty line based on a norm and adjusted for price changes and often referred to as an "absolute" poverty line, and a "relative" poverty line linked to current levels of living. 'The European Community defines poverty as follows: "The poor shall be taken to mean persons, families, and groups of persons whose resources (material, cultural, and social) are so limited as to exclude them from the minimum acceptable way of life in the member state in which they live" (*Council Decision*, December 19, 1984).

3. INDIAN OFFICIAL PROCEDURE

There are two official procedures for estimating poverty lines and poverty ratios in India. One is the approach followed by the Central Statistical Organization (CSO) using the National Accounts Statistics (NAS) and the other is the one based on NSS data collected by the National Sample Survey Organization (NSSO).

(a) CSO Approach

The Task Force (1979) set-up by the Planning Commission defined poverty line as the per capita expenditure level of households at which the calorie norms of 2400K and 2100K cals were set as the basis of the all-India consumption basket for rural and urban households at 1973-74 prices. The poverty line so defined came to Rs. 49.09 and Rs. 56.64 for the rural and urban poor, respectively. For subsequent years, these poverty lines were updated initially by wholesale price deflators and later on by the implicit private consumption deflators available in the NAS. On the recommendations of a Study Group set-up by the Planning Commission *(Perspective Planning Division,* November 1984) in order to arrive at the estimates of population in poverty, the Planning Commission used a device to adjust the NSS data, so that the aggregate private consumption expenditure as given in the NSS is exactly equal to the aggregate private consumption expenditure estimated as a residual in the NAS. In other words, the NAS estimate of the consumption aggregate is distributed into selected household's per capita expenditure categories using the population estimates of NSS as weights. The old NAS statistics were used for deriving the adjustment factor for estimates earlier to 1983, and thereafter, the new NAS series were used. The population in poverty was estimated by applying the updated poverty line to the corresponding NSS distribution of households.

(b) The NSS Approach

This approach was used by Minhas and others (1991) in which the base period consumption basket was retained as before, that is, when the poverty line was defined as Rs. 49.09 and Rs. 56.64 for rural and urban distributions. Then, at the all-India level, two alternative approaches were made to estimate poverty: one that used an all-India poverty line and the associated all-India distribution of per capita total consumption in value terms, and the other, combining the poverty ratios of the state distributions using the State populations as weights. The price adjustments for poverty line updating involved the consumer price index for industrial workers and for non-manual employees for urban areas. This method is almost similar to the one recommended by the Lakdawala Committee.

4. A BAYESIAN APPROACH TO POVERTY MEASUREMENT

As already noted, poverty is a multivariate concept involving several dimensions. In a purely economic sense it may be regarded as the state or condition in which some goods and services essential to maintain an acceptable minimum standard of living are lacking. However, a precise definition of poverty will have to differ from society to society, as the concepts of subsistence, deprivation and income adequacy vary across the regions within a country and between different countries. In India, for example, poverty is understood and interpreted as the lack of the very basic energy required for subsistence. The underlying assumption here is that the consumption pattern of households will ensure that when the food intake reaches the desired level, other essentials like clothing, housing and health would also be available. Initially, protein was considered crucial for ensuring nutritional adequacy, but later on it was established that calorie intake is the most important criterion to be considered for purposes of measuring poverty *(Gopalan, et. al,* 1971; *Gopalan,* 1983; and *Sukhatme,* 1977, 1982). For Indian conditions, an ideal requirement of 2400K cals for the average sedentary male adult has been prescribed *(Gopalan and Rao,* 1968; *Indian Council of Medical Research,* 1980). Calorie norms for other categories of people were linked to this average.

Calorie intake is not directly and easily available, and further, there may be inter and intra-individual variations in calorie consumption within a household, quite unrelated to the poverty level. Hence, it becomes necessary to translate the calorie norm into a more readily observable economic indicator such as the household per capita monthly consumption in money terms. The Planning Commission in India first desired a minimum per capita calorie norm and then took as the poverty line a central measure like the mean, mode, or the median of the per capita total expenditure class for which the mean calorie intake exactly matched the fixed norm. Using this procedure, the Planning Commission (1979) estimated the poverty lines for 1973-74 as Rs. 49.09 per month for the rural calorie norm of 2400K cals daily and Rs. 56.60 for the urban calorie norm of 2100K cals per day. A subsequent Sub-Group of the Planning Commission made estimates of similar poverty lines for later years for different States of India.

There are obvious limitations to this procedure. Firstly, the area covered is too large for either calorie norm or the poverty line to serve any practical purpose. Secondly, for this large area, a rather general occupational profile was considered, which is necessarily inaccurate and probably unrepresentative. Consequently, applying these poverty lines in a specific region for identification of the poor becomes an exercise fraught with dangers of misclassification. This possibility is clearly brought out in Iyengar and Gopalakrishna (1985).

Iyengar, Joshi and Gopalakrishna (1992), in their Karnataka study, used a novel approach based on Bayesian methodology, which departed from other traditional methods where conditional measures were used to estimate the consumption threshold and formulated the poverty line as follows: If y is the per capita consumption of a household in rupees and x is the corresponding per capita calorie intake per day, the poverty line is defined as the minimal y^* which guarantees the availability of the predetermined minimum calorie intake level of x^* cals with probability arbitrariliy close to one. They assumed a familiar log-linear relationship between y and x, and adopted the Bayesian approach for estimating the poverty cut-off so defined. Extensive computations using the available official statistics for the Indian state of Karnataka revealed that poverty was considerably *underestimated* by traditional methods employed by official agencies.

5. OTHER ISSUES IN POVERTY ANALYSIS

Iyengar (1989) surveyed some of the literature on poverty in India. Currently, there is a new emphasis on fighting urban poverty, and the government's new "reforms with a human face" bears testimony. A new form of debate on anti-poverty measures will ensue, demanding a closer examination of the various concepts and techniques of measurement. Critics of the official approach, in very recent years, have raised the issue of "thin" *vs.* "full" sample. The relevant question then will be: If poverty ratio declined during the crucial period 1991-93, as revealed by NSS data, could it be attributed to the economic reforms which were initiated in mid-July 1991? Before attempting a formal answer to this question, one has to begin with a careful analysis of the observed changes in the poverty ratios, which are only *estimates.* In such analyses, sampling errors become crucial for all pair-wise comparisons, over time or space, as the information contained in a sample is both incomplete and inaccurate because of large non-sampling errors, both conceptual and statistical. It is only after the significance of the difference between the two estimates is established by standard tests of significance, then only the question of explanation of why inter-temporal or inter-spatial differences occurred. One can perhaps look for the underlying causes for the observed changes.

If the number of households in a sample is larger than 30 and the variability in the population is not large, the sample is to be considered as large enough to carry out a large sample test for the poverty ratios, which uses the familiar normal distribution. For small samples, a t-test can be used under standard assumptions. However, there are many economists and statisticians who believe that standard methods of hypothesis testing that are generally applicable to random samples, may not strictly apply to the NSS-type situations in which a multistage probability design is employed, which is more complicated than simple random sampling, particularly when it comes to the question of calculating the standard errors. It is perhaps for this reason that Mahalanobis had to introduce the practice of interpenetrating sub-sampling in NSS, which recognizes the presence of both sampling and non-sampling errors in the estimates of various aggregates, averages, ratios and rates, and also facilitates the computation of margins of error for purposes of inter-temporal and spatial comparisons. The modern methods of Fractile Graphical Analysis was especially designed by Mahalanobis (1960) for comparing economic size distributions, using the generalized concept of distance. However, the sub-sampling aspects of the NSS are ignored in current practice. It is ironical that the nation spends large amounts of its limited intellectual and material resources on gathering of information, while a very little of the information so collected is actually utilized for drawing valid scientific inferences. The main user of NSS data are the economists who demand quick tabulations and convenient results, and the meek statisticians often oblige without cautioning the users about the dangers of loss of reliability and validity of their quick estimates. The result is confusion and unending debate. Probably, it is time that our statistical system also undergoes a reform in a manner similar to the economic reforms.

6. POVERTY AND INEQUALITY

Generally, inequality refers to the uneven distribution of income and wealth as well as status and power. It is a common feature of all economies irrespective of economic development, political system, social and cultural values. Poverty and inequality are closely related phenomena, and their interrelationship can be easily demonstrated analytically by choosing an appropriate model of income distribution. In fact, it turns out that policies designed to reduce inequalities are precisely those which will also serve as instruments to reduce poverty. Exploiting this basic idea it is possible to provide a simple definition of poverty that is almost price invariant. An outline of this new approach to measuring relative poverty is given below.

Let us assume that the relevant indicator, such as per capita total consumption in current prices or income of households, has been selected for classifying the ultimate survey units (households) in an ascending order from poor to rich. Let the distribution of the variable indicator (X) be denoted by its density function, $f(x : \theta)$, where θ is the unknown parameter vector. The mean (μ) and the inequality (L) are functions of the elements of θ. One can take for the inequality the co-efficient of variation (c), or the Lorenz ratio (L), which are independent of the monetary units in which x has been expressed. Let us further assume that the poverty line can be defined as a simple fraction of the mean of the distribution, i.e. $x^* = k\mu$, where k lies between zero and one. Here, k is arbitrary and may be left to be determined by a parliamentary decision. For example, k may be fixed as 50 per cent, so that whatever be the mean income or consumption the relative poverty line is just one-half of that income or consumption. When rapid development takes place, the policy-makers may fix a higher proportion of income as the poverty cut-off. This way of defining relative poverty has its own merits. It can be easily tried without demanding any additional data from NSS.

Let us assume that the distribution of income or consumption levels of households closely follows the Law of Proportionate Effect. According to this famous Law, like the celebrated Pareto's Law, the income or wealth status of a household is determined by a multiplicity of random influences, including inheritance, windfalls, etc., each contributing an infinitely small share. It implies that households which are already rich have better chances of improving their rich status in a market-driven economic system in the absence of effective state intervention. This Law has been extensively tested and fairly well established for India using published data from NSS (*Iyengar,* 1960, 1964, 1967; *Bhattacharya,* 1978; *Suryanarayana,* 1987; for example). One implication of the Law of Proportionate Effect is that households' incomes or per capita expenditures when measured in natural logarithms, follow the famous

Gaussian or normal law of distribution (*Cramer*, 1954, *Aitchison and Brown*, 1957).

A random variable (x) is said to be log-normally distributed with parameters θ and λ, if $ln\ x$ is normally distributed with mean θ and standard deviation λ. The mean of the distribution (μ) and the Lorenz measure of inequality (L) are, respectively

$$\mu = \exp(\theta + \lambda^2/2); \quad L = 2\ \phi\ (\lambda/2) - 1 \tag{1}$$

where $\phi\ (u)$ is the cumulative distribution function of the standard normal variable with mean zero and standard deviation one. The cumulative distribution of x is given by:

$$F\ (x) = \phi\ (ln\ x - \theta)\ \lambda/2 \tag{2}$$

If x^* is the poverty line, then the poverty ratio is simply $F\ (x^*)$. If we assume that $x^* = k\mu$ and use this definition in equation (2), we obtain the poverty ratio as

$$F\ (x^*) = F\ (\mu/2); \quad \phi\ [\lambda/2 + (1/\lambda)\ ln\ k] \tag{3}$$

Thus, the relative poverty is dependent upon the policy parameter *(k)* and the degree of inequality *(L)*, as reflected in λ. Incidentally, the co-efficient of variation for the two-parameter log-normal distribution is given by

$$c = \exp(\lambda^2) - 1 \tag{4}$$

which also entirely depends on the single parameter λ. It is easy to show that the poverty ratio increases as inequality increases, and *vice versa*. Also, empirically, it is not difficult to estimate the inequality parameter from the available grouped size distribution data published by NSSO using the technique of concentration curves developed by Iyengar (1960). Appropriate standard errors can also be computed for the poverty estimates assuming large samples under realistic assumptions (*Iyengar and Nadig*, 1993).

7. POVERTY IN DEVELOPING AND OECD COUNTRIES

The World Economic Review (Vol. 5, May 1991) contains several papers which examine the nature and magnitude of poverty in Eastern Europe and China, besides OECD countries, USA, Canada, and Australia, particularly in the wake of worldwide reforms after the fall of socialism. Some of these papers are of high methodological value and others are substantive, dealing with case studies in the developed as well as in some of the developing countries. Studies comparing poverty across countries usually contain an evaluation of their past policies for reducing poverty. If comparisons are to be a valid foundation for such assessments and, in particular, if they are to serve as a guide to effective allocation of public funds, the underlying concepts must be thoroughly examined. Atkinson (1991) lists four important issues that are critical in this respect, the choice of poverty indicator, the determination of poverty line, the unit of analysis and the choice of equivalence scale. He provides stimulating examples from the case studies, on poverty in the OECD countries—France, Spain, Italy, United Kingdom, Germany, Portugal, Greece, Ireland, Netherlands, Belgium, and Denmark. He also makes reference to practices in other industrially advanced countries like USA, Australia, Canada, Norway, and Sweden. Ravallion and Huppi (1991) describe a number of tools available for empirical analysis which allow researchers not only to test the sensitivity of poverty assessments measurement assumptions but also to decompose observed changes in aggregate poverty in terms of the underlying changes in the regional and demographic variables. These authors, like Indian scholars, base their poverty measures on the distribution of household consumption per person, after adjusting for inflation using the consumer price index, though modifying the expenditure weights to accord most closely with the spending patterns of the poor.

Poverty comparisons have been made in terms of income in France, Britain and Germany by taking the poverty standard as 50 per cent of the national average income. One of the two studies for UK uses households below average income as poor. According to a study by UK Department of Social Security (1990), in 1984-85, 9.2 per cent of households lived with incomes below 50 per cent of the mean. In France, in 1984-85, 10.9 per cent of households had incomes below 50 per cent of the median. In Germany, in 1983, 7.0 per cent of the population lived in households with income below 50 per cent of the mean. Of course, these comparisons will have to be qualified, since the methods followed in these countries are not quite the same.

8. CONCLUDING REMARKS

From the foregoing discussions it follows that poverty, in spite of all its diversities, will continue to engage the attention of many gifted scientists, economists and statisticians, and national governments will be deeply concerned with elimination of poverty as an important goal. Since budgetary resources are always a constraint in all developing countries, it is most important to develop appropriate concepts and measurement techniques utilizing the available allocations. Government policies and instruments need to be streamlined, so that funds allocated to the poor reach the deserving poor. Large leakages and unproductive costs of administration and deficiencies in the delivery system must be discouraged. Perhaps, a more vigilant public and press could play a more constructive role in this matter. In the meantime, the present system of rewards and penalties for economic performance also calls for review and reform, so as to ensure full returns to the new policy of economic reforms.

REFERENCES

Acharya, Shankar (1995): *The Economic Consequences of Economic Reforms.* The Indian Institute of Bankers, Bombay.

Aitchison, J. and J.A.C. Brown (1957): *The Log-normal Distribution with Special Reference to Its Uses in Economics*, Cambridge University Press, Cambridge.

Atkinson, A.B. (1991): "Comparing on Poverty Rates Internationally: Lessons from Recent Studies in Developed Countries", *World Bank Review*, 5, I, p. 3.

Bhattacharya, N. (1978): "Studies on Level of Living in India." A *Survey of Research in Economics* (eds.) Iyengar, N.S. and N. Bhattacharya, Vol. 7, *Econometrics*. Bombay: Allied Publishers, pp. 231-51.

Cramer, H. (1946): *Mathematical Methods of Statistics*, pp. 219-20. Princeton University Press, Princeton.

Council of Economic Advisers, U.S. (1964), *Economic Report of the President*, Government Printing Press, Washington, DC.

Gupta, S.P. (I995): "Recent Economic Reform and Its Impact on the Poor", *Artha Beekshan*, 4(1), pp. 13-66. Also *Economic and Political Weekly*, June 3.

Gopalan, C. (1983): "Measurement of Undernutrition: Biological Considerations", *Economic and Political Weekly*, XVIII (15), p. 591.

Gopalan, C. and B.S. Narasingha Rao (1968): *Dietary Allowance for Indians*, Special Report # 60, Indian Council of Medical Research, New Delhi.

Gopalan, C., B.V. Rama Sastry, and S.C. Balasubramanyam (1971): *Nutritive Value of Indian Foods*, National Institute of Nutrition, Hyderabad.

Iyengar, N.S. (1960): "Oh a Method of Computing the Engel Elasticities from Concentration Curves", *Econometrica*. 28 (4), pp. 882-91.

—— (1964): "As Consistent Method of Estimating the Engel Curve from Grouped Survey Data", *Econometrica*, 32 (4), pp. 591-618.

—— (1967): "Some Estimates of Engel Elasticities Based on National Sample Survey Data", *Jour. Roy. Stat. Soc.*, 150 (1), pp. 84-101.

—— (1989): "Recent Studies on Poverty in India: A Survey", *Jour. Quant. Econ.*, 5(2), pp. 223-37.

—— S.N. Joshi, and Mallika Gopalakrishna (1991): 'A Bayesian Approach to the Measurement of Poverty in India", *Bayesian Analysis in Statistics and Econometrics* (eds.) Prem K. Goel and N.S. Iyengar, pp. 379-87, Springer Verlog, New York.

—— and Mallika Gopalakrishna (1985), Appropriate Criteria for the Measurement of Levels of Living", *Indian Economic Review*, XX(2), pp. 191-229.

—— and Manjula Nadig (1993): "A Test for Expenditure Elasticity Estimates from Survey Data," *Indian Journal of Applied Economics*, I (3&4), pp. 42-52.

Government of India (1979): Report of the *Task Force on Projections of Minimum Needs and Effective Consumption Demand*, Planning Commission, New Delhi.

—— (1984): *Recommendations of the Working Group on Construction of Poverty Lines for Different States of India*, Central Statistical Organization, New Delhi.

—— (1993): *Report of the Expert Group on the Concepts and Estimation of Proportion and Number.*

—— (1994): Report *of the Study Group on the Concepts and Estimation of Poverty Line*, Planning Commission, New Delhi.

Mahalanobis, R.C. (I960): "A Method of Fractile Graphical Analysis," *Econometrica*, 28(2), pp. 325-57.

Minhas, B.S., *et. al.* (1991): "Declining Incidence of Poverty", *Economic and Political Weekly*, July.

Poduluk, J.R. (1967): *Incomes of Canadians*, Dominican Bureau of Statistics, Ottawa.

Rowntree, B.S. (1901): *Poverty: A Study of Town Life*, p. 117, Macmillan, London.

Ravallion, M. and Monica Huppi (1991): "Measuring Changes in Poverty: A Methodological Case Study of Indonesia during an Adjustment Period," *The World Economic Review*, 5(1), pp. 57-82.

Suryanarayana, M.H. (1987): *The Problem of Distribution in India's Development: An Empirical Analysis*, Doctoral Thesis, Indian Statistical Institute, Calcutta.

—— (1996): "Reform and Its Human Face", *The Hindu*, Madras, February 16.

Sukhatme, P.V. (1977): *Poverty and Malnutrition*, Lal Bahadur Sastri Memorial Lecture, New Delhi.

—— (ed.) (1982): *Newer Concepts in Nutrition and their Implications for Policy*. Maharashtra Association for the Cultivation of Science Research Institute, Pune.

Times of India (1996): Quotation from Prime Minister's Speech in the Rajya Sabha, Bangalore.

Tendulkar, S.D., K. Sundaram and L.R. Jain (1993): *Poverty in India, 1970-71 to 1988-89*, ARTEP Working Paper, December.

UK Department of Social Security (1990): *Households Below Average Income: A Statistical Analysis, 1981-87*, Department of Social Security, London.

2

On Nutrition and Poverty

N. SREENIVASA IYENGAR

May I thank the organizers of this conference for conferring upon me the honour of delivering the first Dr. Panduranga Vasudeo Sukhatme Memorial Lecture at the joint conference of the Indian Society for Medical Statistics and the International Biometric Society (Indian Region) in Bangalore. In honouring a teacher they have indeed honoured themselves and the great researchers who laid the foundation of statistics in India in the early thirties. My thought naturally goes back to the pioneering contributions of the late Professor Prasanta Chandra Mahalanobis, who put India on the world map of Statistics. Indian statisticians are recognized internationally for their theoretical contribution in many fields of statistical application: sample surveys, experimental designs, estimation and hypothesis testing, to mention just a few. These led to new and highly useful results of practical importance in a variety of statistical investigations, extending to diverse branches of human activity. At a national level, the Indian Statistical Institute at Calcutta, founded by Mahalanobis, became the centre of all statistical activities in India. Research, training, and extension were the main functions of the Institute. Later, new research units were added, and the Biometric Unit was one of them. For some time, its research activities were led by the internationally well-known zoologist, Professor J. B. S. Haldane. One of the main disciples of Mahalanobis, Professor Calyampudi Radhakrishna Rao, who had already achieved great distinction as a statistician, had published a highly technical work entitled *Advanced Methods in Biometric Research* (*Rao*, 1952), which highlighted the Fisherian approach to hypothesis-testing and statistical estimation in biology, genetics, and physical anthropology. In the meantime, another great Indian

* Based on the First Dr. P.V. Sukhatme Memorial Lecture, National Institute of Mental Health and Neuro Sciences, Bangalore, India, December 3, 1999.

statistician, Dr. Panduranga Vasudeo Sukhatme, closely associated with Professor R.A. Fisher at the Galton Laboratory of the University College, London, during the mid-fifties, further popularized Fisherian techniques in India through extensive experiments and field studies in the broad areas of public health, nutrition, and poverty. His well-known work (P.V. Sukhatme), *'Diet, Disease and Development'* (Macmillan, 1993) demonstrates the power of statistical analysis and sound reasoning which is essential in the design and implementation of programmes for social development. After his return from London in 1940, Sukhatme worked as a statistician in the Statistics Unit of the Indian Council of Agricultural Research (ICAR), New Delhi. It was here that he made his most notable contribution in educating the agricultural scientists on statistical methods to estimate crop yields from farm data. The pilot studies at ICAR led to his famous technique of crop-cutting experiments on random rectangular plots selected from the farmer's field for estimating the yield rates of major cereal crops. Several Asian and African countries have adopted his novel procedures for estimating their agricultural production. However, in India, the ISI-led crop-cutting experiments using smaller random circular cuts challenged the official ICAR procedures on grounds of cost and efficiency. The debate probably still continues, resulting in a flood of research papers and discussions, and vastly enriching the Indian literature on statistical sampling (Murthy, 1967).

As some of you are aware, I was trained at ISI Calcutta during the later fifties under the guidance of eminent teachers including P.C. Mahalanobis, C.R. Rao, G. Kalyanpur, R.R. Bahadur, D. Basu, D. Des Raj, T.P. Choudhuri, J. Roy and P. Sarbadhikari. My training included a short stay at the Indian Institute of Agricultural Statistics, New Delhi, then headed by Sukhatme's distinguished successor, Dr. V.G. Panse. This gave me an excellent opportunity to go through some of the ICAR's statistical literature. Of course, Sukhatme's contributions impressed me most. However, I could not pursue the study of design and sample surveys after my return to Calcutta. Instead, I joined the Planning Division of the Institute under the guidance of Professor Mani Mohan Mukherjee. My interest naturally shifted to planning and econometrics. I had the good fortune of participating in some of the *ISI Studies on Planning for National Development*, which eventually brought me my M. Stat. and Ph.D. degrees from the Institute (1962, 1964). R.A. Fisher gave the first ISI Convocation Address on February 12, 1962. I distinctly remember the rich tributes he paid to Indian statisticians for their contributions to statistics. He did not fail to mention the name of Sukhatme. I take this opportunity to pay my humble tribute to the memory of Dr. P.V. Sukhatme.

Sukhatme joined the FAO of the United Nations after his ICAR assignment. During his 20-year service in Rome, he turned his attention to problems of food and nutrition, particularly in the developing countries, and published several research reports and technical papers on hunger, which attracted world attention. After his retirement from FAO, Sukhatme chose to settle down at his native place in Pune, working for the Maharashtra

Association for Cultivation of Science. The social scientist carried out many important and socially relevant research projects on protein-calorie malnutrition and energy requirements of the Indian population. He employed standard statistical models of the first-order auto-regressive type to study the protein problem, which is known as the Sukhatme-Margen hypothesis. He stressed the need for taking into account the intra-individual variation to estimate the energy of protein consumption of a given individual. He regarded individuals as dynamic in nature and under homostatic control. With genetic considerations, this important study of Sukhatme gave rise to the concept of 'intra-individual heritability'. A most important discovery of Sukhatme during the early sixties was that in a healthy living system, the week-to-week variation in the intake is significantly larger than the within-week variance component in the same individual, indicating that the day-to-day observations are serially correlated. This is a reason why inter-individual variation remains wide and cannot be reduced by averaging to the extent it would be if the genetic-physiological process of energy metabolism had remained the same each day. This result had an important bearing on the poverty line estimation in India from a nutritional angle in the early eighties.

There has been growing interest in measuring the incidence of poverty in India. The various measures proposed to measure poverty differ widely in respect of their definition, data used and the manner in which the 'poverty line' is determined. In estimating the extent of poverty on the basis of nutrition, Iyengar and Gopalakrishna (1985) adopted the minimum requirement of 2400k calories per 'equivalent consumption unit' instead of per capita,[1] as recommended by the Nutrition Expert Group (Gopalan *et al.*, 1971), but reduced it by 100k calories to adjust for possible underestimation over and above what may be due to the exclusion of the Group V items. This 2300k calories cut-off coincides with the FAO, 1973 recommendations and endorsed by Sukhatme (1977). The IG indicator is the average over 30 days' consumption of all members within a household and takes into account the intra-individual differences in the calculation of equivalent consumption units. This per unit calorie measure reflects the actual consumption of calories in relation to the needs of the household. One can use it to identify the inadequately nourished and hence poor households. Using the norm of 2300k calories per consumption unit per day, IG estimated the poverty lines separately for rural and urban Karnataka as Rs. 52.72 and Rs. 65.00 for the year 1972-73 at current prices. The percentage of the households below the poverty lines was then estimated.

The Indian Planning Commission and the Central Statistical Organization in 1985-86 set-up two independent Expert Groups to examine the state of methodology and the data requirements for poverty estimation. Sukhatme was an active and valued member of both these groups. I had the good fortune of being a member of those groups. Several interesting suggestions emerged from their deliberations. The Planning Commission (1986) tried to construct poverty lines in monetary terms for different states and sectors of India. However, their approach has serious limitations, as pointed out by Minhas *et al* (1987). There has been a debate and even some controversy over the method of determination of poverty lines that ignores the demographic and occupational variables. For instance, Dandekar *et al* (1971), Krishnaji (1981a, 1981b), and Sukhatme (1978, 1981a, 1981b) took the view that the requirement of man in energy equilibrium maintaining normal body weight varies not only from day-to-day but also from week-to-week, with stationary variance. Most individuals in normal health have a calorie intake between $\bar{R} - 2\sigma$ and $\bar{R} + 2\sigma$. $\bar{R}$ refers to the mean requirement of the reference adult and σ denotes standard deviation. The proportion of individuals below the lower limit is taken as the index of incidence of undernutrition. The coefficient of variation of requirement is approximately 15 per cent. Krishnaji's (1981) point is that Sukhatme's measure underestimates the magnitude of malnutrition, as it specifies a lower minimum requirement than is logically appropriate. Instead, he suggests $\bar{R} - 2\sigma_w$ and $\bar{R} + 2\sigma_w$, where $\bar{R}$, as before, refers to the mean requirement of a standard unit and σ_w, for the intra-household variability. The two estimates may not differ very much when the intra-individual variation is due to environmental factors. But the available evidence suggests that this is not quite so.[2]

As already pointed out, there is more than one concept of poverty. One of the most common practices, however, is to relate poverty to nutritional adequacy.[3] In this case, poverty is defined in terms of a cut-off point y^*, for the low calorie intake level predetermined by the nutritionist. The basic problem of economic interest is to determine a minimal cut-off level, x^*, for the consumption level in monetary units corresponding to y^*. So far, various research workers in India and the Planning Commission tried to relate x and y assuming one or other familiar statistical models and to estimate x^* using ordinary tools of descriptive statistics, such as the conditional mean, mode or median. However, Iyengar, Joshi and Gopalakrishna (1992) reformulated the poverty line as follows: Let x be the per capita monthly consumption of a household in rupees, and y the corresponding daily calorie intake per equivalent consumption unit. The poverty line may be defined as the minimal x, that is x^*. Graphical tests show that the semi-logarithmic specification,

$$y = \alpha + \beta \ln x + u \tag{1}$$

is to be preferred to the other simple linear and double logarithmic models used by IJG. A standard assumption here is that the u's are independently and normally distributed variables with mean zero and positive standard deviation, σ. The model has three parameters: α, β and σ to be estimated from data. For the y's to be positive, the threshold for x has to be above $exp\ (\alpha/\beta)$. The requirement that

$$Pr\ (y \geq y^*) \geq 1 - \eta \tag{2}$$

where η is positive and arbitrarily small, gives the following expression for x^*

$$x^* = exp\ [(y^* - \alpha + \sigma\ z_\eta) / \beta] \qquad (3)$$

where z_η is the standard normal abscissa corresponding to a pre-determined level of confidence as reflected by η. In equation (3), y^* and η are pre-determined, but the parameters (α, β, σ) are unknown. IJG (1992) have proposed a Bayesian method to estimate these parameters under some mild but realistic assumptions about the prior distributions of the unknown parameters and used a generalized maximum likelihood principle. The expected value of the posterior distribution is the Bayes estimate of the required parameter. According to this procedure, a typical household in rural Karnataka needed Rs. 134.84 per head per month to meet the minimal daily intake of 2400k calories. During the same period (1973-74), the urban counterpart needed Rs. 218.92 to attain the same normative level of nutrition. The threshold level of consumption was Rs. 7.38 in the rural areas, while it was Rs. 6.51 in the urban areas in 1973-74 rupees. Perhaps, using the IJG definition, one might also determine the poverty line through a graphical approach. Suppose one has the cross-classified data of sample households according to x and y in grouped form. Then one computes the probability of y exceeding y^* for different levels of x. This probability is a monotonic increasing function of x. Suppose this probability is arbitrarily fixed at P. Corresponding to this level of probability, one can get a poverty line estimate by simple interpolation. Admittedly, this procedure is crude.

The Planning Commission (1986) gave the required bivariate frequency data on (x, y) for many Indian states for the year 1977-78. As a starting point, the data for rural Andhra Pradesh, available from the 32nd round of the National Sample Survey, was analyzed. Assuming the norm of 2400k calories for y^*, which appears in the interval (2375-2425) and using linear interpolation, the corresponding poverty line (x^*) was estimated to be Rs. 175, which corresponds to the probability level of 91 per cent. Still better estimates could be obtained for the poverty line by choosing a higher value for probability. Our analysis shows that official estimates are on the lower side of the Rs. 175 limit for the same period.

Before closing my address, I would like to raise the following questions for closer examination of all social scientists, including the statisticians:

- Should poverty be defined in terms of income adequacy and not in terms of expenditure? Should it be related to the capacity to buy and subsist for oneself and one's dependants?
- Poverty is measured in terms of a mean, and not in terms of a minimum. However, since the minimum in any size distribution is of equal importance, why not estimate it first by any means?[4]
- What about the Bayesian approach to poverty measurement? In this case, poverty line assumes a new definition linked to a standard calorie norm. Is there a better formulation, which minimises the probability of miscalculation of the poor and non-poor households?

- In most economic analyses based on survey data, should one bother about the sampling errors? Can one apply the traditional methods of statistical inference to grouped data and draw valid conclusions?
- Finally, what are the determinants of poverty? Would a decomposition analysis help in finding them?
- The treatment of prices and comparisons over time and across regions assumes crucial importance for poverty analysis. Do we have an adequate database on prices relevant for such an analysis?

Notes and References

1. Per capita takes household size implicitly into account. Taking household size explicitly amounts to making separate analyses for each household size group, as was done by Iyengar, Jain and Srinivasan (1968).
2. It may be possible to argue that increased mechanization of agriculture reduces human labour inputs and hence reduces the calorie needs of the rural households mainly dependent on agriculture. But this hypothesis requires a separate in-depth study.
3. Here, a question may arise: should poverty be defined in terms of nutritional adequacy? This question was first raised by Sukhatme at a time when most other research workers, like V.M. Dandekar, were using a calorie-based definition. Sukhatme's point was that nutrition-based poverty measures are scientifically testable, given the fact that intra- and inter-individual variations in nutrition requirements in India are statistically significant. It appears, however, less controversial to employ a stochastic approach involving comparisons of the cumulative distributions of income/expenditure distributions. Indeed, this was the approach followed in the preliminary study of the changes in the distribution of expenditures of rural and urban households, based on NSS data, which was highly quoted in the report of the Mahalanobis Committee on Distribution of Income and Wealth.
4. In any systematic study of distributional changes, it is customary to confine oneself to the standard parameters like the *mean* and the *standard deviation*, which are used for computing the coefficient of variation often used as an inequality measure for comparative purposes. What is not so common but yet very important from a societal point of view is the concept of *threshold*. It is the level of income or expenditure, for instance, below which no member of the society can exist. If this minimum parameter shows a decline through time, the entire society is declining. It is the weakest link in the chain, and this poorest of the poor can be characterised by the threshold parameter. Suryanarayana and Iyengar have examined trends in the distributions of consumption in rural and urban India, with and without adjustments for price movements.

References

Dandekar, V.M. and N. Rath (1971), *Poverty in India*. Indian Institute of Political Economy.

Gopalan, C.B.V. Rama Sastry, and S.C. Subramaniam (1971). *Nutritive Value of Indian Foods*. Hyderabad: National Institute of Nutrition.

Iyengar (1989). Recent Studies on Poverty in India: A Survey. *Journal of Quantitative Economics*, Vol. 5(2): 223-37.

Iyengar, N.S., S.N. Joshi, and M. Gopalakrishna (1992). A Bayesian Approach to Measurement of Poverty in India. In P.K. Goel and N.S. Iyengar (ed) *Bayesian Analysis in Statistics and Econometrics*. New York: Springer-Verlog, pp. 379-87.

Iyengar, N.S., L.R. Jain and T.N. Srinivasan (1968). Economies of Scale in Household Consumption: A Case Study. *Indian Economic Journal*, Vol. 15: 465-77.

Krishnaji, N. (1981a). On Measuring the Incidence of Undernutrition—A Note on Sukhatme's Procedure. *Economic and Political Weekly*, XVI (22): 989-92.

——— (1981b). On Measuring Incidence of Undernutrition—What is Consumer Unit? *Economic and Political Weekly*, XVI (37): 1509-10.

Minhas, B.S., L.R. Jain, S.M. Kansal and M.R. Saluja (1987). On the Choice of Appropriate Consumer Price Indices and Data Sets for Estimating the Incidence of Poverty in India. *Indian Economic Review*, 22: 20-49.

Murthy, M.N. (1967). *Sampling Theory and Methods*. Calcutta: Statistical Publishing Society.

Rao, C.R. (1952). *Advanced Statistical Methods in Biometric Research*. New York: John Wiley.

Sukhatme, P.V. (1977). *Nutrition and Poverty*. Lal Bahadur Sastri Lecture. New Delhi: IARI.

——— (1978). Assessment of Adequacy of Diets at Different Income Levels. *Economic and Political Weekly*, XIII (31-33):1373-84.

——— (1981a). Measuring the Incidence of Undernutrition—A Comment. *Economic and Political Weekly*, XVI (23): 1034-36.

——— (1981b) On Measurement of Poverty. *Economic and Political Weekly*, XVI(32): 1318-24.

——— (1993). *Diet, Disease and Development*. London: Macmillan.

Suryanarayana, M.H., and N.S. Iyengar (1984). On Poverty Indicators. *Economic and Political Weekly*, XIX: 897-902.

APPENDIX

In the Bayesian approach, the analyst assumes the probabilities $p(\theta)$ *a priori* and obtains additional information about the occurrence of the status of nature θ in the state space Θ. He then incorporates the sample evidence x and formulates the corresponding likelihood function, $f(x \mid \theta)$, of $\theta \in \Theta$. Now he applies *Bayes Theorem* to combine his initial beliefs represented by his prior probability function, $p(\theta)$, to select an optimal action in his action space A. Let $f(\theta \mid x)$ be the posterior (revised) probability distribution function. Then, the theorem states:

$$\textit{revised probability} \propto \textit{a priori probability} \times \textit{likelihood} \tag{1}$$

Bayesians normally assume a quadratic loss function of the type

$$L(d, \theta) = c(d - \theta)^2, \tag{2}$$

where c is a constant and d is the decision function. Then, the mean, $E(\theta \mid x)$, of the posterior distribution $f(x \mid \theta)$, given the sample observation x, minimizes the loss function and when it exists, it is known as the Bayes estimate of θ. The expected *opportunity loss* in using this estimate is proportional to the variance of the posterior distribution.

Generalized Likelihood Estimate (GLE): Consider the method of maximum likelihood estimation *(MLE)* which is widely used in statistics. The classical method involves determining the estimate $\theta^* = z(x)$, after observing the sample x that maximizes the likelihood function $f(x \mid \theta)$. That is, if for each $\theta \in \Theta$, $L_x(\theta) = f(x \mid \theta)$, then the classical statisticians search for an estimate θ^* such that for all $\theta \in \Theta$, $L_x(\theta^*) \geq L_x(\theta)$. The estimate θ^* is called the *MLE* of θ. On the other hand, the Bayesians derive the revised probability function $f(\theta \mid x)$, such that for each $\theta \in \Theta$, given the sample observation x, and finding an estimate θ^{**} such that for all $\theta \in \Theta$, the *GLE* θ^{**} satisfies the condition $f(\theta^{**} \mid x) \geq f(\theta \mid x)$. The same is true in obtaining the regression parameter β and the error variance in the standard regression model, $y = X\beta + \varepsilon$.

From a Bayesian point of view, a hypothesis testing problem can be defined as: H_1: $\theta \in \Theta_1$; H_2: $\theta \in \Theta_2$, where $\Theta_1 \cup \Theta_2 = \Theta$ such that $\Theta_1 \cap \Theta_2 = \emptyset$. Also, there is an opportunity loss function $L(a, \theta)$ defined on, $A \times \Theta$ where, $A = \{a_1, a_2\}$ such that a_1 is the action 'accept the null hypothesis' and a_2 is the action 'reject the null hypothesis'. The opportunity loss function satisfies the following properties: $L(a_1, \theta) = 0$ for $\theta \in \Theta_1$; $L(a_2, \theta) = 0$ for $\theta \in \Theta_2$; $L(a_1, \theta) > 0$ for $\theta \in \Theta_2$ and $L(a_2, \theta) > 0$ for $\theta \in \Theta_1$. Correspondingly, we have a decision function d that maps sample outcomes in the sample space S to action in A as follows: $d(x) = a_1$ for $x \in S_1$ and $d(x) = a_2$ for $x \in S_2$, where $S = S_1 \cup S_2$, such that when $\theta \in \Theta_1$, $\alpha(d, \theta) = p_\theta\{x \mid d(x) = a_1\}$ (Type I error) and $\beta(d, \theta) = p_\theta(x \mid d(x) = a_2$ when $\theta \in \Theta_2$ (Type II error). Based on this representation, the Bayesian approach determines the optimal test.

The classical approach does not allow this kind of formalism, but recognizes the dangers of committing Type I and Type II errors. However, since it is not possible to minimize both these errors simultaneously, the classical statisticians prefer to fix α (level of significance or size of the test) and find the test that maximizes the power $(1 - \beta)$ of the test. One might argue that the selection of $\alpha\ (d, \theta)$, the probability of committing Type I error, is personalist. Also, the classicals assume that $L\ (a_1, \theta) = 1$ for $\theta \in \Theta_2$ and $L\ (a_2, \theta) = 1$ *for* $\theta \in \Theta_1$. In a sense, this may also be considered a subjective choice on the part of the classical statisticians. For detailed references, see Iyengar (1989); Iyengar (with Joshi and Gopalakrishna, 1992).

Poverty, Income Inequality and Growth: An Analysis with Illustrations from Indian Data

N. SREENIVASA IYENGAR

1. INTRODUCTION

The concern for growth and social justice has become really genuine with the realization that the much expected "trickle-down" on which so much hope for poverty alleviation is based, has not come about. While this is true in general about most of the developing countries of the world, the problem has become particularly acute in the case of India, where nearly four decades of economic planning has not caused any substantial amelioration of poverty. In fact, doubts still persist about the kind of strategy adopted, growth achieved, and the net benefits growth.

However, the impact of the efforts made to achieve "growth with equity" should finally get reflected in the material conditions of living of the people. This is particularly true of India where, with low earnings, any increment to income goes largely to augment consumption rather than saving.

In this study, an attempt is made to examine some of the issues arising from growth and inequality, on the basis of the published National Sample Survey (NSS) data on household consumption. An attempt is also made to construct inequality indices for the unobserved income distributions using some simplistic assumptions. An index of poverty, closely related to Rawl's concept of social justice, is also developed and illustrated. In the regional

* Institute for Economic and Social Change, Bangalore. I wish to thank Anita and Srinivasa V. Giri for providing valuable technical support for this paper.

analysis, an attempt is made to analyze the inter- and within-state variations in levels and distributions of household consumption and income, over a period of time. Changes in rural and urban sectors are separately analyzed.

This study, like all other bold attempts, also suffers from a number of limitations: the rather restrictive assumptions, incomplete and inaccurate data that are known to contain large but unknown errors of measurement. Such errors impose severe limitations on our result, which are briefly mentioned in the concluding section.

2. EARLIER STUDIES

Most of the research on distribution in India is currently based on the NSS consumption data (See Iyengar, 1978). This is not to say that we do not at all have any estimates of income distribution for India. In fact, there are both derived and direct estimates, prepared by the National Council for Applied Economic Research (NCAER). For derived estimates, references can be made to early works by Lydall (1960), Iyengar and Mukherjee (1961), Ahmed and Bhattacharya (1972), Iyengar and Jain (1974), Ojha and Bhat (1974), and Iyengar and Suryanarayana (1996), which were based on indirect estimation of income distribution.

Once the National Sample Survey Organization (NSSO) started publishing its reports on household consumption expenditures, the focus was shifted primarily to studies on consumption. This is because of at least three reasons:

(a) the NSS estimates are comparable over time and across space;
(b) consumption is a better and direct measure of the level of living and hence a dependable indicator of social welfare; and
(c) consumption is a better proxy for permanent income compared to measured income (Permanent Income Hypothesis).

Most of the Indian studies using NSS data have been concerned with measuring the degree of and trends in inequality in the distribution of household consumption and the incidence of mass poverty. A detailed review of some of the important studies can be found in Srinivasan and Bardhan (1974). Almost all these studies established a broad decline in the extent of inequality in the nominal consumption distribution in rural India. However, Ahluwalia (1978) presented convincing statistical arguments for the decline. Studies by Radhakrishna and Sharma (1976) pointed out a similar declining trend in the urban areas.

Earlier studies (Mahalanobis, 1962; Iyengar and Bhattacharya, 1965; and Vaidyanathan, 1974) argued that the price-unadjusted consumption distributions are unlikely to reveal the underlying trends in real consumption distributions, since price movements have differential impacts on the poor and non-poor segments of the population. Iyengar and Jain (1976) demonstrated that the inter-decile price movements were such that the poorer sections were affected by inflation more adversely than the rich were during the period, 1963-64 to 1973-74. Interestingly, Vaidyanathan (1974) observed that the decline in the Lorenz ratio between 1957-58 and 1967-68 was smaller in real terms than at current prices. Radhakrishna and Sharma (1976) established that inequalities in living levels, after adjustment for prices, started widening during the period beginning from 1963-64.

The relative inequality in nominal consumption across the states of India has been studies by some researchers. Following Iyengar (1964), Vaidyanathan (1974) computed the Lorenz ratios on the basis of NSS data for four Rounds and found that the extent of inequality had no strong, systematic relationship with per capita consumption, the relative levels of inequality being virtually unstable over time. Using the same methodology, Ahluwalia (1978) extended the analysis to all 14 States of India, covering the period from 1956-57 through 1973-74. His conclusions were:

(a) Significant trend decline in the States of Andhra Pradesh, Assam, Karnataka, Madhya Pradesh, Punjab, Haryana, Tamil Nadu, and Uttar Pradesh;
(b) No significant trend decline in Bihar, Gujarat, Maharashtra, Orissa, Rajasthan, West Bengal; and
(c) No significant trend increases in Kerala.

Chatterjee and Bhattacharya (1974) found that the rural-urban differentials at the national level declined between 1951-52 and 1967-68. Their study also showed a decline in inter-state disparities in nominal per capita consumption. They ranked the States on the basis of per capita consumption for various rounds and found the ranking rather insensitive to inter-temporal shifts, to project a fairly stable picture. Another important purpose of their study was to make adjustments for the inter-state differences in prices and to examine the relative positions of the States. After price adjustment, they found that Madhya Pradesh, which had a consumption level below the national average before adjustment, stood above the national average. Just the reverse was the case with Tamil Nadu and West Bengal.

However, most of the studies in the literature being based on one or more rounds of NSS at different points of time, it is not easy to make any precise statements about the type of improvement achieved, either in the size of the consumption cake or in its distribution.

3. THE PRESENT APPROACH

Let c be the household monthly consumption in rupees per capita, as defined by the NSSO. It is a measure of the welfare that accrues to the household, and varies from one household to another, depending upon the size and composition, location and region, season, occupation, and several other social demographic factors. It can be treated as a random variable, with a distribution function $F(c)$ or a probability mass function $f(c)$ which is the first derivative of *F*. The distribution function may be broadly characterized by two parameters which are of economic interest—the mean consumption level (M_c) and an inequality or dispersion parameter (L_c). Changes over time in the value of M_c indicate growth or decline, depending on the sign. Similarly, an increase or decrease in L_c over time can be interpreted as deterioration or improvement in the distribution of aggregate consumption. For the dispersion parameter, it is preferable to use the Lorenz measure rather than the variance or the coefficient of variation. Moreover, these dispersion parameters are comparatively less sensitive to different types of inter-household transfers (Sen, 1973) and more affected by grouping of the individual observations (Prasad and Iyengar, 1984). The Lorenz Ratio and the Lorenz curve are easily constructed and interpreted for comparing economic size distributions. They are least affected by grouping of observations and appear most appropriate as tools of analysis for the NSS grouped data that are readily available. Among the other important advantages are the decomposability and analytical facility in cases of linear transformation of data.

The Lorenz Curve always lies below the line of equal distribution, and the Lorenz Ratio is twice the area bound by the Lorenz Curve and the line of equality. This ratio is designed to lie between 0 and 1, and expressed as a percentage independent of the currency in which incomes and consumption are observed. The ranking of income or consumption distributions on the basis of the Lorenz Ratio is not necessarily the same as the ranking based on the coefficient of variation. Interestingly, the Lorenz Ratio has an upper bound. It is possible to compute the Lorenz Ratio for the income distribution on the basis of an observed distribution of consumption using the well-known identity, $y = c + s$, where y and s represent the income and saving of households respectively, and c, the residual, is consumption. Appendix A gives supporting mathematical justification for choosing the Lorenz Ratio in our present analyses. The Lorenz Box diagrams serve as a useful descriptive tool for studying inter-temporal and spatial shifts in size distributions. When these statistical tools are applied to sample survey data, it is customary to attach the margins of error to our conclusions. It is possible to estimate standard errors for all estimated Lorenz Ratios in large samples (Iyengar, 1960), based on realistic assumptions.

As already mentioned, the NSS estimates of consumption and its distribution are available in current prices. But changes in consumption valued in current prices do not reveal the real magnitudes, particularly in a context marked by inflation. Also, making judgments about changes in the distribution becomes rather difficult because of differences in consumption patterns between consumption groups and changes in relative prices. This problem is to be overcome by differential price mechanism using separate price indices for each consumption group. For this purpose, we need appropriate price indices for each sector in each State. However, in the absence of reliable retail price indices for all commodity groups at national and State levels, one prefers to use Vaidyanathan's (1974) procedure in preference to that of Iyengar and

Jain (1978) in constructing the required price indices. Accordingly, we can use the All-India Wholesale Price Indices with base 1961-62 as 100, in the construction of the consumption-specific price indices. For this purpose, the weighting diagrams are obtained from the respective NSS distributions, for the base year. Given the relevant data, the price deflator for the ith fractile in the tth year is given by

$$d_{it} = \Sigma_j \, p_{jt} \, w_{if} \qquad \dots (1)$$

The summation goes from j = 1 (cereals and cereal substitutes) to j = 11 (other non-food items); for t^{th} round of NSS, p_{jt} denotes the price index for the pth commodity group and w_{if} is the weight of commodity groupy in the aggregate price index, assumed fixed on the basis of the 1961-62 survey. For illustrative purposes, we consider the following commodity groups for the construction of differential price deflators:

1. Cereals and cereal substitutes
2. Pulses and pulse products
3. Milk and milk products
4. Fish, egg, and meat
5. Edible oils
6. Sugar
7. Fruits, vegetables, and nuts
8. Other food items
9. Clothing
10. Fuel and light
11. Other non-food items

The relevant wholesale price indices for these groups have been taken from the Reserve Bank of India's annual reports on currency and finance (For details, see Suryanarayana, 1980). It may also be noted that we have used linear interpolation to convert the distribution of consumption available in fixed-interval form into equal-frequency distributions.

4. MAIN FINDINGS

The estimates of per capita consumption *(M_c)* and the Lorenz Ratio *(L_c)* based on current price distributions are given separately for the rural and urban sectors of India for the period from 1961-62 to 1973-74 in Table B-1 in Appendix B. We find a marked difference in levels of living and improvement in their distributions in both the sectors. This may tempt us to conclude that there was indeed a marked increase in welfare levels in either sector.

The 'within inequality' was also estimated using the NSS class intervals 0-8, 8-11, 11-13, 13-15, 15-18, 18-21, 21-24, 24-28, 28-34, 34-43, 43-55, 55-75, 75 and above. The estimates show that grouping bias is generally within 5 per cent of total inequality (see, Suryanarayana, 1984c). Table B-l gives estimates of per capita consumption and the Lorenz Ratio based on current-price distributions: India (rural and urban), 1961-62 to 1973-74. Table B-2 shows estimates based on deflated distributions. A closer look at Tables B-1 and B-2 reveals that the movements in the estimates at current prices are different from those indicated by the price-adjusted estimates. Further, it may be noted that:

(i) During the period 1961-62 to 1973-74 taken as a whole, there was no significant trend in per capita real consumption in either of the two sectors;

(ii) Per capita real consumption generally fell in the early phase of the study period and rose more or less steadily from around 1967-68 in both rural and urban areas;

(iii) Per capita real consumption in the terminal year, 1973-74, was generally no higher than that in the initial year in both the sectors; and

(iv) The Lorenz Ratios also did not show any consistent trend; they fluctuated around a stagnant trend irrespective of the sector.

Thus, on the whole, it appears that with stagnant consumption and inequality levels, there was neither growth nor reduction in inequality in the two sectors at the national level during the period 1961-62 to 1973-74.

5. THE POOREST OF THE POOR

The Rawlsian criterion of justice requires that the appropriate strategy should be one of *maxmin*. Operationally, justice is considered to have been delivered if improvement takes place at least for the 'poorest of the poor". Accordingly, we adopt a positive concept of poverty and measure changes in levels of living of this poorest household using the three-parameter log-normal framework. (For further details, see Iyengar and Suryanarayana, 1984). The per capita consumption of the poorest households, denoted by c_p, measured in 1961-62 rupees, are given in Appendix Table B-3. We also measure the distance between the average household consumption (M_c) and the consumption level of the poorest household, i.e. $M_c - c_p$. The mean poverty ratio may be defined as $(M_c - c_p)/M_c$ or $I - \gamma$, say. The γ-parameter shows movements in c_p in relation to M_c. It can be seen that the poorest household's consumption level also deteriorated up-to the mid-sixties and recovered marginally in the late-sixties in both the sectors. The mean poverty gap broadly shows that the poorest experienced relatively faster deterioration (improvement) than the average household during periods of decline (growth) in overall consumption levels. Thus, it appears that the poorest household still continues to be the most vulnerable part of the society. The estimates of the subsistence level and the mean poverty gap are reproduced from Iyengar and Suryanarayana (1984, 1996) and shown in Appendix Table B-4.

6. SECTOR ANALYSIS

In this section we propose to consider the regional dimension of poverty and inequality in India. The Fifth Five Year Plan (Perspective Planning Division, Planning Commission, Government of India, 1973) had specifically stressed the need for increasing rural consumption levels at a much faster rate than the urban in order to reduce the rural-urban disparity. However, there is no way of verifying how far this target of reducing the inter-sector disparities has been achieved. We are, again constrained by the non-availability of information about the inter-sector price differences. Hence, we have to look at the behavior of inter-sector disparities in nominal per capita consumption, which shows a high degree of fluctuation over time (Appendix Table B-5).

Another way of examining the question of inter-sector equity would be by examining the pattern of movements in their consumption levels. However, we do not find any strict relation in the pattern of fluctuations in real consumption levels in the two sectors. But it appears that the declines in consumption levels have been of a much higher order for the rural sector than for the urban in the initial years. This cannot be a firm evidence for making any definitive statements though. Yet, they seem to indicate a situation where the living levels are relatively more stable in the urban sector than in the rural, even though neither of them experienced any significant improvement.

7. INCOME INEQUALITIES IN INDIA

A direct comparison of the means and inequalities in the *income* distributions could be of considerable interest, and hence worth attempting. However, it is not easy in the absence of any comparable data on personal income distributions for India. The scanty NCAER data on households' income and saving have very limited use for any inter-temporal or inter-state study in real terms. However, a few crude attempts have been made from time to time by Indian scholars, using an indirect approach and combing published aggregate data on consumption and savings with standard macro-economic identities. See, Iyengar (1978), for a survey of economic literature on income distributions in India. In what follows, we present a somewhat different approach, based on an early study by Iyengar and Suryanarayana (1996), for estimating the *income* inequality. In this approach there is no need to assume any model of income distribution.

Suppose we have an empirical estimate of the linear consumption function,

$$c = \alpha + \beta y \qquad \text{... (2)}$$

where the variable c is consumption, as already defined, and y is household's disposable income; c and y are household variables. The Greek letters α and β are unknown parameters. The Lorenz-Gini index of income inequality (L_y) is given by

$$L_y = [2\,M_y]^{-1} \int_0^\infty \int_0^\infty |u - v|\; dF(u)\, dF(v) \qquad \text{... (3)}$$

where M_y is the mean disposable income. From Appendix A it is easy to establish the following property:

$$L_c M_c = \beta\, Ly\, M_y \qquad \dots (4)$$

If one has direct estimates of M_y, M_c, and β, then L_y could be easily derived. These computations are shown for 11 successive rounds of NSS, which provides the basis for estimating M_c and L_c. For M_y the Central Statistical Organization's National Income Statistics were used. A *consistent* estimate of β was obtained by applying Wald's method, rather than the standard least squares, in fitting the straight line, $c = \alpha + \beta y$, since both the variables c and y are subject to unknown errors of estimation. For basic data, see Appendix Table B-7. The main limitations of pour approach may be stated as follows:

We ought to have estimated the parameters of the consumption function using cross-section data for each year. But, constrained by the non-availability of such information, we have sought an easy way-out by using the time series data. This approach may have two implications: One, the income inequality is always a constant multiple of the consumption inequality, which, on *a priori* grounds, may appear unrealistic. Further, it implies that whatever may be the changes in the structure of income distribution, it is always related to consumption distribution according to a fixed relationship which is time-invariant. Two, the estimate of the slope parameter β (marginal propensity to consume) depends upon the sample size chosen. Hence, for the same consumption inequality, one may get different estimates of income inequality, depending on the number of observations in the sample. However, these limitations appear rather minor in the context of the social importance attached to income inequality estimates when they are not readily available.

8. INTER-STATE ANALYSIS

For the inter-state analysis, we consider trends in per capita consumption and disparities, in nominal and real terms, and try to compare the 'welfare levels'.[1] For purposes of analyzing state disparities, we consider the following 14 states of the Indian Union: (1) Andhra Pradesh, (2) Assam, (3) Bihar, (4) Gujarat, (5) Karnataka, (6) Kerala, (7) Madhya Pradesh, (8) Maharashtra, (9) Orissa, (10) Punjab-Haryana, (11) Rajasthan, (12) Tamil Nadu, (13) Uttar Pradesh, and (14) West Bengal. The estimates of per capita consumption at current prices for the rural and urban sectors for each of the selected States in Appendix Tables B-5 and B-6. As expected, they show significant improvements in levels of living. However, for analytical purposes, we construct growth indices of consumption in current prices for all the States, by sectors. With 1961-62 as the base, we construct these indices just for two years 1967-68 and 1973-74. This is because of our finding at the national level that consumption in real terms declined up-to 1967-68 and recovered in the later years. Such growth rates are presented in It can be seen that for the rural sector of all the States, consumption grew at a much faster rate during the second period, 1968-69 to 1973-74. The growth has been particularly faster in the rural areas of Andhra Pradesh, Bihar, Kerala, Maharashtra and Rajasthan. We find a similar picture of growth for the urban sector also. The second period analysis shows particularly marked growth in the States of Assam, Bihar, Karnataka, Kerala, and Punjab-Haryana. However, given that prices tend to move at a faster rate in the urban areas, the above statements would imply a situation where the rural-urban disparities in consumption have declined at least in the second group of States. The estimated coefficients of variation of per capita consumption are shown for all the States, in Tables B-8 and B-9 in Appendix B. They show a tendency for inter-State disparities to widen over time in the rural sector. The per capita consumption estimates (see, Tables B-8 and B-9 in Appendix B), after deflation for price changes, do not show much improvement in levels of living. The all-India pattern of decline in real consumption upto mid-sixties and recovery thereafter, was determined for the rural sector of Andhra Pradesh, Gujarat, Karnataka, Kerala, Madhya Pradesh, and West Bengal. The urban sector of any State does not show such pattern. Rather, it exhibits frequent fluctuations. A comparison of the terminal year results reveals that in most of the States, the real standard of living had remained either stagnant or declined. Coming to inequality in current and fixed prices, we find some improvement in the distributions over time in almost all of the selected States. However, the inter-State disparities do not show any significant trend. The State rankings on the basis of the Lorenz Ratio estimates do show some degree of consistency as judged by their rank correlation. The Lorenz Ratio estimates based on re-constructed consumption distributions in 1961-62 prices are shown in Tables (Appendix B). As expected, they show no improvements in the distributions. In fact, we find significant trend increase in inequality in rural West Bengal and trend decrease in the rural sectors of only four States—Assam, Karnataka, Punjab-Haryana, and Tamil Nadu. On the other hand, we find a declining tendency, though not significant, in urban Punjab-Haryana. We find definite signs of deterioration, particularly in urban Kerala and Tamil Nadu.

We also examined how the distributions behaved *vis-a-vis* per capita consumption over time in each State. The correlation between the two appear significant only in the rural sector of Andhra Pradesh and Assam; it is significant also in the urban sector of Assam and Bihar. The correlation is positive and, hence, implies that whenever there is increase in average per capita, the distribution of total consumption deteriorates and *vice versa*. The coefficient being positive for both rural and urban sectors of Assam, it appears that in the entire State, the benefits did not percolate to the poorest sections to the same extent as to the rich in periods of growth. Significantly enough, it would also imply that during years of hardship the poorer sections suffer less compared to the better-off. The coefficients are found to be negative though not significant for a few other State sectors. That only indicates a mild tendency for distributions to improve during periods of growth in consumption and *vice versa*.

9. GROWTH AND EQUITY: A STATE-WISE ANALYSIS

In this section, examine the performance of each State sector on the growth and distribution front during 1961-62 to 1967-68, 1967-68 to 1974-74, and 1961-62 to 1973-74. We may interpret the numbers as follows:

(i) Assam is the only State where growth occurred in terms along with an improvement in the distribution, between 1961-62 and 1967-68. The worst combination of a decline in living level and a worsening of the distribution occurred in the States of Gujarat, Kerala, Madhya Pradesh, Maharashtra, Orissa, and Uttar Pradesh,

(ii) During the second period, the States of Bihar, Gujarat, Karnataka, Madhya Pradesh, Orissa, Punjab-Haryana, Rajasthan, Tamil Nadu, and Uttar Pradesh experienced growth and equity. Assam fell into the worst case,

(iii) Between 1961-62 and 1973-74, Andhra Pradesh, Bihar, and Rajasthan experienced growth with equity while West Bengal saw decline and deterioration,

(iv) In the urban sector, between 1961-62 and 1967-68, no State experienced growth with equity, while as many as eight States suffered decline and deterioration,

(v) The second period saw a majority of States, with the exception of Assam, decline in consumption and deterioration in distribution, and

(vi) Between 1961-62 and 1967-68, Karnataka, Madhya Pradesh, Punjab-Haryana experienced growth and equity, while Tamil Nadu, Maharashtra, Orissa, and West Bengal saw decline and deterioration.

10. SUGGESTIONS FOR FURTHER WORK

Our analysis though based on limited set of data, points to the fact that growth defined as a sustained improvement in the levels of living has yet not taken place in India. Official policies and programs to contain excessive consumption and income inequalities seem to have arrested the tendency for inequalities to widen in rural areas, but urban inequalities in income distributions are slightly on the increase.

We find that it is the poorest of the poor who constitute the most vulnerable section of the society. In rural areas, the poorer sections appear to have benefited more as compared with the affluent sections during the years of general improvement. However, in the years of decline, it is also the poor that suffered more.

At the regional level, the picture differs from one State to another, and even within a State, between rural and urban sectors. However, one common feature in their development is that none of them really experienced any significant growth in consumption in real terms, let alone improvements in their consumption distributions. However, the picture in Punjab-Haryana is quite different. In this State economic development was accompanied by a narrowing of inequalities. In rural West Bengal, on the other hand, there was a marked deterioration in the distribution of consumption. A similar deterioration is discernible in the case of urban Tamil Nadu.

The inter-State data on mean consumption levels and extent of inequality, suggest that there is no clear-cut evidence for the Kuznets hypothesis of inverted U-shaped development. This might, perhaps, because of the narrow range of observations on consumption levels available for India.[2]

Our conclusions are, no doubt, subject to a number of limitations, arising from inaccurate or incomplete data and conceptual errors with regard to prices. In our pursuit of egalitarian goals, it is necessary to define the degree of inequality, which is optimal from the points of view of efficiency and social justice. Of course, this concept is normative. We have not succeeded in studying this and other related aspects of policy affecting the Indian economy.

Finally, the calculation of income inequality, even after effecting appropriate corrections for grouping bias, may be questioned on the ground that the *marginal propensity to consume (mpc)* was imported from an entirely different source. To overcome this objection, it might have been appropriate to use the estimates of *mpc* computed from the same source. However, this is not feasible in practice unless the NSSO or other Survey Organizations periodically collect and publish regular data on both consumption and income, along with other relevant household variables.

NOTES AND REFERENCES

1. The social aggregate welfare (W) can be considered as a convex function of the two parameters (M_c) and (L_c), appearing in the distribution of c. W increases with M_c but decreases as L_c increases. Mathematically, we may write $W = \psi(M_c, L_c)$, with the partial derivatives $\partial\psi/\partial M_c$ and $\partial\psi/\partial L_c$ moving in opposite directions. It may be possible to view this as a neoclassical production function from which the merits of the growth strategy *vs.* redistribution policy. The highest level of welfare, if it exists, occurs for the optimal combination of M_c and L_c. The Indian States can be ranked on the basis of M_c and L_c, and the inter-state disparities in their development graphed. Perhaps, the Kuznets hypothesis may also be checked from Table B-7.
2. In recent years the NSSO has come up with more detailed published reports, extending upto 1993-94, so that it is definitely possible to update our conclusions, to cover both pre- and post-Economic Reform periods.

REFERENCES

Ahmed, M. and N. Bhattacharya (1972): "Size Distribution of per capita Personal Income in India: 1960-61 and 1963-64," *Economic and Political Weekly*, Special Number, Vol. VII, Nos. 31, 32, and 33, pp. 1581-88.

Ahluwalia, M.S. (1978): "Rural Poverty and Agricultural Performance in India", *The Journal of Development Studies*, Vol. XIV, No. 3, pp. 298-323.

Bardhan, P.K. (1974): "The Pattern of Income Distribution in India: A Review" in T.N. Srinivasan and P.K. Bardhan (Ed.) *Poverty and Income Distribution in India*, Statistical Publishing Society, Calcutta, pp. 103-38.

Chatterjee, G.S. and N. Bhattacharya (1974): "On Disparities in per capita Household Consumption in India" in TNS-PKB (Ed.) (*op. cit.*), pp. 183-214.

Eapen, M. (1970): "Some aspects of the Unemployment Problem in Kerala", *Working Paper No. 79*, Centre for Development Studies, Trivandrum.

Iyengar, N.S. (1964): "Contributions to Analysis of Consumer Expenditure", *Doctoral Thesis*, Indian Statistical Institute, Calcutta.

Iyengar, N.S. and M. Mukherjee (1961): "A note on the derivation of size distribution of personal household income from a given size distribution of consumption expenditure", Paper presented at the Second Indian Econometric Conference, Waltair.

Iyengar, N.S. (1989): "Recent Studies on Poverty in India: A Survey", *Journal of Quantitative Economics*, Vol. 5, No. 2, pp. 223-37.

Iyengar, N.S. (1978): "Size Distribution of Consumption and Income" in *ICSSR: A Survey of Research in Economics*, Vol. VII, Allied Publishers Pvt. Ltd., Bombay, pp. 277-316.

Iyengar, N.S. (1997): "Poverty Concepts and Measurement: A Review", *Artha Beekshan*, 6, pp. 40-49.

Iyengar, N.S. (2002): "Inequality and Relative Poverty", *Indian Economic Journal*, 49, pp. 125-28.

Iyengar, N.S. and M. Mukherjee (1961): "A note on the derivation of personal household income from a given size distribution of consumption expenditure", Paper presented at the Second Indian Econometric Conference, Waltair.

Iyengar, N.S. and N. Bhattacharya (1965): "On the effect of differentials in consumer price index on measures of inequality", *Sankhya*, Series B, Vol. 27, pp. 47-56.

Iyengar, N.S. and L.R. Jain ((974): "A Method of Estimating Income Distributions", *Economic and Political Weekly*, Vol. IX, No. 51, pp. 2103-09.

Iyengar, N.S. and L.R. Jain (1976): "On Inflation and its Differential Effects", *Indian Economic Review* (New Series), Vol. 11, No. 1, pp. 69-83.

Iyengar, N.S. and M.H. Suryanarayana (1983): "On Poverty Indicators", in S.P. Gupta (Ed.) *Regional Dimensions of India's Economic Development*, Uttar Pradesh State Planning Commission, Lucknow, pp. 310-28. Also in *Economic and Political Weekly*, Vol. XIX, Nos. 22 and 23, pp. 897-902.

Iyengar, N.S. and M.H. Suryanarayana (1986): "On growth and equity in Indian Planning during 1961-62 to 1973-74," *Indian Economic Journal*, Vol. 33, No. 4, pp. 53-83.

Kakwani, N.C. (1980): *Income Inequality and Poverty*, Oxford University Press, London.

Kuznets, S. (1955): 'Economic Growth and Income Inequality", *American Economic Review*, Vol. SLV, No. 1, pp. 1-26.

Lydall, H.F. (1960): "The Inequality of Indian Incomes", *Economic Weekly*, Special Number, Vol. 12, Nos. 23-25, pp. 873-74.

Mahalanobis, P.C. (1962): "A Preliminary note on the Consumption of Cereals in India," *Bulletin of International Statistical Institute*, Vol. 34, No. 4, pp. 53-56.

National Sample Survey Organization (2002): *Household Consumer Expenditure and Employment-Unemployment Situation in India, 2001-02*, Government of India: Ministry of Statistics and Programme Implementation, New Delhi.

Ojha, P.D. and V.V. Bhat (1974): "Pattern of Income Distribution in India, 1953-55 to 1963-65" in TNS-PKB (Ed), *op. cit.*, pp. 163-66.

Perspective Planning Division (1973): *A Technical Note on the Approach to the Fifth Plan of India: 1974-79*, Planning Commission, Government of India, New Delhi.

Prasad, Shailaja and N.S. Iyengar (1976): "A Note on the Effect of Grouping of Data on Inequality Measures", Paper presented at the 22nd Indian Econometric Conference, Bangalore.

Radhakrishna, R. and Atul Sharma (1976): "Inflation and Disparities in Levels of Living," *Indian Economic Journal*, Vol. 23, No. 4, pp. 364-373.

Ramakrishnan, M.K. (1984): "Some Results on Gini Ratio," Discussion Paper, Stat-Math Unit, Indian Statistical Institute, Bangalore Centre.

Sen, A.K. (1973): *On Economic Inequality*, Oxford University Press, Bombay.

Vaidyanathan, A. (1974): "Some Aspects of Inequalities in Living Standards in Rural India" in TNS-PKB (Ed.), *op. cit.*, pp. 214-41.

APPENDIX

The standard definitions and related mathematical properties of the Gini-Lorenz measure are given in Appendix A. The numerical results of analysis are presented in a series of Tables in Appendix B.

APPENDIX A

Let $F(y)$ be the distribution function (DF) of $y \geq y_o > 0$, so that F raises from 0 to 1, as y moves up from y_o to ∞. It remains 0 in the interval $(0, y_o)$, as there is no household in the population that can exist below the critical minimum (y_o). For this reason, it may be called the "threshold" or "subsistence" level. In Rawl's theory of social equilibrium it assumes great importance as the weakest link in a gold chain. To determine the level of y_o empirically is just as important as determination of inequality. The two other parameters in F that are of economic interest are, as already stated, the mean or growth parameter (M_y) and the inequality parameter (L_y). The Gini-Lorenz index of inequality is defined by

$$L_y = [2M_y]^{-1} \int_u \int_v | u - v | \, dF(u) \, dF(v) \qquad \text{... (A.1)}$$

This can also be written as

$$M_y L_y = \int_t F(t) [1 - F(t)] \, dt \qquad \text{... (A.2)}$$

where M_y is the mean of y. This formula can be useful in decomposition of inequality as between and within sectors. Let F_1 be the first incomplete moment of y, i.e.

$$F_1(y) = [M_y]^{-1} \int_t^y dF(t) \qquad \text{... (A.3)}$$

As a matter of fact, $F_1(y)$ is the cumulative proportion of total income of all the households receiving an income not exceeding y. In empirical contexts, it is represented as the vertical axis of the Lorenz curve. The horizontal axis represents $F(y)$, so that a typical point on the Lorenz curve is represented by (F, F_1). The following properties may be noted:

(a) $F_1(y) \leq F(y)$ *for all* y. ... (A.4)

In other words, the Lorenz curve always lies below the line of equality or the leading diagonal, $F_1(y) = F(y)$. This appears to be the case for all positively skewed distributions, like income.

(b) $L_y = 1 - 2 \int_t F_1(t) \, dF(t)$ ... (A.3)

(c) $L_y \leq CV(y) / \sqrt{3}$,

CV being the coefficient of variation of y. ... (A.4)

A.4 asserts that the Lorenz Ratio has an upper bound. Finally,

(d) $L_{\alpha+\beta y} = \beta M_y L_y / [\alpha + \beta My]$ ... (A.5)

From the above equations, it follows that ranking of income distributions on the basis of their Lorenz Ratio is not necessarily the same as ranking based on the coefficient of variation. Property (A.5) gives the rule for computing the Lorenz measure for linear functions of income, such as the consumption function often employed in Keynesian macro-economic analyses.

It would be interesting if we can assume a standard model for the personal income distribution $F(y)$ and derive various results therefrom. This could be the only way for determining the threshold y_o, which may be of interest to social scientists who may be concerned with the poorest of the poor. Their rehabilitation should receive highest priority from Indian scholars and policy-makers.

The empirical Lorenz Ratios were obtained using the familiar trapezoid rule

$$L = 1 - \Sigma (p_i - p_{i-1}) (Q_i + Q_{i+1}) \quad \text{... (A.6)}$$

where the summation goes from $i = 1$ to k, k being the number of class intervals into which the sample households are grouped on the basis of the per capita consumption; p_i is the cumulative proportion of households in the first i groups and Q_i is their share in the aggregate consumption. These ratios can be estimated both in current prices and constant prices. *Total inequality* is the sum of the "between group inequality" and the "within group inequality". The latter arises from grouping of households and is expressed as

$$\Sigma (p_i - p_{i-1}) (q_i - q_{i-1}) L_i \quad \text{... (A.7)}$$

where L_i is the Lorenz Ratio for the distribution of households within the y-class interval (y_{i-1}, y_i). Suppose we assume a uniform distribution for the distribution within the income class interval Δy_i. Then

$$L_i = [\Delta y_i]/3 (y_i + y_{i-1}), \forall \text{ i} = 1, 2, \ldots, k. \quad \text{... (A.8)}$$

and, when y_k is not finite, $L_i \to 1/3$. (see, Ramakrishnan, 1984).

If PL is arbitrarily defined as the poverty line based on a minimal budget for buying the household needs like food, clothing, housing, education, and health care, then $F(PL)$ is the poverty ratio; it is also referred to in Indian poverty literature as the head-count ratio, where $F(.)$ is the distribution function of the household per capita expenditure or any other economic size variable like income. Relative poverty, in contrast to absolute poverty, does not depend upon the "poverty line" so defined. Here, poverty line is assumed to be proportional to the mean of the distribution. However, the constant of proportionality is arbitrary, varying between zero and one. That is to say, the relative poverty ratio is simply $F\ (k\ M_c)$, when one is using household per capita consumption c as his size variable. It makes sense to assume k as one-half. One may link poverty with inequality assuming plausible parametric forms for the observed distributions as shown in Iyengar (1997, 2002).

APPENDIX B

TABLE B1

Estimated per capita Consumption and Inequality in Current (Constant) Prices: Rural and Urban India: 1961-62 to 1973-74

Year	*Per capita consumption (Rs. Per month)*		*Inequality (Lorenz ratio)*	
	Rural	*Urban*	*Rural*	*Urban*
1961-62	21.73 (21.73)	30.86 (30.86)	0.3130 (0.3100)	0.3566 (0.3566)
1963-64	22.37 (20.31)	32.96 (30.24)	0.2974 (0.3000)	0.3596 (0.3630)
1964-65	26.44 (20.88)	36.03 (29.51)	0.2936 (0.3080)	0.3492 (0.3640)
1965-66	28.40 (20.84)	36.65 (27.90)	0.2972 (0.3090)	0.3385 (0.3540)
1966-67	30.90 (19.78)	41.54 (27.94)	0.2934 (0.3120)	0.3368 (0.3620)
1967-68	33.40 (18.80)	44.82 (27.19)	0.2908 (0.3150)	0.3324 (0.3650)
1968-69	33.29 (19.49)	46.04 (28.58)	0.3051 (0.3260)	0.3292 (0.3550)
1969-70	34.70 (19.45)	50.39 (29.75)	0.2928 (0.3140)	0.3403 (0.3640)
1970-71	35.31 (19.30)	52.85 (30.14)	0.2831 (0.3010)	0.3265 (0.3490)
1972-73	44.17 (20.58)	63.33 (32.96)	0.2993 (0.3220)	0.3410 (0.3710)
1973-74	53.01 (21.51)	70.77 (30.60)	0.2758 (0.2990)	0.3013 (0.3460)

Source: Suryanarayana (1984).

TABLE B2

Estimates of "Total" Inequality of Consumption, Subsistence Level, and Mean Poverty Gap: *1961-62 to 1973-74* *(in contant prices of 1961-62)*

Year	*Inequality*		*Subsistence level*		*Mean poverty gap*	
	Rural	*Urban*	*Rural*	*Urban*	*Rural*	*Urban*
1961-62	0.3160	0.3621	3.84	8.64	0.8235	0.7200
1963-64	0.3019	0.3685	4.78	6.61	0.7646	0.7814
1964-65	0.3085	0.3707	3.72	6.82	0.8218	0.7689
1965-66	0.3117	0.3616	2.27	7.44	0.8911	0.7333
1966-67	0.3143	0.3707	0.92	5.54	0.9535	0.8017
1967-68	0.3204	0.3796	1.28	6.81	0.9319	0.7495
1968-69	0.3285	0.3663	1.64	8.23	0.9159	0/7120
1969-70	0.3178	0.3852	4.21	7.97	0.7835	0.7321
1970-71	0.4043	0.3732	5.71	5.44	0.7041	0.8195
1972-73	0.3243	0.3780	6.44	7.60	0.6871	0.7694
1973-74	0.3046	0,3443	3.33	3.85	0.8452	0.8742

Source: Iyengar and Suryanarayana (1984).

TABLE B3

Estimates of Inequality in Distributions of Income and Consumption: All-India, 1961-62 to 1973-74 in Current Prices

Year	*Full and partial inequality as measured by the Gini-Lorenz ratio**			
	Consumption Inequality		*Income Inequality*	
	Partial	*Full*	*Partial*	*Full*
1961-62	0.3315	0.3347	0.4069	0.4108
1963-64	0.3216	0.3248	0.3948	0.3987
1964-65	0.3069	0.3115	0.3767	0.3824
1965-66	0.3107	0.3149	0.3814	0.3865
1966-67	0.3094	0.3146	0.3798	0.3862
1967-68	0.3042	0.3104	0.3734	0.3810
1968-69	0.3201	0.3267	0.3929	0.4010
1969-70	0.3137	0.3213	0.3851	0.3944
1970-71	0.3063	0.3144	0.3760	0.3858
1972-73	0.3116	0.3166	0.3825	0.3886
1973-74	0.2898	0.2965	0.3557	0.3639

*The full Gini-Lorenz ratio is normally computed from grouped size distribution data, using the groupweights and group means. Usually, the trapezoidal rule of numerical integration is employed to compute the area of concentration. This ratio captures only the inter-group variations in the group means, but cannot reflect the intra-group inequality. The latter cannot be ignored, since it introduces a negative bias in inequality estimation to some extent.

TABLE B4

Estimates of Rural per capita Consumption by State (in current prices)*

(*In Rs.*)

State	*Year*										
	1961-62	*63-64*	*64-65*	*65-66*	*66-67*	*67-68*	*68-69*	*69-70*	*70-71*	*72-73*	*73-74*
Andhra Pradesh	20.11	20.76	26.45	27.66	29.14	30.46	31.47	34.54	34.35	39.79	50.57
Assam	22.23	26.43	29.30	30.66	36.83	41.53	37.57	37.69	40.37	41.67	52.03
Bihar	19.00	21.31	26.60	30.31	29.02	33.36	29.78	33.65	33.15	41.20	56.01
Gujarat	22.58	22.69	26.98	26.57	28.99	31.35	34.53	34.38	36.64	51.70	54.49
Karnataka	25.33	20.43	25.23	26.42	29.29	31.93	31.21	31.08	35.89	44.53	52.32
Kerala	21.07	20.36	22.30	21.80	24.56	28.54	36.18	31.07	36.12	42.19	55.35
Madhya Pradesh	21.46	23.37	26.30	28.07	29.57	31.77	31.15	33.68	32.88	40.72	50.39
Maharashtra	19.91	21.72	25.16	27.74	28.33	30.66	32.04	33.22	36.39	41.55	52.27
Orissa	17.40	19.35	20.61	21.50	26.20	30.24	28.24	28.70	28.86	34.96	42.66
Punjab-Haryana	32.76	28.66	37.52	37.05	44.82	45.01	52.36	53.93	53.97	72.62	74.16
Rajashtan	23.48	23.13	30.55	32.98	37.14	38.42	41.06	41.26	35.39	51.98	64.01
Tamil Nadu	22.53	23.39	24.55	24.57	28.59	29.61	30.02	32.08	29.98	37.70	47.74
Uttar Pradesh	22.73	21.51	27.09	29.46	33.15	35.14	35.09	34.00	29.98	37.70	47.74
West Bengal	20.83	21.69	23.18	26.71	28.98	32.63	29.85	32.86	33.32	38.46	47.50
**Coefficient of Variation (%)	16.25	11.10	15.38	13.88	17.04	14.34	18.42	17.58	16.54	21.17	14.27

* At present, India has more than 14 States. The new States are (15) Haryana, (16) Jammu & Kashmir, (17) Tripura, (18) Jarkhand, (19) Chatisgarh, (20) North-Eastern States, and (21) Group of Union Tetritories. The NSSO 56th Round Report (2002) gives detailed data for the year 2000-2001. See, Government of India (2002).

** The variation is across the States and may be taken as a measure of regional inequality.

TABLE B5

Estimates of Urban Monthly per capita Consumption by States in Current Prices

(in Rs.)

State	*Year*										
	1961-62	*63-64*	*64-65*	*65-66*	*66-67*	*67-68*	*68-69*	*69-70*	*70-71*	*72-73*	*73-74*
Andhra Pradesh	25.19	28.16	31.78	34.65	37.34	40.49	44.44	47.68	49.27	56.32	65.30
Assam	39.20	46.64	42.66	42.23	60.44	58.70	55.93	60.52	64.24	60.75	72.78
Bihar	34.96	29.89	32.41	33.86	38.95	44.23	44.14	47.15	51.02	59.91	68.36
Gujarat	31.73	33.03	31.19	33.59	38.35	42.42	40.21	44.24	48.83	57.78	66.76
Karnataka	27.21	25.88	32.44	33.84	34.25	38.33	42.90	45.60	50.71	57.89	66.50
Kerala	25.82	27.29	30.11	24.93	35.45	34.81	38.39	44.11	47.63	58.27	68.93
Madhya Pradesh	26.70	29.93	34.44	32.86	40.08	40.20	44.35	45.77	50.37	61.88	65.50
Maharashtra	36.66	37.24	44.48	46.87	49.46	50.34	52.06	62.20	63.60	74.34	79.78
Orissa	33.71	31.92	31.79	34.35	41.98	47.21	48.26	54.66	52.75	62.35	70.09
Punjab-Haryana	29.27	34.33	36.95	36.48	44.12	47.35	51.69	55.30	62.02	75.00	79.58
Rajasthan	28.92	32.53	34.21	34.37	39.93	44.60	46.49	46.72	54.13	63.87	68.76
Tamil Nadu	29.74	31.47	34.34	34.11	35.31	41.22	40.68	43.70	44.69	54.02	64.78
Uttar Pradesh	25.40	29.17	30.05	31.97	38/87	42.67	41.08	42.55	45.17	53.55	60.81
West Bengal	38.42	41.66	41.13	42.77	48.31	51.94	53.52	59.32	60.69	68.23	80.76
Coefficient of Variation (%)	15.83	17.42	13.50	16.63	16.96	13.78	11.92	13.83	12.65	10.98	8.81

TABLE B6

Rural Monthly per capita Consumption by States in Constant Rupees of 1961-62

State	*Year*										
	1961-62	*63-64*	*64-65*	*65-66*	*66-67*	*67-68*	*68-69*	*69-70*	*70-71*	*72-73*	*73-74*
Andhra Pradesh	20.11	18.85	20.98	20.28	18.62	17.22	18.45	19.35	18,82	19.55	20.80
Assam	27.23	23.74	22.74	22.04	23.04	22.42	21.61	20.84	21.60	19.71	19.90
Bihar	19.00	19.96	23.93	25.85	21.75	24.41	20.71	18.62	17.67	24.22	26.85
Gujarat	22.58	20.68	21.39	19.57	18.66	17.74	20.17	19.33	19.75	25.06	21.57
Karnataka	25.33	13.57	20.01	19.60	18.98	18.26	19.20	17.52	19.77	21.67	21.05
Kerala	21.07	18.60	18.05	16.47	16.26	16.97	22.29	18.05	20.42	21.70	23.77
Madhya Pradesh	21.46	21.21	20.70	21.95	18.87	17.85	18.29	18.91	18.01	19.20	19.84
Maharashtra	19.91	19.73	19.95	20.53	18.47	17.48	19.12	18.78	19.97	20.53	21.42
Orissa	17.40	17.49	16.04	16.97	16.39	16.63	16.23	15.89	15.69	16.69	16.71
Punjab-Haryana	32.76	26.32	30.72	28.11	30.14	26.91	31.50	31.15	30.11	36.76	31.53
Rajasthan	23.47	21.19	24.58	24.53	24.34	22.28	24.46	23.42	19.47	25.61	25.57
Tamil Nadu	21.72	21.21	19.47	18.12	18.36	16.82	17.70	18.01	16.44	18.57	19.57
Uttar Pradesh	22.72	19.35	21.41	21.68	21.35	19.84	19.61	19.28	19.40	19.94	20.59
West Bengal	20.83	21.47	18/17	19.43	18.32	18.15	17.27	18.34	18.15	18.71	19.14

Source: Suryanarayana (1984).

TABLE B7

Urban Monthly per capita Consumption by States in Constant Rupees of 1961-62

State	*Year*										
	1961-62	*63-64*	*64-65*	*65-66*	*66-67*	*67-68*	*68-69*	*69-70*	*70-71*	*72-73*	*73-74*
Andhra Pradesh	25.19	25.70	25.68	25.98	24.59	23.97	26.97	27.51	27.58	28.59	27.52
Assam	39.20	42.45	34.64	35.39	40.11	35.31	34.43	35.81	36.48	30.94	30.36
Bihar	34.96	26.94	26.94	27.60	29,65	29.91	27.83	29.88	32.24	28.67	31.45
Gujarat	31.75	30.38	25.45	25.51	25.65	25.50	24.72	25.82	27.49	29.76	28.52
Karnataka	27.21	23.61	26.33	25.67	22.88	22.85	25.99	26.32	28.42	29.73	28.53
Kerala	25.82	25.00	24.81	19.16	24.13	21.33	23.93	25.92	27.08	30.92	30.99
Madhya Pradesh	26.70	27.44	28.06	24.91	26.85	24.12	27.33	26.89	28.60	31.83	28.11
Maharashtra	36.66	34.30	36.93	36.19	33.93	31.43	33.08	37.63	37.05	39.99	35.46
Orissa	33.71	29.21	25.87	26.45	28.13	28.47	30.01	32.66	30.47	32.61	30.45
Punjab-Haryana	29.27	31.73	30.35	27.88	29.73	28.72	31.56	32.22	34.75	38.44	34.03
Rajasthan	28.92	29.87	27.85	25.94	26.54	26.51	28.07	26.90	30.14	32.44	29.06
Tamil Nadu	29.74	28.65	27.90	25.86	25.57	24.66	24.90	25.39	25.15	27.83	27.75
Uttar Pradesh	25.40	26.75	24.46	24.24	26.00	25.54	25.23	24.93	25.61	27.58	26.13
West Bengal	38.42	38.24	33.85	32.16	32.59	31,86	33.45	35.41	34.99	35.90	35.04

Source: The estimates for Kerala, Punjab-Haryana, and Tamil Nadu are from Suryanarayana (1980) and those for Karnataka are from Suryanarayana (1984).

TABLE B8

State-wise Coefficient of Correlation between per capita Consumption and Consumption Inequality, Computed from NSS Inter-round Variations

State	Sector		State	Sector	
	Rural	Urban		Rural	Urban
Andhra Pradesh	0.5746*	0.2607	Maharashtra	0.1722	0.1364
Assam	0.5720*	0.5232*	Orissa	(–) 0.1380	0.1053
Bihar	0.4038	0.5398*	Punjab-Haryana	0.2661	(–) 0.1593
Gujarat	(–) 0.0626	0.0593	Rajasthan	(–) 0.0246	0.4971
Karnataka	0.4564	0.0006	Tamil Nadu	0.4362	(–) 0.3161
Kerala	0.4850	0.4598	Uttar Pradesh	(–) 0.1590	(–) 0.1146
Madhya Pradesh	(–) 0.1350	(–) 0.0962	West Bengal	0.1033	(–) 0.0409

*Significant at 10 per cent level for a two-tail test.

Source: Estimates for the rural sector are from Suryanarayana (1984).

TABLE B9

Growth and Inequality Changes between 1961-62 and 1973-74 in Indian States

Growth	*Rural Distribution*		*Urban Distribution*	
	Improvement	*Deterioration*	*Improvement*	*Deterioration*
Positive	Andhra Pradesh Bihar Rajasthan	Kerala Maharashtra	Karnataka Madhya Pradesh Punjab-Haryana Uttar Pradesh	Andhra Pradesh Kerala Rajasthan
Negative	Assam, Gujarat, Maharashtra, Karnataka Madhya Pradesh Punjab-Haryana	West Bengal	Assam, Bihar Gujarat	Maharashtra Orissa Tamil Nadu West Bengal

SECTION II

POVERTY: CONCEPTUAL AND ANALYTICAL ISSUES

The Economy of Dependency and Sustained Poverty

SUNIPA DAS GUPTA AND RANESH KUMAR RAY

INTRODUCTION

Let us begin this discussion with a summary of the budget speech delivered by Jaswant Singh, which reflects upon the fact that poverty is an well accepted fact in India:[1]

> " . . . the core of the country is releasing national creativity and further accelerating the reform process to eradicate poverty—a moral and economic issue of our time. . . ."

What then is poverty ? —A fall out of total financial collapse that strikes the conscience of the society ? Since 1970s the issue of poverty has been at the focus of academic debates and discussions. But the truth lies in the fact that poverty imparts sense of embarrassment amongst the better-off, and thereby compels an academic quest into its definition and complex nature.

TWO CONCEPTS OF POVERTY

Poverty may exist in both absolute and relative senses. While absolute poverty refers to lack/absence of subsistence income/consumption expenditure/medical facilities, relative poverty is said to be related to property rights and distributional aspects. From this point of view relative poverty is not only a problem of the third world, but also that of the developed countries where private ownership of property and inequality in wealth may exist. In this context it is interesting to note the fact that relative and absolute poverty may co-exist in a society. For example, primitive societies revealed a low standard of living and hence poverty and distress in absolute sense. But with the evolution of modern society, standard of living improved, private property rights evolved. Growth could heal absolute poverty, leaving behind traces of relative poverty, as in the cases of advanced countries. But the myth of growth and non-sustainability of poverty in absolute terms broke as per the backward economies. Here relative poverty feeds absolute and in turn gets fed by it, thereby generating a vicious cycle of poverty where the backward economy gets entrapped.

The formidability of poverty looms large on the backward economy, as the size of the cake is small. As Monimohan Mukhopadhay[2] points out that the smallness of the size of the cake barely leaves any share for the lowest decile of the population to survive. A.K. Sen too feels that some people starve because there is not enough food for their consumption, i.e., there are some others who are getting relatively more for consumption. Herein private ownership becomes pertaining to impoverishment. Here poverty is not the common/general outcome, but comes specific for those who are deprived of certain scopes and facilities. The distinction between rich and poor becomes valid. However, Sen feels that of different causes of poverty, starvation, malnutrition etc. are also important. He tries to define poverty in the context of subsistence/lack of it given the prevalence of absolute poverty in the backward block. And growth here is no panacea to the malady.

Our purpose is to study why poverty is sustained in a dependent economy, like India and the hypothesis of poverty eradication with sustained growth gets denied.

We can begin our discussion with the analysis of the plunder of the Indian economy during colonial rule causing persistent poverty.

India in the Process of Colonization: To begin this subsection let us quote from Life of T. Munro[3], which would bring forth our contention,

> "The consequence of the conquest of India by British arms would be, in place of raising, to debase the whole people." This brings us to the history of colonization through de-industrialization and economic drain in India.

India and Britain got integrated to the world capitalist system almost at the same time. But while Britain developed, India underwent a process of de-development. However in the precolonial phase India was no less developed than Britain, if no more. In fact Indian industry and agriculture were far more advanced. Though British economists try to attribute the backwardness of the Indian economy to the traditional, self-sufficient rural economic system, Marx criticized colonial exploitation and plunder to be its sole reason. Marx knew that the primary condition for the transformation of a pre-capitalist system into mature capitalism is the process of primitive accumulation. As capitalism develops, industrialization occurs. The focus of the economy shifts from agriculture to industry. Population pressure on agriculture diminishes. Organized production replaces handicrafts and cottage industries. Productive capacity persistently develops, and surplus value replaces primitive accumulation.

But this transformation process got hindered by British subjugation. No surplus value could be generated either from industry or from agriculture for India. Instead the primitive was drained out to Britain to feed the factories emerging out of the Industrial Revolution. It fed British capitalism at home. De-industrialization catered to this propagation of under development. Imperialism did not allow independent capitalism to develop in the colonies. But converted the latter into appendages of the imperialist system.

East India Company not only opened up trade in India, but also gradually took control over the produce of Indian industry, agriculture and trade. Prior to 1765 the company carried out its operations with the capital that they brought from home. But after obtaining the Diwani in 1765 they started making use of the revenue collected from India for trading here, and remitted a considerable portion of the profit home, i.e., they appropriated the surplus value of their Indian subjects through trade activities. It is interesting to note that the source of profit was no longer restricted to trade, rather it was embedded in land revenue system. Land revenue got integrated to the foreigners' profit and was utilized for the domestic economy. Productive capacity gradually dried up. The colonial economic relationship provided the major network for drain of surplus from Indian agriculture and industry.

The colonial power operated with two objectives in view:

1. to get a market for British manufactures in India; and
2. to plunder natural resources from India to Britain to feed the British industries at home.

With the transference of power from the Company to the Crown, the pattern of foreign trade between India and Britain got distinctly reverted. Indian textiles succumbed to the aggressive competition faced from British textiles in India. In 1815 British cotton textile imported in India was of 0.40 million gauge. In 1839 it increased steeply to 100.05 million gauge. In 1849 the total volume of cotton yarn and thread exported from India to England was around 0.69 million pounds; while imported textile use in India increased by as much as 3 times in 1860. W.H. Wilson directly accused the British policy to have destroyed Indian looms. Manchester textile mills were saved at the cost of a 50 to 60% price cut on Indian raw materials exported to Britain, along with a 70 to 80% export duty on Indian finished goods exported to Britain.

The introduction of railways striked the final nail to the coffin. Indian markets were completely subjugated. By 1846-55, 9.15% of British imports were targeted for the Indian market. This within 1876 to 1885 shot up to 12.6%. As commented by Ifran Habib, traditional Indian handicrafts has no other way but to collapse in the face of such indiscriminate import aggression. By the end of the 19th century most of the traditional industries in India were destroyed. Even the controlled development of modern organized industry could not compensate for this heavy loss. Nationalist economists attributed the destruction of traditional industries as the cause of pauperization and unemployment in the economy. These accelerated with the pace of de-industrialization. Romesh Dutt finds de-industrialization to mark the beginning of an epoch of abysmal distress in the history of India. This process of 'flight of capital' from India was a desired outcome of British economic policies and has been referred to as the "economic drain" by Dadabhai Naoroji. This colonial interface created a vicious circle of under development in the colonies, which can be represented by the following figure:

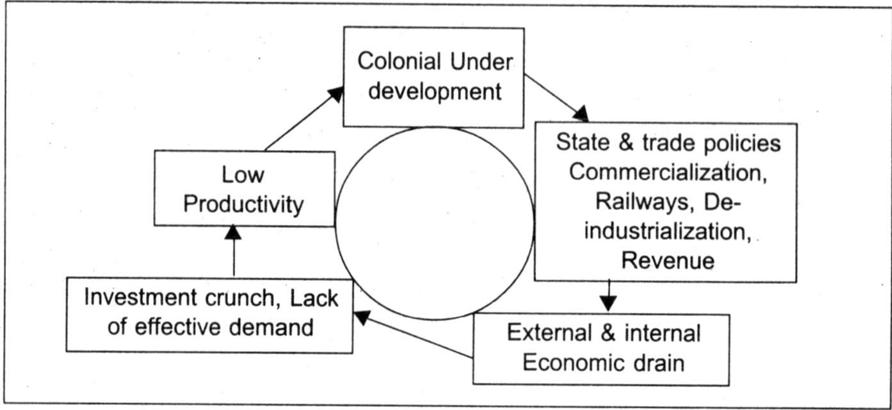

Let us now try to explain the growth retarding process under commercialization and surplus expropriation in the Simple Keynesian income-expenditure equation[4]:

$$Y = C + I + X - M - T$$

where taxes reduce the disposable income left for consumption alone, we get:

$$C = c\,(Y - T) \text{ and } M = m\,(Y - T)$$

Therefore, $Y = c\,(Y - T) + X - m\,(Y - T) - T$
$= cY - mY - T\,(1 + c - m) + I + X$

or, $(1 - c + m)\,Y = -T\,(1 + c - m) + I + X$

Differentiating we get the loss of income due to unit increase in taxes as:

$$dY/dT = -\,(1 + c - m)/(s + m)$$

The above case can be offset by a unit increase in exports which would change income as follows:

$$dY/dX = 1/(s + m)$$

It is no denying that with increase in the pace of commercialization of agriculture there was short-run expansionary effect generated through export.

But according to the fiscal arrangements in colonial India net exports, dX, were completely dampened by equivalent net rise in taxes, dT, so that we get the net change in income as:

$$dY/dT + dY/dX = (m - c)/(s + m) = 1\ (1/m - c + 1)$$

This explains the rather paradoxical result of growth retardation in the face of short-run expansion of export surplus. Under a situation where export revenues are withheld from circular flow of income within the country, through net taxes, the country will experience a foreign trade multiplier effect which is larger/smaller depending on the relative value of the marginal propensity to consume (c) and the marginal propensity to import (m). Clearly, the income generating effect of such an economy's export sector operates in reverse gear since the economy has to transfer abroad by political necessities, the entire value of net export earnings.

In our attempt to identify the flow of unilateral transfers from India, we find that these financial transfers were more than a sacrifice of short-run command over external resources, but also initiated the process of contraction in money supply and credit squeeze within the domestic economy.

THE COUNCIL BILL MECHANISM

India's trade and exchange links with the rest of the world appeared to have achieved a fair degree of sophistication by the 1890s. The decade witnessed the emergence of a network of banks and business nouses in India, largely controlled by Europeans, which supported official attempts to achieve a smooth flow of remittances to England on account of overseas liabilities. By the turn of the century these liabilities were as large as the sum spent to meet official liabilities in India. The Council Bills (CB) drawn on the Indian treasury appeared as the formal device employed by the British rulers to siphon-off sterling proceeds of India's export surpluses to England. By the Act of 1905, CBs were allowed to exceeds home charges and were thus sold up to a value which was acceptable in the market. This in turn provided a route for retaining in England the entire amount of India's export surplus which could now even build up externally held assets for the India office in London, under the directives of the Bank of England, which soon gained authority over the financial policies of the Indian government. The process, in terms of the Simple Keynesian model implied a leakage in the income stream. Compounded with the monetary squeeze and credit strigencies, this made the colonial economy encounter a sluggishness in demand and related depression in growth.

Mode of remittances between India and England can be represented on next page.[5]

CBs sold by the India office to exchange banks served as a device to retain in London India's sterling revenue from net export earnings abroad. In India the treasury paid to the exchange banks an equivalent amount in rupees against the CBs. The rupee payments were the counterpart funds to sterling

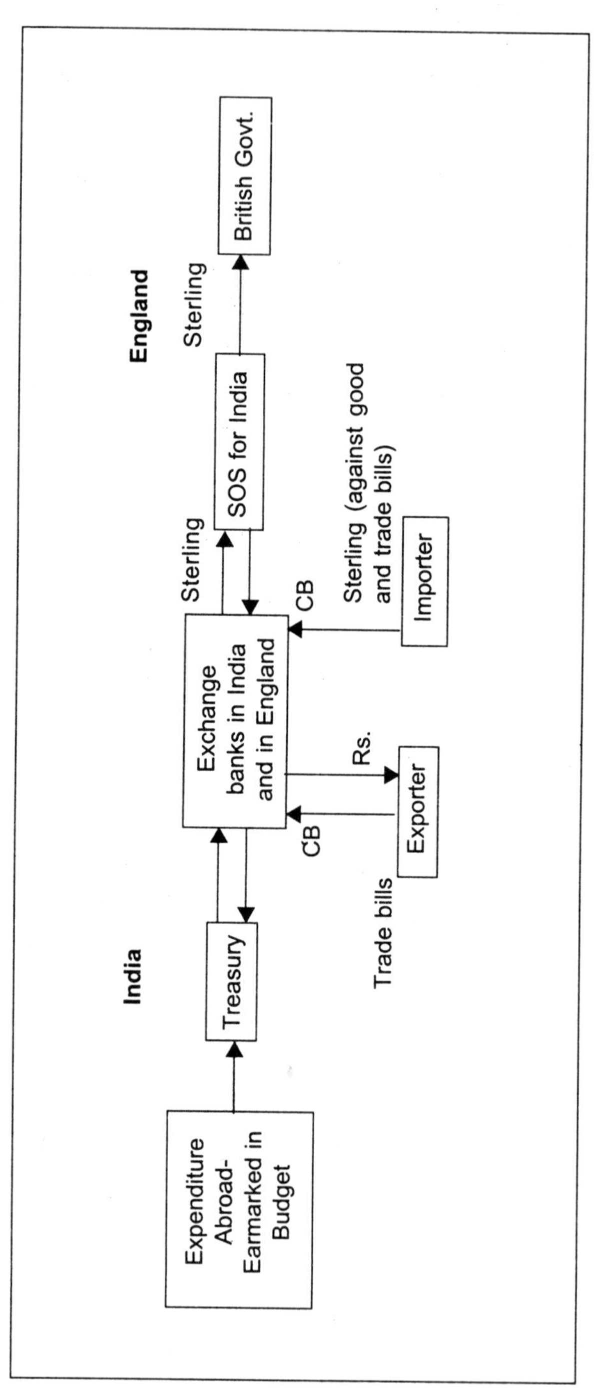
England
India
British Govt.
Sterling
SOS for India
Sterling
Sterling (against good
and trade bills)
CB
Importer
Exchange
banks in India
and in England
Rs.
Exporter
CB
Trade bills
Treasury
Expenditure
Abroad-
Earmarked in
Budget

disbursed under the budgetary head of Expenditure Abroad. About the middle of the 19th century, a new stage set in for English capitalism. With capital investment at home reaching its saturation point, the export of capital began in earnest and British 'nèt investment' in the colony reached as much as 114%. British capitalism gradually converted itself into monopoly capitalism during this period on facing impending competition from Germany and the USA. international supremacy of British imperialism gave birth to a protectionist colonoialism particularly after 1870. In such a context the CB network provided a handy tool to the finance department of the India government to further strengthen the unilateral transfers. In 1830 it closed the mint to free coinage on public demand, on recommendation of the Royal Commission on Indian currency. This on one hand increased the demand for CBs in England, as a form of remittances. On the other hand, it de-linked the rupee rate from the market fluctuations in silver prices. Rupee coins worth Rs. 10 million were melted off without any new coinage, causing a net withdrawal of Rs. 525 million from circulation in 1893-98. As an institutional set-up for financial transfers from India were tightened up, during the subsequent periods net remittances were met through CB network. As a consequence the India office received a regular flow of sterling remittances from India's trade surplus and other sterling receipts in London. After 1905 the SOS permitted the sell of CBs not only to cover the current and capital expenses, but also up to that limit which could be absorbed by the market. Soon bills actually sold by the SOS by and large exceeded the sum earmarked as the annual budgetary estimates of CB sales. The additional amount accumulated could add up to the foreign assets of the SOS, ordinarily maintained as non-interest bearing deposits with the Bank of England and/or as sterling securities invested in England, thereby easing out the financial flows to the SOS. Thus the aforesaid discussion makes it clear to us that though the phase of capital export might reveal a partial reversal in the pattern of capital flow, but it was of course, superficial. The principal and returns on this capital belonged to Britain and not to India and would only swell in time the size of the Indian tribute. According to Romesh Dutt,[6] taxation in India by the British rule was

> ". . . but the moisture raised from the Indian soil . . . now descends as fertilizing rain largely on other lands, not on India."

India in the Process of Pauperization

The First World period evidenced an aggressive market capturing race on part of Britain in India. During this period much of capital inflow in India was preeminently for railway construction. But railways failed to suffice as the forerunner of development in India, because neither was there any proletariat uprising in England, nor could India broke-off from the yoke of foreign servitude. Instead the construction of railways in India was profitable in two ways:

1. next to Australia, India became the largest consumer of Britain for locomotive, reaping high profits for Britain; and
2. railway construction was geared to the political exigencies of British in India.

Thus within 1875-76 to 1897-98 and 1898-99 to 1913-14 expenses on "Army and Marine" staggered up highly. These expenses falling within the unproductive budget category was clearly encouraged by the provision for notional transfers incorporated in the budget. In this context let us take a look at the pattern of overseas expenditure under home charge from 1861-62 to 1913-14. Quantitatively, the weight of debt service charges in respect of railway and irrigation loans appear to predominate aggregate overseas expenditure during this period. These loans were chargeable under productive heads. And the railways alone attributed for 47% of total expenses on home charges. Though Vera Anstey commented that ". . . the money could not have been as cheaply elsewhere as in London", it is worth-mentioning at this point that this cheap borrowing practice in the name of public work was but a camouflaging of the imperialist ploy. With notional transfers incorporated in the budget, revenue earmarked to finance public work, was in effect used to subsidize unproductive expenditure by canceling old unproductive debt, hence a natural tendency on part of the government was to continue with its unproductive expenditure in both countries and covering them up by taxes and loans raised from the market. Moreover, sterling loans contracted against public work expenditure in India, being statutory under the Select Committee recommendation, increased liquidity held by the India Office in England, as a part of the public work expenses in India were met in rupees. Adoption of this procedure led to a steep rise in the size of productive debt held as a proportion of total debt in rupee and sterling. This was the outcome of a policy contrived by the colonial rulers to finance politically sensitive and economically unviable expenditures of the government thus while in countries like Western Europe and America, railways acted as catalyst of industrial, in India it became a device of economic drain and pauperization.

On the other hand, during this period the sum of British overseas and domestic investment ($I_d + I_t$) was actually smaller than the sum of savings at domestic origin and investment income from abroad (S_d + i). Looking at the data for 1870 we get:

I_d: 64 million, I_t: 55 million, S_d: 111 million, i: 35 million, all payable in sterling.

The excess of (S_d + i) over aggregate invesment ($l_d + I_t$) was used to supplement domestic consumption in Britain, particularly of the working class. Indirect evidences of such distinct improvement has been provided by Sunanda Sen[7]:

"Aggregate consumption of items like tea, which had a low income elasticity of demand went up—a fact which indicates that tea entered the consumption basket of a wider section of British people, a large section of whom were presumably from the upcoming working classes."

The picture conforms to a mirror image for colonies—especially India. In so far as capital invested in railways helped to subjugate the Indian market for British industry, it inhibited the export of capital for other sectors.

Tariffs were so manipulated as to make India an utterly unprotected economy and apart from plantation and jute industry no other branch of the economy could attract British capital with any expectation of high returns. Simultaneously the railways aggravated the onslaught of British imports by their ability to furnish exports in return. Between 1878 to 1901, the total value of exports rose from 67.43 to 12 crore, being comprised of food grain, raw cotton, hides and skin, opium, tea and oilseeds. Thus a real shift took place in Indian agriculture—a shift in relative acreage to non-food and food crops meant for exports. Thus the ploy was no longer to levy direct tribute through land revenue, but the exploitation of India as market and source of raw material. Such ruthless seizure of markets more than sufficed to crumble down old craft industries. But there was no prospect for new industries to develop and offset the corresponding output and employment loss.

The implementation of this policy was largely helped by a general price rise during the second half of the 19th century. This in turn led to enhancement of rents, while land revenue to be paid by the zamindars to the government remained stationary throughout the entire settlement Thus to fulfil its purpose of forced commercialization the government sided with the large proprietors and repressed the peasants. At the same time the role of usury too became very important in facilitating the subversion of small peasant cultivation and the growth of landlord and rich peasant agriculture. It was parasitically feeding up on the growth process by the moneylender being a claimant to a large share of the rural surplus, excluding the mass.

PAUPERIZATION OF RURAL INDIA

By the second half of the 19th century the alliance formed between the modern Indian landlord and imperialism polarized the rural population and pauperized millions. Pauperization found its reflection through famines that striked the frequently and on large scales, culmination into the great famines of 1896-97, 1899-1900 and the Great Bengal Famine of 1943; with the last being attributable to British War-time policies, apart from other reasons.

The Bengal famine was essentially a rural phenomenon. Urban areas like Calcutta saw it mainly in the form of influx of rural destitute. This desitution can be understood in terms of shifting exchange entitlements. This period evidenced a drastic decline in the exchange rate against agricultural labor. While there was a sild upsurge in rice price, there was no matching movement in wage rate. When price index rose to 221 by November, the wage rate fell in absolute terms and the index of exchange declined to 38. By July 1943 it was below 30 for three months in succession. Besides, the exchange rate of a number of commodities *vis-a-vis* rice fell. Of these fish and bamboo umbrellas, milk, haircuts etc. can be mentioned. According to Prof. A.K.Sen, rice was not short in supplies,—rather it was unavailable to those who lacked the purchasing power.

On the other hand, the famine saw the emergence of a class of 'middle man' who made high profits from the war-time inflationary condition and therefore had a vested interest towards the continuum of the price spiral. As already mentioned the government was in alliance with them to achieved its imperialist target. Bengal during this time saw an unprecedented scale of civil and military expenses which were financed by priting notes; though a substantial part of it was recoverable as sterling balances owned by British. But it was this recoverable expenditure which tended to have a stronger inflationary effect, than India's expenditure on her own account, given the fact that under the Indian monetary system the RBI was 'entitled to print notes worth about two and a half times their total value'. Thus the famine was a 'boom famine' related of Western autocracy in the colonies. Hence it is no surprise that the Bengal famine was never officially declared as a 'famine' which would have brought in obligation to work programs and relief operations specified by the 'Famine Code'.

An important aspect of the famine was an uneven expansion in the income and purchasing power, particularly of those in military and civil defense work, in army, in industries and commerce stimulated by war. The economic position of agricultural labourers, fishermen, artisans and other workers in unorganized production was weak due to their relative abundance. Their large scale destitution or switching over to occupations like husking paddy, which is much below subsistence revealed the deep wound of relative poverty from which the society suffers even today.

From the above discussion it become clear that the intention of British policies in India had been to keep alive the semi-feudal class relations to aid to their objective of drain of the colonial resources. Semi-feudsl class relations in Indian agriculture not only keeps it backward, but it also implicitly points out to the fact that absolute and relative poverty lie intertwined in Indian economy. Class relations in India are important determinants of the pattern of accumulation, which in turn reflects the destitution and relative deprivation of the vulnerable mass, exploited through the nexus of the proprietary classes.

POVERTY IN INDEPENDENT INDIA—A LEGACY OF THE PAST

Note that the transfer of power in India was simply a compromise that the British were compelled to make, finding themselves already weak in the changed co-relation of forces in the international arena, after the Second World War, and being repeatedly thwarted by unforeseen revolutionary upsurges of different classes of people in India. But the compromise was purposefully made with the Indian 'comprador bourgeoisie'—a class created by the imperialist power to serve to its ends. This brings home the fact that it would require more than a revolution in India to destory the vestiges of imperialist aggression.

By the late 19th century imperialism underwent immense changes in modalities and instrumentation. In the post-Word War period scenario as the return on capital investment fell, capitalism adhered to a monopolistic policy in the home industries and searched for new investment fields abroad. Now trade, aid, and operations of the MNCs, TNCs, became the tools of the imperialist conquests. This marked the beginning of a new epoch of finance capitalism, designed to appropriate primitive surplus from the colonies. The Process was further eased out through the purposive power dealing which created a complex class matrix within the colonies:

1. a landed gentry to deploy much of the potential surplus from land through luxury consumption and purchase of landed property;
2. merchants extracting surplus through commercial speculation; and
3. bureaucracy indulging in foreign investment leading to drainage of local surplus.

Thus the Indian economy after independence found itself in the twilight of feudalism and capitalism, both with their negative consequences.

Under development persisted in India as a sequel to the actual surplus falling short of the potential surplus, under the new governments policies, which were more in conformity with the foreign investors' interest than that of indigenous development. The best example in this regard can be provided by the government's much advertised Green Revolution. An analysis of the trend in output revealed that between 1960-61 to 1968-69, other than wheat, the compound growth rates of major agricuultural commodities had been much lower than that in the fifties. In fact long-term compound growth rate of food grain output was alarmingly outpaced by increase in population during this phase. More significantly, on the other hand, for major commercial crops like oil seeds, cotton, etc. which called for increasing volume of foreign investment, growth had been practically nil during this time. This marked a dangerous trend for the agricultural economy and its industrial growth.

Situations further worsened and the government's budgetary operations both at the central and the state level reflected it. Fear of accelerating inflation was looming large over the economy. And this rising trend in prices continued to grow steeper with a spending spree on defense. The distrubutive effect of such price rise accentuated inequality. It is abundantly clear that the large proportion of the less favorable places, i.e. agricultural laborers, middle and lower paid employees, rural artisans and tenants suffered the most. But the most disturbing factor in the balance of payment had been the continuous growth of heavy investments, leading to an increasing drain of our resources. The high rates of interest on loans, the growing burden of loot in the form of profits, payments on royalties, technical know-how and various other forms, adopted by the international finance capital, led to a phenomenal growth in foreign exchange payments under investment income and amortization.

This phenomenon interestingly points out to the fact that industrialization in India has had been a consequence of foreign capital under the disguise of aids. It had adopted various forms to control the growth of Indian industries. This is clearly discernable from the method of giving direct loans to Indian industries and by assessing the importance of its role in the establishment of new industries like Hindustan Aluminium in the expansion of established industries like TISCO, IISCO, Indian Aluminium. But the most significant means adopted so far, was the policy of aiding Indian Financial Corporations (IFC). IFC were set-up in India since 1947 for promotion of India's independent industrial growth. The imperialist ploy however had been to use these institutions as bases for a quick and extensive penetration of foreign monopolies into Indian industries. According to the Industrial Licensing Policy Enquiry Committee, the total financial assistance sanctioned and distributed by the IFC during 1956-66 were largely biased toward large industrial houses like ACC, Birla, J.K. Singhania, Mafatlal, Tata, Bajaj, Kirloskar, etc. India gradually improved the prospects for foreign capital and by the end of the period under discussion had established a conducive 'climate'.... A most important factor towards this objective had been the various institution established by the government of India to assist the development of private sector. Of these ICICI, deserves special mention. On the basis of the extensive loans that the India government funneled into the pipeline, and the that the World Bank continued to pump in, ICICI became a major source of capital for foreign investment. Subsequently ICICI's assistance helped big business to grow bigger so that the assistance accounting for companies controlld by large industrial houses was Rs. 85.4 crore, and formed 49.7% together with their second tier companies, the share of these large industrial houses was 52.7% and for foreign controlled companies and large independent companies this was 13.2%.

Thus despite of the government's declaration of industrialization to be the strategy governing planning, the reality conformed to something else after ten years of planned development.

Percentage Distribution of Population in Different Sectors[8]

Year	*Agriculture*	*Trade and Commerce*	*Transport and Communication*	*Other*	*Industry*
1901	67.53	6.05	1.12	8.46	16.84
1951	69.74	5.25	1.53	10.49	13.00
1961	69.53	4.04	1.59	10.38	14.45

Data reveal that relative concentration of population in agriculture has had been larger than it was 60 years ago under the British Raj. More striking is the fact, that the relative number of people employed in 'other services' revealed a rising trend. This latter sector is in the nature of boondoggles adding very little to the productive capacity of the economy. This simply revealed that the planning efforts had failed to alter the disproportionate relationship between different sectors of the stunted and deformed economic structure— which are inheritances from the colonial days. The legacy continued even in the production sphere, where the country remained agricultural predominantly. In fact fifteen years of planning efforts led to an increase in taxation of people, growing inflation, rocketing of prices, public debt, and foreign debts and stagnation in economic growth. In 1981-82 the proportion contributed by the manufacturing sector to NDP was 15% (at factor cost and 1970-71 prices). Here it is remarkable to notice that the contribution of the registered part of the manufacturing sector had been lower than that sector categorized in the National Income accounts as hotels, trade and restaurants. As already seen that the situation was so at the beginning of the fifties and it continued thus even in the eighties. In fact the estimated growth rate of the manufacturing sector recorded a statistically significant deceleration during this period.

GROWING UNEMPLOYMENT

This economic crisis led to a total liquidation of the planning and resulted in unbearable growth of unemployment. At the end of each of the first three five year plans the backlog of unemployment rose steadily from 5.3 million at the end of the 1st five year plan to 7.1 million at the end of the 2nd plan. This back log was 9 to 10 millions at the beginning of the 4th plan, of whom three-fourth were in rural areas. Registered unemployment in 1968 was 30.1 lakhs in 1969, 40.7 lakhs in 1970 and an alarming 47.1 lakh by July 1971. However, such figures are largely underestimated as only a small portion of educated enemployed do register as much. The immensity of educated unemloyed is discernable from the fact that by July 1968 there were 83,000 qualified engineers without jobs. Needless to mention how pathetic the condition of the uneducated force will be. Obviously the other side of the coin exhibited an alarming growth of poverty.

GROWING POVERTY

Yojana, in its issue of April 1966 published the dramatic statement that "*. . . at the current rate of growth in per capita income, India will take another 135 years to reach the present Japanese level of income*". But only low per capita income in a country like India does not provide the real state of poverty since the National Income is not distributed equally amongst all. In case that the average annual income is distributed equally to every Indian, a reasonably balanced diet will be available to all, provided they "*consept to go naked, live out of doors all year round . . . and have nothing else except raw* food." Thus it reveals clearly that the basic minimum considered is not sufficient for civilized human existence. So it requires no mention that in the presence of stark inequality in income distribution, this minimum has been perpetually denied to the vast majority, who continued in an abhorrent state.

The hazard of poverty on life can be illustrated by the incidents of consumption of 'Kesari Dal', the excessive consumption of which can cause paralysis particulars in young adults. But over the years this has been an important food item entering the diet of landless labourers in M.P., U.P., Bihar, Orissa, and West Bengal. It was found that labourers employed by landowners and big cultivatiors in these states were paid Kesari Dal in lieu of wages. On the basis of the NSS data, the *Economic Times*, October 1970, concluded that per capita expenditure of masses in India, whether urban or rural, did not experience any improvement over the twelve years, ending in 1963. 5% of the population lived on less than Rs. 3.2 per month, 10% lived on Rs. 6.2 per month, and 50% on Rs. 14.6 per month, i.e., less than a rupee per day. Planning Commission dismally concluded that on the basis of such progress something like a two-third of the population would live below the poverty line in 2000. Thus even today cases of mortgaging children for food is common in India. This brings home the fact that in India human labour is valueless, but kindness to animals and 'cow societies' are abundant.

GAME OF MODERNIZATION

Modernization never occurred as a voluntary process in India, rather it was imposed on the nation's weak shoulders to cater to the imperialists' motive. Soon the comprador bourgeoisie found its vested interest in the outcome. Thus modernization became the dominating strategy in the uneven game between the starved mass and the aggressive imperial power and its agents.

In this respect it is worth-mentioning that capitalism was and is a worldwide system because of its very nature. On the one hand in must expand its market to ever wider frontiers; on the other, it gives pre-capitalist societies only two options ; either to become capitalist or be absorbed in the capitalist system as colonies/semi colonies. It was therefore not an accident/historically exceptional that India was integrated into world capitalism without enjoying much of its fruits. Thus country was modernized and yet remained under developed at the same time. In fact the degree/intensity of under development/backwardness are precisely determined by the level of this integration and colonial modernization. It is perhaps because of this intricate dependency on the world capitalist system that India, the classic colony, the most developed to attain the 'take-off' *vis-a-vis* countries like China, who could completely break loose from capitalism. India's integration with the capitalist system had been tightened up by the uprising of the comprador bourgeoisie, who in the due courses took up to an expansionist. Just as India took over from Britain all its policies in relation to the neighbouring small countries— also the Indian ruling class took over from the British imperialists the concept of India as the 'center of Asia' and soon tried to step into shoes of the evacuating colonial power, particularly in the various Afro-Asian countries. This trend was clearly in a study by the Federation of Indian Chamber of Commerce and Industry, which listed 125 industrial projects located in other countries in which Indian bourgeoisie were collaborating/Proposing to collaborate with the entrepreneurs and government of the Afro-Asian ventures covered a wide range of products from manufacturing of textiles, hard board, rolls, pipes to chemical and pharmaceutical products and different engineering items. Repetitive collaboration with foreign finance in such industries which already existed in the country pointed out to the fact that the Indian entrepreneurs were playing the role of smoke screen for foreign capital which used India as a jumping-off ground for penetrating in the newly liberated Afro-Asian nations. In this process bourgeoisie played the role of a subsidiary to the foreign finance capital. They expected to reap benefits from investments not only by way of dividends etc., but by creating a market for themselves in these nations. Imperialism thus had been spinning its network not only by exploiting India through monopoly capital investment but also by using it as a seaboard to penetrate into other dependent nations. Hence dependency perpetuates even today and mainly in collaboration with the subservient bourgeoisie.

The political economy of reforms in India reveals the fact that the economic role of the state, planning and public sector did not however amount to a commitment to socialism by the nationalist movement as a whole. In fact the early nationalists and later the right wing nationalists did their entire thinking within the framework of a capitalist mode of production. Similarly, the capitalists actively espoused the cause of private enterprise even shine being willing to correct and compensate for its willingness through active state role and social intervention in general. By even those committed to socialism, being aware that the anti-imperialist movement required the unity of diverse social classes and ideological trends did not insist on the adoption of socialism by the national movement and the immediate objective.

Thus in due courses the public sector became a profitable pasture for private sector at the cost of the nation. In this context the government's policy of producing furance oil and promoting its use under the influence of foreign oil companies can be cited. This completely discouraged the use of coal leading to its under production, closure of pits, and increasing unemployment. The classic examples of loss to public sector and profit to private sectors, can be provided by the State Electricity Boards. In 1966-67 the Uttar Pradesh Electricity Board suffered a loss of Rs. 103.67 lakhs, due to under assessment of charges for power supplied to Hindustan Aluminium Company of the Birlas—one of the biggest industrial giants in India, with U.S. funds—at a role of Rs. 1.99 per unit, a price much lower than the cost of production. Mainstream in October 1971, informed that the public sector company, Indian Drugs and Pharmaceuticals Ltd. sold bulk drugs to a predominantly foreign owned drug industry who stamped tablets, packed and distributed the drugs at rates of profits often touching 200% of production cost. While the public sector helped to mobilize scarce financial resources for the foreign monopolies, produced output to be siphoned-off into private marketing channels to yield super normal profit for private capital, it claimed to make India self-reliant in defense production, but an article in the *Times of India*, October 1971, reported certain important facts which brought out our reliance on foreign powers and finance capital in defense sector and revealed the futility of the claim. Thus Gunnar Myrdal rightly commented that

> "... interest of private business does not normally conflict with expansion of public sector in big business."

Similarly public sector in India has no anti-imperialist/anti-monopolist character. It is but a weapon in hands of foreign monopoly and Indian big business—a combination of foreign monopoly capital and bureaucratic capital. Instead of supplementing government revenue and mop up purchasing power, the public sector functioned to inflate private profit. In India the state power ultimately falls in the hand of the comprador bourgeoisie in alliance with the landlords. This class could not alienate itself from its vested interest in land as well as foreign finance, thereby rendering land reforms meaningless.

WESTERN AID AND MULTI-DIMENSIONAL LOOT

The main feature of western aid in India is its purposive allocation as industrial loan. As it grew in volume, production on one hand was concentrated in foreign dominated industries, while on the other hand in caused drain in the name of import requirements. According to the *Patriot*, July 1968,

> "Most of our collaboration agreements are pretences to convert India into a market for immediate American and Western surpluses."

In fact the new industrial development in India was mostly based on imports to such an extent that the Hindu Survey of Industries in 1966 pointed out that:

> "... the dependence on maintenance of imports has been much more than was originally foreseen ... 80% of imports are now obtained utilizing U. S. aid. American materials are costlier 25 to 40% than those from U.K., Germany or Japan and devaluation accentuated the problem."

In fact foreign manufacturing firms in a wide range of industries prefer a high revenue from sales to their Indian branches to high profits, since such profits are non-cognizable. Thus western aid and capital investment usually came with exorbitantly high price tags. According to the *Indian Express*, May 1970:

> "Royalty payments and fees for technical knowhow do involve a drain

of foreign exchange; actual outgo amounts to about Rs. 50 crores annually."

In this context the public sector companies were as criminal as private sector companies. *Economic Times* spoke of 'deliberately inflated prices of sale of share of foreign companies involving large transfer of foreign exchange,' which were not accounted for. The amount of material loss to India is unaccounted. There continued over-invoicing and under-invoicing of various forms and the process is exactly identical to that under the British rule phase of 1861 to 1914. Transactions at deliberated inflated prices imply deliberate over payments to the foreign bank accounts. This led to significant repatriation of profits. Thus the foreign capital could easily divert domestic savings from India to wards the economic growth of the west through the foreign banks and their scheme of the 'Participation Certificate'. This rendered resorting to RBI for marginal accommodation needless and restricted the role of the government financial institutions in bolstering the deposits of the foreign banks. Soon the foreign capital along with the bureaucratic capital in a well co-ordinated way took control of 30% of India's external trade and created a multinational industrial empire in India.

POLITICAL ECONOMY OF REFORMS IN INDIA

In his memorandum of June 1939, to the NPC, Jawaharlal Nehru laid down that the ideal of the foundation of our plan was not socialism, but the creation of an egalitarian society in which all citizens have equal opportunities and a '. . . civilized standard of life . . . so as to make the attainment of this equal opportunity a reality'. Laying the basis of a mixed economy, he wrote in August 1940:

> "Private enterprise has certainly not been ruled out but it has to strictly controlled and co-ordinated to general plan."

In other words, capitalist entrepreneurs were to remain the main agent of development. But though the national movement did not accept socialism as a social objective on the whole, from the beginning it had a pro-poor orientation and a reformist program, which was further strengthened after 1918 with the advent of Gandhiji and the growth of the left. Moreover it continued to define itself in a more and more radical direction. Increasing freedom was defined in radical socio-economic terms based on growing social justice and greater social and equality and a refusal to accept economic privileges. Later the NPC, and the Bombay Plan, favored large measures to social welfare such as an employment policy based on the right to work and full employment, the guarantee of a minimum wage, greater state expenditure on housing, waster, sanitation, free education, social insurance to cover unemployment and sickness, and the provision of utility services such as electricity and transport at low cost through state subsidies. Above all states planning was to be based on the objective of removal of gross inequalities in income and productive assets, among classes and individuals. Inequality was also undesirable because it tended to restrict the domestic market. As the Bombay plan puts it, "*the large increase in production which is postulated in the plan, would be difficult to achieve if the present disparities in income are allowed to persist.*"

But complex class matrix in Indian society rendered state planning unfruitful. In spite of resource mobilization largely through indirect taxation and transfer of savings from household sector through nationalized financial institutions, the bulk of these resources have been frittered away in current expenditure leaving not enough surplus to finance massive public investment programs, particularly for coal, transport, power and irrigation, needed to boost the rate of economic growth above its low level equilibrium level. When diverse elements of loose and uneasy coalition of dominant proprietary class pull in different directions and none of them are individually strong enough to dominate the process of resource allocation, one predictable outcome is the proliferation of subsidies and grants to placate all of them, with subsequent reduction in resources for public capital formation. The conflict of proprietary classes clearly distinguishes a heterogeneous class alignment in India, which is largely attributable to the historical process of weak development of capitalism here. So the industrial capitalist class could not be strong enough to undermine the economic importance of class of rich farmers or absorb them in giant capitalist agro-business enterprise; not could it succeed in colonizing the bureaucracy and molding it towards the capitalist goal. Besides the ethnic and regional diversity of Indian society militate against the emergence of a single dominant class whose writ can be enforced throughout the country. The co-existence of such contending classes had important implications for the pace and pattern of economic growth.

The three proprietary classes identifiable in India comprising of the traders, rich farmers and the professionals in the public sector, all belong roughly to the top two deciles of the population, and the social and economic gulf between them and the bottom half of the population living in abject poverty in deep indeed. But the Indian style of politics is deceptively consensual providing scope for intense bargaining and hard fought apportionment of benefits among the different partners of the dominant coalition.

In the agricultural sector, in some of the states like Punjab, Haryana, Gujarat, and Karnataka the strong rich farmer lobbies have succeeded in obtaining the major benefits of support prices, subsidies and low taxes on agriculture. But this associated agrarian growth with deceleration in the seventies, and an increasing part of agrarian savings were siphoned-off to usurious purpose, and a large amount was disbursed as export subsidies, there was no corresponding rise in net foreign exchanges earnings.

Phenomenal expansion of subsidized credit from public leading agencies, were mainly in the form of political boondoggle. Lending targets, were often set-up by partisan political parties, without any consideration of maximum social returns. Some of the bigger loan scandals involving the nationalized banks originated essentially in the politicized public banking. Consequently it represented a deplorable record of loan repayment. More significantly in the industrial sector, subsidized credit was often being used to nurse sick private industries. Outstanding bank credit to large sick units alone amounted to about Rs. 15 billion by December 1981. Lame duck private companies tried to place themselves on this sick list; in some states such sickness reached epidemic proportions.

Thus Indian public economy assumed an elaborate network of patronage and subsidies. The heterogeneous proprietary classes fight and bargain for their share in the spoils of the system, and often strike compromises in the form of 'log rolling' in the usual form of pressure group politics.

THEN WHAT HAPPENED TO THE OBJECTIVE OF REDUCING POVERTY AND INEQUALITY?

The objective of economic planning in India has been growth with justice. The Indian planners aimed at increasing national income and P.C.I. on the assumption that rise in income would eventually remove poverty and misery and rise the standard of living of the masses. But poor development of capitalism led to the perpetuation dependency on finance capital and broke the myth of sustainable growth and poverty eradication—the country itself caught in a low level-equilibrium trap with mass dwelling in abject poverty. India has been mortgaged to monopoly capitalism that allowed the creation of new East India Companies in the country, which militate against her economic independence. Thus from the fourth plan onwards poverty alleviation was assigned separate priority in the planning process. But the popular method of explaining poverty in India has been to use the concept of poverty line, which tries to measure the absolute poverty level in terms of different indicators like—PCI, per head consumption, infrastructural facilities, nutrition, etc. Thus the problem of inequality or relative poverty, which too is acute for the country, is ignored accepting inequality as natural. As a result, poverty alleviation programmes are a one way track pouring the top to the bottom as mere charity which denies the right and prestige of the poor. It also helps to hide the fact that poverty is a results of exploitation and deprivation. This is made possible by the fact that political democracy has also its way of building up pressures for state subsidies from a growing number of groups even beyond the confines of the aforesaid dominant coalition. Some section of unionized workers, small traders and some other small propertied interest taking advantage of their large numbers are increasingly vocal in electoral politics for a large share of the pie. Regional and sectarian pressures for increased claim to federal money also build up. While from time to time a significant number of crumbs have to be thrown at these clamoring groups banging at the gates just outside the periphery of the dominant coalition;

equally expensive is the process of manning and securing those gates and of controlling the crowds if they ever look threatening. Thus very little of the Government expenditure do reach the real poor. In these large complicated bargaining counters, there has emerged a group specializing as brokers, who act as agents for different bargaining interest group and of course take a cut for themselves for the services rendered. These gangs are led by a large number of M.L.As, M.Ps and political middlemen, who over the years have specialized in these professions. Their brokerage fees and services and usually unaccounted in the official statistical book-keeping, contributing to the thriving of underworld of 'black money'. As elections have more expensive and as their professional expertise in brokerage increased, it skimmed-off the surplus of the economy in the form of annually multiplying fees. Thus keeping all heterogeneous elements of the dominant coalition happy, guarding the fortresses and alternatively coaxing and coercing the intermediate groups all contribute to mounting non-developmental expenditure in the budget and leave for the state a dwindling share of the revenues to be reinvested in public capital formation. This in due courses led to a 'fiscal crisis' blocking the necessary accumulation function of the state.

Our discussion so far points out to the fact that poverty sustains in an economy with direct or indirect foreign intervention. Subservience on monopoly capital in India on one hand filtered away much of the re-investible profits as interests and amortization on external assistance. But simultaneously it could generate an internal fiscal crisis through heterogeneous class conflicts, giving birth to a class of comprador bourgeoisie, working as the agents of monopoly capitalism. The economy is entrapped in a 'dept-trap' and its dependency on finance capital gets multiplied. Dependency distorts growth from catering to the objective of social justice and equality. Thus it is believed that in a pervasive economy like India, independent economic growth in the only panacea to poverty.

REFORMS AND QUESTION OF INDEPENDENT GROWTH

The second-generation reforms in India, with globalization, liberalization and privatization as the basic objective, make this question more relevant. This issue has been at the focus of all relevant economic debates. With the scope of our paper being limited, we shall not be able to go into the depth of it-but we shall try to hint to those aspects, relevant to bring forth our contention and sufficiency to open up the scope of a much vivid discussion in some near future.

It is noteworthy here that liberalization in India has been a crisis-driven response, rather than being a long-term policy measure. Lack of economic insight throughout the last few decades brought the country within a hair's breadth of default. With pressure of liquidity crunch ever mounting and options being more or less exhausted the Congress Government in office was bound to negotiate a stand by adjustment with IMF and structural adjustment loan with the World Bank as short-term macro-management. IMF to India was not merely the lender of the last resort but was important for its imprimature to restore international confidence in India's capacity of repayment. This imprimature however came with a high price tag as IMF and World Bank are far from charitable institution.

While the IMF policy package provided the rationable for a sharp reduction in the fiscal deficits of the government, adoption of tight monetary policy and subsequent devaluation of rupee, the structural reforms of the World Bank type is the almost exclusive concern of the supply side. It seeks to:

(i) Shift resources from non-traded to goods sector,
(ii) From government to private sector,
(iii) Improve resource utilization by improving the degree of openness of the economy, and
(iv) Changing the structure of incentives in favor of private initiatives against state intervention.

In conformity with such increasing reliance on market forces, government of India by following the Washington Consensus embarked on a wide range of policy regimes in July 1991, encompassing:

(1) The Industrial Sector
(2) Public Sector
(3) Trade Regime
(4) Financial Sector
(5) Foreign Investment
(6) Foreign Technology

But such marco-management policies are far from being simple:

(i) By no means it is certain that fiscal austerity and monetary discipline will translate lower demand to reduced current a/c deficit if there is deflation affecting non-traded goods largely than traded goods.
(ii) Reduced demand may lead to lower production as the size of the market shrinks. This would have adverse impact on income and employment.
(iii) A tight monetary policy combining a credit squeeze with high interest rate is likely to dampen investment.

Thus in an economy where wages and prices are rigid and the impact of compressing demand falls on output and employment rather than prices, the deflation associated with stabilization may lead to contraction of output and not prices. Moreover, in the short-run a devaluation may escalate inflation directly by cost of impact that enter domestic production/ consumption. If monetary wages fail to keep pace with inflation a consequent not in real wages may decrease real income leading to a fall in demand and output, i.e. stagflation. Low level equilibrium trap gets strengthened and reliance on external assistance gets multiplied. In such a context removal of regulations brings large conglomerates in closer proximity to monopoly capitalism, which in due courses help them to pre-empt competition. Finance capital strengthens its stranglehold, gets fed by repatriated profit and continues its aggressive marketing strategy through its satellite agents. Is not the story repeating itself?

It may be true that India has been able to repay its obligations to the IMF, but what about its increased dependence on private foreign investment ? Since financial sector liberalization. NRI remittances and foreign portfolio investment have been swelled up India's foreign exchange house—there is nothing to be overjoyed at the sight, because deep reflection will suffice to bring out the fact that private capital has woven an intricate network to dominate the economy's fate at its pull of the strings.

Keeping the issue open for future academic debate I would like to conclude the paper by drawing attention to the fact that colonization has retarded the capacity of the economic system to insulate economic management from political process of distributive demands, rent-seeking political and patronage disbursement that have crucial impact on economic growth and development, this capacity does not depend on lack on accountability on the public sector management, nor is it a monotonic inverse function of degree of representativeness of the government. But in a polyglot and vastly more heterogeneous and fragmented society like that of India this insulation has been difficult to achieve and maintain alongside a pluralist open polity and thereby the public economy gets exposed.

Thus colonization exposes the economy to aggressive monopolistic intervention of capitalism. It within itself develops a weak capitalist structure with elements of feudalism dominating in their negative sense. Economy undergoes both physical and moral drain and looses sight of its egalitarian motive—thus few prosper by providing brokerage service to the imperial power at the cost of the development and well-being of the numerous who continue dwelling in abject poverty and die by passing the burden as a bequest to the next generation.

Notes and References

1. *Employment News*, April-May, 2003.
2. M. Mukhopadhyay, Bharat or Jatiya Aye, p. 59.
3. Empire in Asia, p. 466.
4. S. Sen, Colonies and The Empire, p. 13.
5. S. Sen, Colonies and The Empire, p. 22.
6. R. Dutt, The Economic History of India, Vol. I, Preface xxix.
7. S. Sen, Colonies and The Empire, p. 50.
8. 1961 Census Papers No. 1.

REFERENCES

Colonies and the Empire, India 1890-1914—Sunanda Sen, Orient Longman, 1992.

Essays in Indian History, Towards a Marxist perspective—Irfan Habib, Tulika, 1995.

Essays on Colonialism—Bipan Chandra, Orient Longman Ltd., 1999.

India mortgaged, A Marxist Leninist Appraisal—T. Nagi Reddy, Tarimela Nagi Reddy Memorial Trust.

Perspective of Poverty Alleviation—Ronesh Kumar Ray; *Artha Shastra*, Vol. 8, No. 1, 1989.

Political Economy of Development in India—Pranab Bardhan; OUP.

Poverty and Famines: Essays on Entitlement and Deprivation—Amartya Sen; OUP.

Poverty and Un-British Rule in India—Dadabhai Naoroji, Publication Division, Ministry of Information and Broadcasting, GOI.

The Economic History of India, Vol. 1—Romesh Dutt; Do.

The Intelligent Person's Guide to Liberalization—Amit Bhaduri and Deepak Nayyar, Penguin Books India (P) Ltd.

Whatever Happened to Imperialism and Other Essays—Prabhat Patnaik; Tulika, 2000.

Poverty: A Danger to Prosperity

Tapan Kumar Shandilya

Poverty is a multi-facet concept. It is a universal phenomenon. The phenomenon of poverty does not only affect the individual (poor) but is productive of danger to nations. The Philadelphia Chracter has postulated that "Poverty anywhere constitutes a danger to prosperity everywhere".

Poverty is a relative term and it is understood in relation to prosperity. Poverty and prosperity are comparative concepts. Hence from time immemorial, the poor have co-existed with the rich in India as well as throughout the world. Adam Smith says, "Main is rich or poor according to the degree in which he can, which he can afford to enjoy the necessaries, the conveniences, and the amusements of life." The word degree is not equal in all periods and in all places.

Mahatma Gandhi considered poverty as a curse of God as well as a crime. He wrote: "Poverty was the curse of God. It deprived you of everything: food, clothing, shelter, your self-respect, your humanity, even your soul. In poverty, you suffered not only hunger, nakedness, the cruelty of cold and heath, the blind fury of Nature's wild elements: you also suffered from humiliation, loss of human dignity. You were driven to acknowledge defect and overwhelmed by distress and despair. You were compelled to take to crime or beggary for a morsel of bread, women having to sell their bodies and live in sin and shame, and men having to sell their own souls to keep their bodies or those of their wives and children, to keep the wolf from the door, to put an end to their pangs of hunger of thirst." Sri Aurobindo, however, looked at it from the point of view of an organized society. He said: "The acceptance of poverty is noble and beneficial in a class or an individual, but it becomes fatal and pauperizes the life of its richness and expansion if is perversely organized into a general or national ideal. Poverty is no more a necessity of social life than disease of the natural body; false habits of life and an ignorance of our true organization are in both cases the per cent causes of an avoidable disorder."

According to Gillin and Gillin: "Poverty is the condition in which a person, either because of inadequate income or unwise expenditure, does not maintain a scale of living to provide for his physical and mental efficiency and to function usually according to the standards or the society of which he is a member." To Godard, "Poverty is insufficient supply of those things which are requisite for an individual to maintain himself and those dependent upon him for health and vigour."

Poverty is harmful not only to the poor but also to the economy as a whole. The abysmal poverty off the masses in this country and the sharp disparities in incomes and levels of living place severe structural constraints on the generation of effective demand which alone can ensure continuous productive activities in the economy. Accordingly, in India, the structure of production is heavily weighted in favour of higher-income consumption goods, which provide a comparatively more profitable market. But the erosion of middle and poor class income because of continuous inflation and showing down of the generation of new incomes and employment opportunities because of a slowdown in development activities to check inflation have led to a shrinkage in demand, which affects, the class production to the level of under-utilisation of established capacities. This, in turn, has affected adversely the income and consumption levels of the people.

ENVIRONMENT OF POVERTY

The environment of poverty is conditioned by malnutrition, which increases a person's vulnerability to disease and reduces his learning ability, Malnutrition adversely affects fuller mental development, physical growth, productivity, the span of working years, all of which significantly influence the economic potential of men and women. Lack of education increases ignorance and reduces the scope for self-improvement, and generates ignorance of the means to prevent sickness. It also affects the norms and value system of a society. Illiteracy and fertility are a vicious combination. Poor housing with lack of basic amenities create a physical environment, which results in a high incidence of water-borne and air-borne diseases. On the other hand, a conditioned learning environment *inter alia* develops ignorance about food source, diet, food preparation, storage, etc. poor health reduces one's ability to absorb food. The net result of malnutrition, illiteracy, poor housing and poor health is reduced production of basic goods, low skills, lower productivity and lower incomes. Poverty affects the quality and quantity of the human capital, which is the end and means of economic growth.

The environment of poverty stresses the key importance of participation. Low participation constitutes the fifth segment of the circle, demonstrating how, in addition to institutional factors, unsatisfied needs detract from more active participation: work capacities are reduced by disease, poor nourishment, low skill and even poor housing. Reduced participation in turn capacities to produce basic goods and earn incomes, and feeds back into the circle of deprivation. The involution of the poverty environment is thus complete. The key changes capable of transforming this environment obviously consist in the removal of the obstructive factors at the centre. This symbolic representation of the environment of poverty is thus transformed from a vicious into a virtuous circular arrangement, raising levies of satisfaction of needs conjointly and then becomes a self-generating process.

Rural poor population includes landless agricultural labour households, agricultural labour with small holdings, landless non-agricultural rural labourers including village artisans progressively losing their traditional jobs and small land operators with cultivating holding of less than 2 hectares and particularly less than 1 hectare. (Minhas, Burdhan, Dandekar and Rath). The urban poor, according to Dandekar and Rath, "they belong to the same class as the rural poor".

At least 70% of the population is in agriculture, which engages 60% of the work force. Its contribution to GDP is merely 27% and that too is constantly declining from 31.6% in 1987-88 to 26.8% in 1998-99. Out of the 70% of agricultural population 80% of the farmers are small and marginal farmers and 75% of Indian poor are in rural areas. More than 60% of them live in five states, namely, Bihar, U.P., M.P., Rajasthan and Orissa.

Several attempts have been made to estimate purely or the pre and post-reform period. Gupta, 1955; Chandrashekhar and Sen, 1966; Jain, 1996; B. Ozler, G. Dutt and M. Ravallion, 1996; Shenggen Fan, Peter Hazell, S.K. Thorat, 2000 and Bhijit Sen, 2000 are some notable estimates. These studies rural that the rural poverty has constantly reduced during the pre-reform period 1973-74 to 1980-90 and increased significantly during the first two and half years of reform 1991-92, 1992-93 and 1993-94. During this period rural poverty increased by about 2 percentage point while the urban poverty declined by 4 percentagepoint. Tendulkar's estimates of severity of poverty (FGT-index) show that there was a very mild decline in severity for rural areas while a significant decline is found in urban areas. A lower level of FGT index implies less severity of poverty and a high value signifies more server poverty. Following table shows these levels of severity during pre and post-reform period.

The State-wise estimates reveals that four states, namely, Bihar, M.P., U.P. and Maharashtra, together accounted 55% of the rural poor in 1993. Bihar and U.P. together accounted 18% of the total rural poor. These states had the highest incidence of poverty in 1993 with 42.68% of their rural population falling below the poverty line. On the other hand, A.P., Haryana, Kerala, Punjab and West Bengal had only 25 to 35% of their rural population below the poverty line in 1993. The study also reveals that most of the states experienced an increase in poverty after 1990. In Orissa, for example, the poverty ratio increased from 19% to 25% between 1990-93.

TABLE 1

Severity of Poverty During Pre- and Post-Liberalisation Period

Years	*FGT-Rural*	*FGT-Urban*
1970-71	0.773	0.053
1977-98	0.068	0.043
1987-88	0.040	0.038
1989-90	0.035	0.031
1990-91	0.031	0.032
1991	0.031	0.032
1992	0.042	0.033
1993	0.035	0.036
1993-94	0.031	0.026

Source: Mahendra Dew, S. and Ranade, A., Poverty and Public: A Mixed Record in Kirit S. Parich (Ed.) India's Development Report, Oxford 1997 (Table A-2).

The period 1994 to 1998 remained fluctuating. During 1994 to 1997, rural poverty show a declining trend, but increased sharply during 1997-98, Dutt, Gupta and Tendulkar, H-C ratio estimates of rural poverty during 1994-98 are given in the following table:

TABLE 2

Rural Poverty Estimates (H-C Ratio) 1994-98

NSS-Round	*Years*	*FGT-Rural*	*FGT-Urban*
July 1993-June 1994	36.7	37.3	39.7
July 1994-June 1995	41.7	38.0	43.6
July 1995-June 1996	37.2	38.2	40.1
Jan.-Dec. 1997	35.8	38.5	38.3
Jan. 1998-June 1998	N. A.	45.3	44.9

Source: Abhijit Sen, Estimates of Consumers' Expenditure and its Distribution: Statistical priorities after NSS 55th Round, *EPW*, Dec. 16-22, 2000 (Table 1).

These estimates reveal that during 1991 to 1994 and again during 1997-98 rural poverty has increased. Three years 1995, 1996, and Jan.-December 1997, it shows a declining trend.

INCIDENCE OF POVERTY: PRESENT SCENARIO

The Planning Commission has been estimating the incidence of poverty at the national and state level using the methodology contained in the report of the Expert Group on Estimation of Proportion and Number of Poor (Lakdawala Committee) and applying it to consumption expenditure data from the large sample surveys on consumer expenditure conducted by the National Sample Survey Organization (NSSO) at an interval of approximately five years. The latest available large sample survey data on consumer expenditure are for the 55th Round covering the period July 1999 to June 2000 (Table 3).

In the earlier Surveys, the NSSO estimated monthly consumption expenditure on the basis of responses using a 30-day recall period for all food and non-food items. In the 55th Round, the consumption expenditure on clothing, footwear, medical (institutional) and durable goods were collected using a 365-days recall period. In the case of all other non-food items, the 30-day recall period was used as earlier. The data on consumption expenditure on food items were collected using two different reference periods of last 30-days from the same households. The poverty ratios indicated in Table 3 are estimated on the basis of 30-days recall period for 1973-74 to 1999-2000. Poverty at the national level is estimated as the weighted average of State-wise poverty levels.

TABLE 3

Estimates of Incidence of Poverty in India

Year	*Poverty ratio (%)*			*Number of poor (million)*		
	Rural	*Urban*	*Combined*	*Rural*	*Urban*	*Combined*
1973-74	56.4	49.0	54.6	261.3	60.0	321.3
1977-78	53.1	45.2	51.3	264.3	64.6	328.9
1983	45.7	40.8	44.5	252.0	70.9	322.9
1987-88	39.1	38.2	38.9	231.9	75.2	307.1
1993-94	37.3	32.4	36.0	244.0	76.3	320.3
1999-00	27.1	23.6	26.1	193.2	67.1	260.3
2007	21.1	15.1	19.3	170.5	49.6	220.1

*Poverty projection for 2007.
Source: Tenth Five Year Plan, Vol. 1, Planning Commission.

The success of the anti-poverty strategy is reflected in the decline in the combined poverty ratio from 54.9 per cent in 1973-74 to 36.0 per cent in 1993-94. The poverty ratio declined by nearly 10 percentage points in the 5 year period between 1993-94 to reach 26.1 per cent in 1999-00. While the proportion of poor in the rural areas declined from 56.4 per cent in 1973-74 to 27.1 per cent in 1999-00, the decline in urban areas has been from 49 per cent to 23.6 per cent during this period. In absolute terms, the number of poor declined to 260 million in 1999-00, with about 75 per cent of these being in the rural areas.

Wide Inter-State disparities are visible in the poverty ratios between rural and urban areas as also in the rates of decline of poverty among major States, Orissa, Bihar, West Bengal and Tamil Nadu had more than 50 per cent of their population below the poverty line in 1983. By 1999-2000, while Tamil Nadu and West Bengal had reduced their poverty ratios by nearly half. Orissa and Bihar continued to be the two poorest States with poverty ratios of 47 and 43 per cent respectively. In 1999-2000, 20 States and Union Territories had poverty ratios, which were less than the national average. Among other States, Jammu and Kashmir, Haryana, Gujarat, Punjab, Andhra Pradesh, Maharashtra and Karnataka also succeeded in significantly reducing the incidence of poverty.

Apart from an indicative target of an 8 per cent average G.D.P. growth rate, specific monitorable targets for key indicators have been finalized for the Tenth Five Year Plan (2000-07) and beyond. One of these pertains to the reduction in poverty ratio by five percentage points by 2007 and by 15 percentage points by 2012. The poverty reduction target set by the Planning Commission for the Tenth Five Year Plan aims at achieving a poverty ratio of 19.3 per cent for the country as a whole by 2007, 21.1 per cent for the rural, and 15.1 per cent for the urban area.

MEASUREMENT OF POVERTY

The measurement of poverty involves two distinct problems, namely:

(i) The Specification of "poverty line," and
(ii) Determination of the index of poverty.

In India, most of the studies on poverty regard the proportion of people below the line as the index of poverty. This ratio is called the Head Count Ratio. More specifically,

$$H = \frac{q}{n}$$

H = Poverty Index,
q = The number of people below the poverty line, and
n = The total number of people in the community.

According to Sen (1976), H is obviously a very crude Index. This index is highly insensitive to the extent of the aggregate shorfall of the income from the poverty line as well as to the distribution of income amongst the poor. In spite of these limitations, H is still widely used. In the debate on whether or not rural poverty in India is on the increase, Dandekar and Rath (1971), Ojha (1970) and Bardhan (1971) have used this index.

Another common measure is the so-called "poverty gap" which is the aggregate shortfall of the income of all the poor taken together from the poverty line. That is:

$$I = \frac{\sum_{i=1}^{q} g_i}{q^z}$$

where $g_i = z - y_i$.

In the above measure,

z = Poverty line
y_i = Income of the ith.

The above ratio gives up the percentage of their mean shortfall from the poverty level. This measure is totally insensitive to the number of living below the poverty line. Thus, while the head-count ratio (H) is completely insensitive to the extent of the poverty shortfall per person, the income-gap ratio (I) is completely insensitive to the numbers involved. According to Sen (1976), "Both should have some role in the index of poverty. But H and I together are not sufficiently informative either, since neither gives adequate information on the exact income distribution among the poor." Sen (1976) has suggested a measure, which is sensitive to the gaps in the incomes of the poor. His measure is:

$$P - H (I + (l - I) G)$$

where

$$H = \frac{q}{n} + \text{Head-count ratio}$$

$$1 = \frac{\sum_{i=1}^{q} g_i}{q'} + \text{Income gap ratio and G is the Gini coefficient of the}$$

income distribution of the poor.

The index lies in between zero and unity. If P – O, this index shows that every one has as income greater than z, and if P = I, everyone has zero income. In practice of course, P will never taken these two extreme values.

Referring to the problem of poverty, A.K. Sen says that the usual procedure is to identify some level of income, which is required for the recommended balanced diet, and to consider those falling below that level as poor. He has added two more criteria.

(i) We should be concerned not merely with the number of people living below the poverty line but also with the amount by which the incomes of the poor fall short of the specified poverty level, and

(ii) The bigger the shortfall from the poverty measure.

On this basis, Sen develops his P measure of poverty as:

$$p = \frac{2}{(q + 1) xy^*} \sum_{i=1}^{q} (y^* - Y_1 (q + 1 - i)$$

where

N is the population size,

Y is the income of ith individual arranged in the ascending order of magnitude,

Y is the minimum acceptable level of income or the poverty line, and

q is the number of people at or below the poverty line.

CAUSES OF RURAL POVERTY IN INDIA

Poverty has many faces, and its causes vary from one thinker to another and from one environment to another. Henary and George hold that the main cause of poverty is the personal ownership of large acres of land. Karl Marx is of the opinion that "Poverty is the exploitation of the labourers by the capitalist." Malthus, on the other hand, enunciated that the rapid growth of population was the main cause of poverty. He said: "Poverty increases because the food production increases in arithmetic progression, while population increases in geometric progression." However, poverty is the result of multiple causes. Economic, political, geographical, social and cultural factors, individually or collectively, contribute to poverty.

Among the important economic factors, the steady growth of population and the prevalent inheritance laws have resulted in the fragmentation of land. Moreover, the economically non-viable farmers sell their land to big landlords and/or traders or urban dwellers and become agricultural labourers themselves, they have one partial employment. Low income, low productivity coupled with some vices push a large number of people into poverty. The birth rate among the poor is also higher and ignorance is a contributory factor. For example, Family Planning workers in an Indian village demonstrated the use of condoms by unrolling them on a bamboo everyone; the workers left the village with enough stocks of condoms. But when they returned some months later, they were surprised to observe groups of pregnant women, who complained about the ineffectiveness of the new technology. The women, insisted that had followed the instructions to latter. And when the family planning workers visited their homes, they found gathering dust. The poor, because they are poor, often resort to robbery, etc. In short, there is a decline in the value system. Exploitation by the affluent also continues. In other words, poverty strikes the poor, physically, materially, socially and culturally.

In rural areas, land is the principal productive asset. But land is very unevenly distributed.

The problem of poverty has been aggravated by the steady increase in population and the consequent rise in unemployment. By and large, the lower income groups tend to have large families. This fact, to some extent, accounts for the low consumption and high unemployment among the poor. Moreover, they suffer from social disabilities. Most of them belong to scheduled castes/tribes and other backward classes. They are illiterate and are engaged mostly in unskilled occupations, in which the wages are very low.

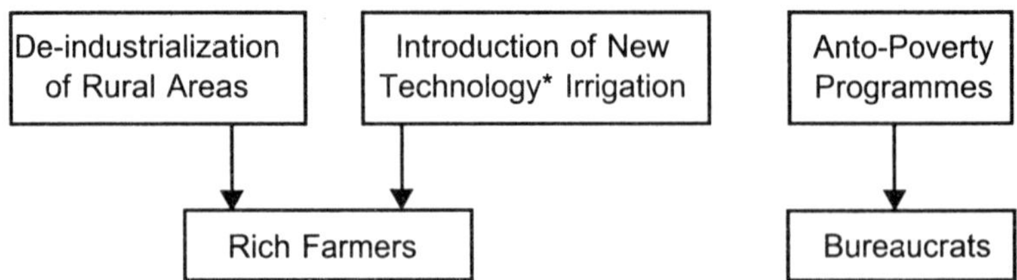

Rural Population Rising at 2.5%
Rural Employment at 0.5
Rural Real Income at 0.8

Most significantly, the perpetuation of rural poverty is ensured by the double strategy of de-industrialising the rural areas and pumping into agriculture resource, which fall into the hands of rich farmers. To make matters worse, the bureaucrats pocket a large proportion of the funds allocated under the so-called anti-poverty programme.

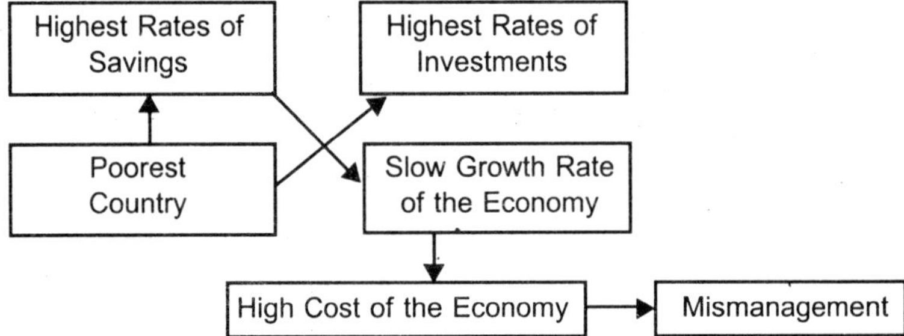

The rural poor are caught in another vicious circle. Whatever little improvement occurs in their incomes or assets in one year is washed away in the line except the incomes of those who have assured irrigation. Drought affects both the rich and the poor farmers. In fact, during the drought period, the crisis overtakes everyone, and ultimately affects industry. All these developments push the poor further down the line. They lose job, they lose incomes; and they cannot buy food.

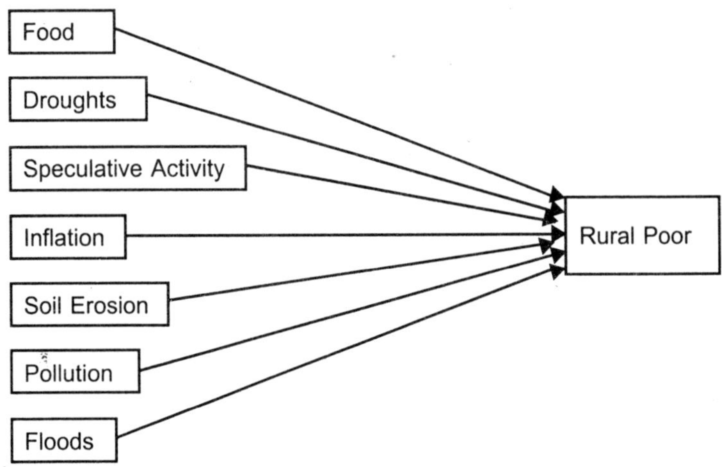

- Destruction of Land
- Animals
- Desiltation
- Lose Jobs
- Health Hazards
- Lose Jobs
- Lose
- Lose Food
- Lose Drinking Water

And when floods come, there is the destruction of other assets. Lands are washed away, Cattle disappear, Houses collapse. The poor are uprooted in the process. They lose jobs, Health hazards for them become serious.

According to a recent study, the cause of poverty are abject poverty (having meager means of livelihood), unemployment (agriculture provides about 175-190 days of work in a year), lack of employment opportunities outside agriculture, political disputes (wrangling over land, women, family feuds or status), corruption at the grass root level, dishonesty and bureaucratic inefficiency, caste system and illiteracy. The inadequacy of civic amenities, inefficient communication facilities, problems of transport and non-availability of safe drinking water accentuate poverty in rural areas.

The causes of poverty are multi-dimensional—they are social, economical, political, managerial, organizational, cultural, psychological, etc. Social inequality is linked to economic inequality—each being the cause and effect of the other. Socialist slogans, however meaningful, are only useful means of winning the votes of the ignorant, illiterate mass to be in power. Under the biggest democracy in the world, vast number of people continue to be born in poverty, live in poverty and die in poverty.

GOVERNMENT INTERVENTION: DIRECT ATTACK ON POVERTY

Alleviation of rural poverty has been one of the primary objectives of planned development in India. Ever since the inception of planning, the policies and the programmes have been designed and redesigned with this aim. The problem of rural poverty was brought into a sharper focus during the Sixth Plan. The Seventh Plan too emphasized growth with social justice. It was realized that a sustainable strategy of poverty alleviation has to be based on increasing the productive employment opportunities in the process of growth itself. However, to the extent the process of growth bypasses some sections of the population, it is necessary to formulate specific poverty alleviation programmes for generation of a certain minimum level of income for the rural poor.

Rural development implies both the economic betterment of people of well as greater social transformation. Increased participation of people in the rural development process, decentralization of planning, better enforcement of land reforms and greater access to credit and inputs go a long way in providing the rural people with better prospects for economic development. Improvement in health, education, drinking water, energy supply, sanitation and housing coupled with attitudinal changes also facilitate their social development.

Rural poverty is inextricably linked with low rural productivity and unemployment, including underemployment. Hence, it is imperative to improve productivity and increase employment in rural areas. Moreover, more employment needs to be generated at higher levels of productivity in order to generate higher output. Employment at miserably low levels of productivity and income is already a problem of far greater magnitude than unemployment as such. It is estimated that in 1987-88 the rate of unemployment was only 3 per cent and inclusive of the underemployed, it was around 5 per cent. As per the currently used methodology in the Planning Commission, poverty for the same year was estimated to be 30 per cent. This demonstrates that even though a large proportion of the rural population was 'working', it was difficult for them to eke out a living even at subsistence levels from it. It is true that there has been a considerable decline in the incidence of rural poverty over time. In terms of absolute numbers of poor, the decline has been much less. While this can be attributed to the demographic factor, the fact remains that after 40 years of planned development about 200 million are still poor in rural India. In 1987-88, the rural poverty line in terms of per capita monthly expenditure was Rs. 131.80. The average incidence of rural poverty conceals wide interstate differences, which suggests that greater attention needs to be paid to the regions, which have a greater concentration of the rural poor. In recent years, several issues have been raised about the methodology of poverty estimation, both by professionals and State Government. An Expert Group appointed by the Planning Commission is looking into these issues relating to the definition and measurement of poverty.

The decline in rural poverty is attributable both to the growth factor and to the special employment programmes launched by the Government in order to generate more incomes in the rural area. Hence, in its more limited interpretation, rural development has been confined to a direct attack on poverty through special employment programmes, area development programmes and land reforms.

India has launched several such programmes, which focus the rural poor. They basically provide employment to targeted poor, enhance their income and generate assets to rural poor families, SGSY, SGRY, PMGY, PMGST, SJSRY, TRYSEM, IAY, MWS, EAS are the few among the series of such programmes. Some details of such programmes are given below.

THE SWARNAJAYANTI GRAM SWAROZGAR YOJANA (SGSY)

SGSY was launched in April 1999 and is the only self-employment programme currently being implemented. It aims at promoting micro-enterprises and to bring the assisted poor families (Swarozgaris) above the poverty line by organizing them into Self Help Groups (SHGs) through the process of social mobilization, training and capacity building and provision of income generating assets through a mix of Bank credit and Government subsidy. The scheme is being implemented on a cost-sharing ratio of 75.25

between the Centre and the States. Since inception of the Scheme upto December 2002 a total allocation of Rs. 3,496.66 crore, to benefit 32.48 lakh Swarozgaris.

SAMPOORNA GRAMEEN ROZGAR YOJANA (SGRY)

The Sampoorna Grammen Rozgar Yojana (SGRY) was launched in September 2001. The schemes of Jawahar Gram Samridhi Yojana (JGSY) and Employment Assurance Scheme (EAS) have been fully integrated with SGRY. The objective of the scheme is to provide additional wage employment alongwith food security, creation of durable community, social and economic assets and infrastructure development in the rural area. The scheme envisages generation of 100 crore mandays of employment in a year. The cost of the programme is to be shared between the Centre and the State on a cost-sharing ratio of 87.5 : 12.5 (including foodgrains component). During 2001-02, 22.00 lakh tonnes of rice and 12.49 lakh tonnes of wheat were allocated under the scheme. Off take upto April 2002 was 13.5 lakh tonnes of rice and 5.64 lakh tonnes of wheat. During the current year the total of foodgrains from the Central pool, under the scheme was 39.22 lakh tonnes upto December 2002. Under SGRY (Spl. Comp.) 47.63 lakh tonnes of foodgrains have separately been released until now, free of cost, to the State Governments for facilitating employment generation programmes in drought prone areas.

PRADHAN MANTRI GRAMODAYA YOJANA (PMGY)

PMGY was launched in 2000-01 in all the State and the UTs (Union Territories) in order to achieve the objective of sustainable human development at the village level. The PMGY envisages allocation of Additional Central Assistance to the States and UTs for selected basic minimum services in order to focus on certain priority areas of the Government, PMGY initially had five components viz., Primary health, Primary Education, Rural Shelter, Rural Drinking Water and Nutrition. Rural Electrification has been added as an additional component from 2001-02.

The allocation for PMGY in 2000-01 was Rs. 2500 crore. This has been enhanced to Rs. 2800 crore for 2001-02. For the year 2002-03, Rs. 2800 crore have been provided.

During the last two annual plans, the six sectoral programmes of PMGY were managed by the concerned Central Administrative Departments. However this programme, New guidelines on the implementation of the PMGY during Annual Plan 2002-03 have been issues to all the State Governments and UTs.

PRADHAN MANTRI GRAMODAYA YOJANA (GRAMIN AWAS)

The scheme seeks to achieve the objective of sustainable habitat development at the village level. Central allocation for rural shelter component of PMGY: GA in 2001-02 was Rs. 406.85 crore out of which Rs. 291.25 crore has been released by Ministry of Finance.

PRADHAN MANTRI GRAMODAYA YOJANA—RURAL DRINKING WATER PROJECT

Under this programme, a minimum 25 per cent of the total allocation is to be utilized to be respective States/UTs on projects/schemes for water conservation, water harvesting, water fedhrage and sustainability of the drinking water sources in respect of areas under Desert Development Programme/Drought Prone Area Programme.

PRADHAN MANTRI GRAM SADAK YOJANA (PMGSY)

The PMGSY, which was launched on 25th December 2000, is a programme to provide road connectivity through good all-weather roads to 1.60 lakh Unconnected Habitations with a population of 500 persons or more in the rural areas by the end of the Tenth Plan period (2007) at an estimated cost of Rs. 60,000 crore. The programme is being executed in all the States and six Union Territories. While the focus of the programme is on providing road connectivity of Unconnected Habitations of stipulated population size, connectivity is being provided to all Panchayat Headquarters and places of tourist interest under the PMGSY irrespective of the population size. Since inception, project proposals for Rs. 7.553.26 crore have been cleared. About 56.200 kms. of rural roads have been taken up under the programme, benefiting about 37,225 habitations. The programme is being executed in all states and six Union Territories. Till December 2002, 10,882 road works have been completed providing connectivity to 12,508 Habitations with an expenditure of Rs. 3,321,059 crore.

The present source of funding for PMGSY is the diesel cess, 50 per cent of which is earmarked for PMGSY. Efforts are underway to raise additional resources for the programme with financial assistance from the World Bank and the Asian Development Bank.

ANTYODAYA ANNA YOJANA

The scheme was launched by the Prime Minister on 25th December 2001. Under the scheme 1 crore poorest families out of the BPL families covered under the Targetted Public Distribution System are identified. 25 kgs of foodgrains were made available to each eligible family at a highly subsidized rate of Rs. 2 per kg for wheat and Rs. 3 per kg for rice. This quantity has been enhanced from 25 to 35 kgs with effect from April, 2002 for a period of 1 year, i.e., upto March 31, 2003. Against an allocation of 19,060 lakh tonnes of foodgrains from the Central Pool, upto December 2002, was 24.08 lakh tonnes.

ANNAPURNA YOJANA

This scheme was launched on April 1, 2002 as a 100 per cent Centrally Sponsored scheme. It aims at providing food security to meet the requirement of those senior citizens who though eligible for pension under the National Old Age Pension Scheme, are not getting the same. 10 kgs of foodgrains per person per month are supplied free of cost. 1062 lakh tonnes of foodgrains (wheat and rice) at BPL rates was allotted to Ministry of Rural Development during 2001-02. Off-take were 0.37 lakh tonnes of wheat and 0.56 lakh tonnes of rice. During 2002-03, 0.87 lakh tonnes of foodgrains have been lifted upto December 2002. The scheme has been transferred to the State Plan from 2002-03.

INDIRA AWAS YOJANA (IAY)

The Indira Awas Yojana (IAY) aims at providing dwelling units, free of cost, to the poor families of the Scheduled Caste, Scheduled Tribes, freed bonded labourers and also the non-ST/ST persons below the poverty lines in rural areas. The scheme is funded on a cost-sharing basis of 75.25 between the Centre and States. The ceiling on construction assistance under the IAY is Rs. 20,000 per unit for the plain areas and Rs. 22,000 for the hilly/difficult areas. Since inception, upto February 2003 about 94-lakh houses have been constructed by incurring an expenditure of Rs. 16.202.25 crore. A major scheme for construction of houses to be given to the poor, free of cost, it has an additional component, namely, conversion of unserviceable *kutcha* houses to semi-*pucca* houses. Further, a Credit-*cum*-Subsidy Scheme for rural housing was launched from 1.4.1999 targeting rural families having annual income up to Rs. 32,000. From the year 2002-03, this scheme has been merged with IAY.

JAI PRAKASH ROZGAR GUARANTEE YOJANA (JPRGY)

The scheme seeks to provide guaranteed employment to the employed in the most distressed districts of the country. Operational modalities for launching of the scheme are being worked out.

SWARNA JAYANTI SHAHRI ROZGAR YOJANA (SJSRY)

The Urban Self-employment Programme and the Urban Wage Employment Programme are two special schemes of the SJSRY initiated in December 1997, which replaced various programmes operated earlier for urban poverty alleviation. This is funded on a 75.25 basis between the Centre and States. During 2001-02 an allocation of Rs. 168 crore was provided for various components of this programme, which was reduced to Rs. 45.50 crore at RE stage. The expenditure was Rs. 39.21 crore during 2001-02. For 2002-03 an allocation of Rs. 105 crore has been provided for various components of this programme. The expenditure during the current financial year, upto January 31, 2003 is Rs. 73.61 crore.

VALMIKI AMBEDKAR AWAS YOJANA (VAMBAY)

This scheme was formally launched by the Prime Minister on the 2nd December 2001. The scheme seeks to ameliorate the conditions of the urban slum dwellers living the poverty line who do not possess adequate shelter. The scheme has the primary objective of facilitating the construction and upgradation of dwelling units for the slum dwellers and providing a healthy and enable urban environment through community toilets under Nirmal Bharat Abhiyan, a component of the scheme. The Central government provides a subsidy of 50 per cent; the balance 50 per cent being arranged by the State Government with ceiling prescribed both for dwelling units/community toilets.

During the current financial year, Central subsidy to the extent of Rs. 138.31 crore has already been released out of the budget provision of Rs. 2,53,085 crore. Till January 2003, a total sum of Rs. 211.87 crore has been released as Government of India Subsidy for the construction/upgradation of 1,06,038 dwelling units, 20,817 toilet seats under the scheme.

EMPLOYMENT FRONT

This is an established fact that the employment intensive acceleration of economic growth facilitates the reduction of poverty in the long-run. In a series of poverty alleviation programmes, employment generation has always been a focal point. But due to reduction in public sector expenditure on welfare programmes during post-reform and the weak implementation and execution of poverty alleviation programmes, as have been discussed in the earlier parts, employment generation targets could hardly be achieved.

Wherever, our schemes fail to touch targets or prove to be weak to fulfil the goals, we in order to make them more effective, redesigned and restructured them. Various schemes have been merged and renamed. Various parts of schemes have been deleted. Various alterations have been made. But inspite of all such exercises, the review reports have always been disappointing. Our IRDP and JRY are the examples. More recently, Jawahar Gram Samridhi Yojana (JGSY) was introduced in April 1999 as a successor of JRY. Similarly, Swarna Jayanti Gram Swarozgar Yojana (SGSY) was also introduced in April 1999, which is the combined and restructured shape of IRDP and allied Programmes along with Million Well Schemes (MWS) into single self-Employment programmes. Employment Assurance Schemes (AES) has been extended to cover all 5449 rural blocks of the country situated in draught prone, desert, tribal and hill areas. The primary objective is the creation of additional wage employment opportunities during the period of acute shortage of wage employment through manual work for the rural poor living below the poverty line. But our past experience reveals that the ultimate results of such changes, alterations, deletions and mergers have been impressive.

TABLE 4

Growth Rate of Employment in Organized Sector: 1991-99 (%)

Year	*Public Sector*	*Private Sector*	*Total Organized Sector*
1991	1.52	1.24	1.44
1992	0.80	2.21	1.21
1993	0.60	0.06	0.44
1994	0.62	0.01	0.73
1995	0.11	1.63	0.55
1996	–0.19	5.62	1.51
1997	0.67	2.06	0.09
1998	–0.09	1.72	0.46
1999	–0.00	0.11	0.04

Source: GOI, *Economic Survey,* 2000-01, p. 192.

The annual growth of employment for the national as a whole during the post-reform period 1991-99 has been quite unsatisfactory. Private sector shown an organized growth in employment during the said period while there was hardly any growth of employment in the public sector. The above Table 4 presents the public and private sector employment growth trend during 1991-99.

The agriculture sector reflects this trend more severely. The estimates of real wages for unskilled workers in poverty ridden States presents a most deplorable condition.

All states except Gujarat shows a deteriorating situation. The level of deterioration is highest in Bihar, which shows no improvement after 1996-97. Assam shown +8.60 per cent change in real wages in 1993-94, but his percentage declined to +4.13 in 1999-2000. Orissa also showed a negative change in most of the years except in 1995-96, 1997-98 and 1998-99 when the range was positive, but it was of very low profile. Gujarat is the only state where this change remained positive throughout the years.

TABLE 5

Annual Percentage Change in Real Wages for Unskilled Agricultural Workers for Selected States: 1993-2000

States	*1993-94*	*94-95*	*95-96*	*96-97*	*97-98*	*98-99*	*99-2000*
Assam	+5.30	+2.71	–1.73	+1.51	+4.3	–3.46	+4.13
Bihar	+5.38	+1.69	–2.73	+15.15	–4.70	–5.70	–3.26
Gujarat	+2.36	+1.27	+2.92	+5.08	–14.43	–7.37	+10.14
M.P.	–3.53	+1.93	+ 1.24	+1.31	+0.83	+0.79	+3.74
Orissa	–0.11	–3.52	+0.55	–0.41	+2.39	+0.61	+0.23
Rajasthan	–7.66	+1.05	–10.33	+17.81	+5.12	–16.26	+16.83
U.P.	–6.77	–2.31	+14.78	–6.39	+17.36	+0.38	–5.61

Source: GOI, *Economic Survey,* 2000-01, p. 193.

A recent study by K. Sundaram: Employment and Poverty in 1990's (*EPW*, August 11-17, 2001) confirms that the over-all rural employment situation in post-reform period has not thousand improved. The crude worker population ratio per thousand reduced from 533 rural males in 1993-94 to 531 in 1999-2000, and the figures for the rural females from 328 to 299. The total figures in terms of rural persons declined from 444 in 1993-94 to 419 in 1999-2000. The industry-wise rural workforce division (males and females) during 1961, 1993-94 and 1999-2000 also shows the same declining trend.

These estimates clearly shows that the rural employment scenario during the post-reform period is no facilitating our poverty alleviation programmes. One should not deny the fact that merely restructuring and redesigning the prevailing programmes or combining them is not the guarantee to make them more effective. For improving the efficiency of these programmes the reed is to reduce the number of programmes so that duplication and fragmentation could be stooped, wastage and corruption could be checked and better targets in terms of relevance to total local needs and priorities could be determined.

TABLE 6

Industries-wise Rural Workforce Division during 1961, 1993-94 and 1999-2000 (Per 1000 Share)

Industry Division/ Group	*1961*		*1993-94*		*1999-2001*	
	Males	*Females*	*Males*	*Females*	*Males*	*Females*
1. Agriculture/ Forestry, Fishing	861	857	784	774	762	749
2. Group Production, Plantation	834	841	718	666	696	643
3. Live-stock	21	14	53	97	49	90
4. Agricultural Services	1	1	—	—	12	12
5. Mining and Quarrying	4	3	6	4	5	3

Source: K. Sundaram, Employment and Poverty in 1990's. Tables 4 and 5, pp. 3043-44.

CONCLUDING OBSERVATIONS

All the discussed above are not helping much in reducing the rural poverty. The growth trend, which is a sound base for eliminating poverty, is proved weak. The achievements of the direct attack measure remained far behind the targets. And as a result NSS indicates that there is little change in the rural poverty rate upto 2002. Our prevailing poverty elimination programmes also need reforms. There is an urgent need of diverting the spending pattern from help-base to growth-base.

Higher emphasis should be placed on the growth of agriculture and small-scale industries and creation of self-employment opportunities. In agriculture, the strategy of growth with employment should bring about extension of irrigation, more specially with the minor irrigation works, in the slow growth areas in the country, changes in crop pattern and development of allied agricultural activities like animal husbandry and fishery, poultry, etc. which are highly employment generation, should also be encouraged. A vigorous programme of rural industrialization with emphasis on processing of agricultural produce, fruit and vegetable processing, industries utilizing agricultural by-products, village handicrafts and cottage industries should be launched. In addition, ancillary and feeder industries should be located in the rural areas. For such a programme of rural industrialization all possible of supporting administrative technical financial and organizational measures should be provided.

6

Poverty—Progeny of Progress

RAM NARESH THAKUR

A study of the poverty of nations has even more urgency than a study of the wealth of nations. Poverty is the key point around which the 'Economics of Development', clusters. Poverty anywhere is threat to plenty (prosperity). Poverty is the weakest point in the whole development sequence of nation. Poverty is the greatest enemy of human right and human development. Poverty elimination is the origin of all human rights. Freedom of all citizens to get food with honour, to lead dignified life is the main thing of all human right documents. But it is impossible without alleviation of poverty from the country at instant and for ever.

POVERTY AND DEVELOPMENT

Whether it is a question of the developing countries or of the industrial economies: (a) there exists an overlap between poverty and in quality and that day are closely related; and (b) incidence of poverty correlates with low levels of health, education and nutrition, inadequate shelter and other unsatisfactory social conditions. It is also an accepted fact that poverty in most of the developing countries despite being urbanized still remains overwhelmingly a rural phenomenon The poor are not only concentrated in countries with low rates of GNP and per capita GNP levels but also in fast growing countries with relatively high rates of GNP. Poverty tends to be concentrated in the areas with little or no access to health, education, and infrastructure services like transport and communications. Poverty *per se* is necessarily associated with crime and related activities. When poverty, including wide disparities and high unemployment rates, gets combined with a perception that the state, on the one hand does not do much for the poor and the poor get highly marginalized, isolated and excluded socially, on the other, there emerge very strong incentives that force disadvantaged poor to crime and violence. Significantly poverty is not seen as an isolated problem, but is the cause of our all other problems. FAO insists that if people are hungry it is because they are poor and cannot afford to buy the food they need. WHO also assures us that if people are disease-ridden and die young it is because they are poor and cannot afford the medicines that would make them healthy. The answer to both hunger and disease is thus the eradication of poverty, which means more development. By defining poverty in purely monetary terms, it assumed that money has always been, and always must be a pre-requisite—as indeed it partly clearly today for satisfying real needs.

Some economists define it as 'Poverty is meant for that social activity in which a part of the society is unable to satisfy their basic necessities and a larger part of the society becomes deprived of minimum standard of living. That is recognized as a token of wide-spread poverty. In India the commonly accepted definition of poverty stresses on the low standard of living in comparison with high standard of living. The absolute level of poverty that is expressed in terms of food grains, milk, cloth, or attainment of calories is measured by present standard of living in any country. The large part of society (low income group), being deprived of basic necessities (facilities) in comparison of luxurious standard of living of high income group, makes the poverty more incisive.

According to poverty such persons are become poor who remain unsuccessful in attaining certain minimum standard of living. But all the experts and economists are not of one view on the point of any one minimum standard of living or income. Planning Commission of India had made the conception of poverty by making "Poverty line" on the basis of certain minimum calories or certain income annually in rural and urban areas specifically.

Marshal Sahlins expresses his idea about poverty: "The world's most primitive people have few possessions, but they are not poor. Poverty is not a certain small amount of goods, nor it is just a relation between people. Poverty is a social status. As such it is the invention of civilization."

Economic Development, in spite of its developing effects on societies and the environments, remains the overriding goal of international agencies, national governments, and transnational corporations that are of course its main promoters and beneficiaries.

This is justified on the grounds that only development, and of course the global free trade that fuel it today can eradicate poverty. Hardly any one in a position of authority today seems willing to question this thesis, even though it is backed by neither any empirical nor any serious theoretical evidence. Since shortly after World War II when world trade and economic development really got underway, the former has increased by nineteen times and the latter by no less than six times—an unprecedented performance. If these processes really provide the answer to world poverty, then it should by now have been reduced to little more than a faint memory of our barbaric and underdeveloped past. However, the opposite is true in Indonesia. Poverty has increased by 50% since

1997, in South Korea doubled during the same period; in Russia, it grows from 2.9% to 32.7% between 1966 and 1998 alone.

Much the same thing has happened throughout South America, as well as the Caribbean. It has also increased in the rich industrial world, where 37 million people are now unemployed and 100 million are homeless. In U.K. the number of adults in households with less than half the average income has increased by a million above the level of the early 1990s and reasonable people, these facts should be enough to discredit the dogma that development eradicates poverty. But for the promoters development merely indicates that it has not proceeded fast enough.

POVERTY TREND

The performance of the Indian economy in recent years in terms of rate of growth of national income is remarkable. "Economic reforms initiated in 1991 would be the cause for such growth. The growth rate of GDP was very stagnant at the mean level of 3.5% before 1980s and at 5.8% during 1980-90 had jumped to 6.1% in 1990-98" (R. Nagraj, 2000:2831).

The economic growth banishes the intensity of poverty and provides relief to the poor by offering various opportunities. Growth helps to reduce poverty because of three central reasons:

(a) It creates jobs that "pull up" the poor into gainful employment.
(b) It provides the revenues (income) with which we can build more schools and provide more health facilities for the poor.
(c) It creates the incentives that enable the poor to access these facilities and also for the advancement of progressive social agendas (Jagdish Bhagwati, 2001:844). The inverse relationship between economic growth and decline in poverty level has been witnessed in Indian economy too. "India's experience in the 1960s and most of the 70s showed that poverty reduction was negligible when per capita GDP growth was below 2%, but it began to decline when per capita growth accelerated to 3% and more in the late 70s and 80s. Generalizing from the experience one should expect that poverty reduction should have occurred" (Montek Singh Ahluwalia, 2000: 1640). However, there is a dispute about the tale of poverty reduction is that N.S.S. stagnation of poverty around 37.38% throughout 1990s (Deepak Lal and others, 2001:1019). Whereas NCAER's (National Council for Applied Economic Research) data reveals significant reduction of poverty along with higher economic growth in the 1990s. That is the story of our nation. What about the case of individual state? Ahluwalia feels that economic performance of the individual states in the post-reform period has received less attention. Liberation has reduced the degree of control exercised by the centre in many areas leaving much greater scope for the state level initiatives. This is particularly true as well as attracting

investment; both domestic and foreign is concerned. Therefore, state level performance deserves more attention.

GROWTH-POVERTY-INEQUALITY SYNDROME

The impact of growth on poverty and income distribution is viewed differently by different studies. (Table 1). The earlier work of Simon Kuznets out a negative relationship between the extent of inequality (wide gap of rich and poor) and the level of growth in the name of growth-inequality syndrome. Some of the recent empirical works in India point out reductions in poverty consequent on higher level growth and certain other studies point out increase in poverty, particularly after 1991 despite greater level of growth. These became reduction in the rural poverty during the post-reform period (Mahendra Dev, 2000). At the same time there became increasing inter-state inequalities measured in terms of per capita SDR. On the other hand, NSS data reveals the fact that the rank concordance index across states does not usually show convergence (Raghvendra Jha, 2000). A worrisome development is that there is greater dispersion in rural poverty across the states, though also the convergence of inequality, poverty, and mean consumption in selected states. The concerned table presents the trend in the magnitude of the rural and urban poverty measured in terms of head-count ratio by different sources. It is found that at All India level; percentage of poor below poverty line (BPL) was nearly 53.07% as in 1977-78 and declined round 39% in I990-9I. However, these same quickly shot up to 45% in 1998. The studies of World Bank as well IGIDR (Indira Gandhi Institute of Development Research) bring out a falling and an urban context too. The magnitude of inequality seems to have widened

TABLE 1

Poverty Estimates in All-India (Head Count Ratio)

Year	*PC*	*WB*	*IGIDR*	*PCWB*	*IGIDR*		*All India*
1977-78	53.07	50.6	50.64	45.24	40.5	40.5	51,.32
1983-84	45.65	45.31	45.31	40.79	86.65	36.65	44.48
1987-88	39.09	39.23	39.52	38	W.2	35.6	39
1990-91	NA	36.43	36.4	NA	—	—	—
1992-93	NA	43.47	43.47	NA	NA	NA	NA
1993-94	37.27	36.66	38.71	32.36	30.51	30.09	35.97
1997-98	38.5	35.78	34.22	NA	NA	NA	NA
1998	45.2	NA	NA	34.6	NA	NA	NA
1999-2000	NA	NA	NA	NA	NA	NA	26.1

IGIGDR = Indira Gandhi Institute of Development Research, estimates Reported in Jha (1999).

Estimated quoted in Deepak Lal etc. at *EPW*, March 24, 2001 (pp. 10-19).

Source: PC = Planning Commission (1997) Estimate based on Expert Committee Estimates, WB = World Bank Reported in Datt (1995).

measured by gini-coefficient, particularly during the decade of reform measures. The gini-coefficient for rural India according to the study of IGIDR was estimated at 33.74 as in 1957-58 and at 35.90 for urban India. The same declined to 27.71 for rural as in 1990-91. During 1990s the gini-coefficient increased to 30.11 and 36.12 for rural and urban India respectively, measured as in 1997-98. This finding was further supported by MISH as well as World Bank and Tendulkar estimates, though there are statistical variations in their estimates (*EPW*, March 24, 2001). This is the short analysis of growth, poverty and inequality (in equality between poor and rich, between rural and urban, between inter-states, between forward class and dalits, backwards etc.).

The data is not related with each other due to methodological differences of the sources. The problem of poverty must be analysed by taking rural on division into account. Then only one can understand the impact of growth on the reduction (or increase) of poverty at all India level or at different regions or areas. The average size of rural poverty is higher in all sources than urban poverty. So there is rural-urban divide in the process of growth (development) in the economy. The inverse relationship between growth and poverty lies in the certain coefficient between per capita income and the level of poverty therein.

The provisions of globalization and liberalization also are going in favour of rich states (as it is going in favour of developed nations on the world level) only. The trend of privatization is on the peak. It is increasing unemployment inequality and poverty every day. The future is very dark. The government factories and industries are being closed. The industrial Progress of all the units of BIMARU states (except Rajasthan) has remained negative. There has become heavy downfall in the establishment of industrial units in Andhra Pradesh, Bihar, and M.P. Although they has become slight progress in the condition of Uttar Pradesh. In the first ten years of liberalization only 17% increase took place in the total number of industrial units. Under the Factories Act the following change took place during 1991-92 and 1999-2000 in the number of industrial units in the country (states-wise). (Table 2)

TABLE 2(A)

Industrial Units in India, (States-wise)

Sl. No.	*States*	*1991-92*	*1999-2000*	*Increase or Decrease (%)*
1.	Bihar	3,671	1.570	–57.23
2.	M.P.	4,163	.4	
3.	Andhra Pradesh	15,972	164	
4.	Karnataka	5,850	52	
5.	Kerala	3,702	+30.87	
6.	Tamil Nadu	15,502	20,249	+30.6
	All India	1,12,286	1, 1,557	+ 17

TABLE 2(B)

Industrial Sickness

Satisfactory Condition	*Very satisfactory Condition*
Northern States Delhi, U.P., Haryana, H.P., J&K and and Nagar Haweli	**Western States** Gujarat, Goa, Maharashtra and Dadar Rajasthan

Industrial development is the most important factor for eliminating poverty. But during the last thirteen years (which remained the period of liberalization and Economic Reform) there became no progress according to expectation in the manufacturing sector due to the effects of liberalization policy During this period (1991-92 to 1999-2000) of economic reform or liberalization, Bihar has suffered the most. There became 57% decrease in the number of industrial units in the stipulated period, in southern state Andhra Pradesh, though it has made progress in information technology sector has been proved its worst in the case of industrial units. The so-called progress made by liberalization has made no impact on the condition of economically backward and so-called BIMARU States. Really their condition has been worsened during past thirteen years due to the LPG Policy (Liberalization, Privatization and Globalization).

NEXUS OF UNEMPLOYMENT AND POVERTY

Poverty cannot be eliminated without continuous process of eliminating it through employment. Providing employment continuously and its position constant and increasing, development is essential continuously. But the must thrilling position is that the growth rate of employment has remained less than 1% decreasingly from more than 20%. In one hand, population is increasing tremendously and on the other hand the opportunity of employment is decreasing. The Prime Minister is deceiving the nation saying that more than one crore employment is being created, counting the whole prospect of increasing all kinds of probable employment (including part-time, temporary and muster roll employment created in roads, projects, etc.) in all the sectors (agriculture, industrial, service, trade, infrastructure, etc.) under private, public or/and joint ownership. This is a very fraud method of cheating the nation en bloc. The employment ratio is decreasing in public sector. The public sector is not in a position to provide more employment due to many reasons (like continuous loss running tendency of the government for public sector retrenchment, compulsory retirement, avoiding new and fresh appointment policies of the government, etc). Once Rajiv Gandhi was being criticized for launching computer and thus decreasing the opportunities of employment. But now due to computers alone, crores of unemployed youths got opportunities of employment. After all what the computers can do alone?

Crores of unemployed are on the roads without bread. According to the previous economic survey, 2,24,000 industrial units are sick in the country. 473 out of 700 licensed sugar mills are in running position any how. 143 out of 271 sugar mills are closed in private sector and remaining are in loss. The cotton mills provided maximum number of employment previously and earned more and more foreign exchange. But almost all big cotton mills are in closed position till decade. 313 cotton mills had become closed up to 31 March, 1999. In the phase of liberalization unemployment took its acute form in developed countries on the record level. This level of unemployment became the largest thereafter 1994. This number became more than 90 lakh there. Now as the record of U.S.A. the rate of unemployment had decreased there. But it is not due to increase in the number of opportunities of employment: it is due to the fall in the number of job-seekers who left the job market out of despair, job was available to them. In June 2002 the rate of unemployment there was 6.4% which became 6.2% now (July 2003). It became due to the fall in number of unemployed persons in the employment exchanges who could not get employment and became out of job market record. Such number of unemployed persons (not being recorded as unemployed) is more than 5.5 lakh there. Such persons are unemployed, but they are not treated unemployed as they became out of register. Besides this in the US economy many persons became prey of retrenchment due to depress such type of retrenched persons (really became unemployed but not recorded as unemployed) were more than 72 thousand in June, 2003 and again more than 44 thousand in July 2003. Maximum retrenchment took place in the construction companies there. Such retrenchment was more than 71 thousand.

50% of population of world spends their lives on the income less than $2 per day. Out of them about 70% are living in the rural areas of Asian and African countries. 23% people of the world are leading lives in acute poverty. But the condition of India is very severe.

POVERTY AND HUMAN DEVELOPMENT

India is leading towards grave economic crisis. Its condition has become worse than 1991. Its growth rate was 6.7% between I992 to 1997, which has lifted up to 4.4% in 2001-02. (World Bank Report quoting data of Planning Commission, India). If India does not control the worsening condition of central as well as states, economic reform does not become welfare and equality-oriented; all its objectives of development-oriented, all its objectives of development and poverty eradication will remain on the paper only. In the urban and rural population the gap of development is increasing in lieu of decreasing. If the new economic policy widened the gap of development between developed and developing countries, it is also increasing the gap of poverty (due to gap of development) between the rich and poor states within the country.

More than half population living below poverty line (BPL) are living in

Bihar, Uttar Pradesh, Madhya Pradesh, and Orissa only. While the condition of Maharashtra, Tamil Nadu etc. is far better. The government poses that its foreign exchange stock has increased up to more than $80 Arab. When investment is not increasing, how did 'foreign exchange stock increase? Our deficit balance of trade has touched up to $152 crore or Rs. 76 thousand crore. We are compensating our trade deficit from surplus stock of foreign exchange.' We will have to pay adversely for it in the near future. The country will not sustain this development regularly. This is the story of one sided, limited, unmanaged, and imperfect (incomplete) development. The joint income of three billionaire of world is more than joint income of most oppressed and poor 6 crore persons of the poor countries. Out of more than 6 Arab persons 20% people have income of less than $1 per day.

The UNDP has ranked India in the year 2003 on the 12@ position (out of 175 nations), when its position was 12th (out of 173 nations) in previous year. There has become downfall in the ranking of human development, whether a slight increase took place in the "Human Development Index." It has been ranked 0.577 in previous year. According to the report of UNDP India is one of such counted countries which have made good contribution in achieving the aim of decreasing the number of poor up to half till 2015 in the direction of attainment of "Global Millennium Development Goal." It has praised specially experiment of decentralization of Madhya Pradesh, Kerala, and West Bengal. The report has also praised the effort of Madhya Pradesh, Rajasthan, Uttar Pradesh, and Bihar (BIMARU states only) in bridging the 'Gender Literacy Gap'.

PROSPECTED POVERTY SCENARIO

Poverty eradication is also one the other objective in the out line of Tenth Five Year Plan (2002-07). In this plan the economic growth rate is targeted 8% per year at national level and different growth rate targets of different states. According to the current data the number of persons below poverty line in 1999-2000 was 26.10%. In 2007 (in the last of Tenth Plan) the poverty ratio (the ratio of persons living below poverty line in the total population) will remain only 19.34%. According to the Planning Commission, in that condition the total number of poor persons in the country will be 22 crore. The maximum havoc of poverty will fall on only two states viz. undivided Bihar (present Bihar, and Jharkhand) and Orissa. The number of poor persons will be 10 crores in those states, which will be about 50% of the total number of poor persons will be 80 persons in joint U.P. (present U.P. and Uttaranchal), Joint M.P. (present M.P. and Chhatisgarh), Maharashtra and West best Bengal in addition to those states (i.e. Bihar, Jharkhand and Orissa). (Table 3)

Prospected after attainment of target of Tenth Five Year Plan. In 2007 Bihar will be the only state to record the increase in the rate of poverty (percentage of population living below poverty line) at the rate of 1.12%.

TABLE 3

Population Below Poverty Line

SI. No.	*States*	*1993-94*	*1999-2000*	*2007*
1	*2*	*3*	*4*	*5*
1.	Andhra Pradesh	NA	15.77	8.49
2.	Bihar (Joint)	54.96	42.60	43.18
3.	Gujarat	24.21	14.0/	2.0
4.	Haryana	25.5	8.74	2.0
5.	Karnataka	33.16	20.04	7.85
6.	Kerala	25.43	12.72	3.61
7.	M.P. (Joint)	42.52	37.43	29.52
8.	Maharashtra	36.86	25.02	16.18
9.	Orissa	48.56	47.15	41.04
10.	Punjab	NA	6.16	2.0
11.	Rajasthan	27.41	15.28	12.11
12.	Tamil Nadu	35.03	21.12	6.61
13.	U.P. (Joint)	40.03	31.15	24.67
14.	West Bengal	40.03	27.02	18.30
	All India		26.10	19.34

DEVELOPMENT COLLAPSED

We all know that neither in planned economic development under capitalist system nor in the condition of free market the solution of unemployment not possible. The most miserable condition of the poor mainly due to the gigantic problem of the unemployment. The remedy of the problem of unemployment is possible in developed countries too under capitalism. In India highly educated person is anxious for getting even a job of a peon. Now about 34 crore people are working (in employment) in which 2 crore 92 lakh only are engaged in organized sector, about 4 crore persons are in self-employment (rich peasants), about 27 crore persons come either in the grade of unemployed or they are facing the misery of under-employment (semi-employment or invisible employment). Most of them are engaged in a different illegal works including crime and violence in effort of earning bread. Can this be called 'development' by anyway?

Either it might be 'controlled economic system (1950-1990) or infrastructure of free market (initiated after 1990)' India is running in direction of development lessness continuously.

WORLD PANORAMA OF POVERTY VERSUS DEVELOPMENT

Now poverty, development, inequality, hunger, disease, unemployment, disparity, etc. have been scrapped from the agenda of world. The war against terrorism and other agendas have taken its place. In 2000 New York has witnessed the 'United Nations Millennium Apex Conference' consisting of 189 countries' administrative heads. In that conference eight objectives of development had decided for performing within stipulated period (up to 2015) the following were main objectives of development in the world conference agenda—

(a) Decreasing the number of maximum poor persons, earning less than $1 a day, to the half, from the level of, 1990 to 2015.
(b) To make it guaranteed that each child is admitted in primary schools and he completes the education.
(c) The gender gap should be abolished in primary and middle school completely up to 2005.
(d) Two-third decreased should be made between 1990 to 2015 in the infant death-rate below the age of five.
(e) The three-fourth decreased will be made in the maternal death rate in this stipulated period.
(f) There will be effort to control over the expansion of the epidemics like HIV/AIDS, T.B. and malaria within 1990-2015.

The availability of guaranteed pure water and reducing the number of the deprived persons to the half etc.

The administrative heads of 189 countries had made some promises with the more than one Arab poor hungry, unemployed, sick and deprived persons of the world. But the situation had been changed in such a way that the developed countries like USA and Great Britain, in spite of fulfilling those aims and objectives are trying for new war of their supremacy over the countries again and again on the name of war against terrorism (although it may be the vital problem too) without any hesitation to refuse and disobey the identity, existence, authority and dignity of even UNO (Besides most of the countries of the world opposed of the war against poverty and employment).

The UNDP through the Annual Human Development Report, 2003 again had tried and reminded the world to bring poverty, hunger, unemployment and disease, etc. is the agenda of world. The UNDP thus is trying to show of mirror to the world for seeing its own reformatted face. The change in the agenda of the world developed countries (visual, UK, etc.). It is less hoped that the target of millennium can be achieved up to 2015 till the problem of hunger, poverty, disease, disparity, and unemployment does not become the first priority in the agenda of world in place of terrorism as well as developed and rich countries do not perform their obligations towards the poor people of the world. If there will be same speed of progress in achieving the target in the twenty countries of Sub-Sahara region of the African Sub-continent there will be 125 years span of time (till 2129) to fulfil the aim of universal primary education, it will be up to 2147 to make the number of poor persons to the half. In this way it will be not less than 6165 to cut down the two-third ratio of infant mortality rate. The countries of Sub-Sahara region are considered as the most poor and most backward (in respect of development) country of the world. But the progress report of rest under developed and developing countries, except some counted developing countries, is not less serious or non-alarming. This decade of globalization (decade of 90s) is considered as the 'decade of despair in economic prosperity or boom' but that decade was proved as the 'decade of despair and breakage of dream' for most of the countries of the world. The UNDP report has unveiled the mystery of the decade of 'jump in economic prosperity'.

In the Decade (1990-2000)

(1) Fifty-four countries have witnessed increase in the number and rate of persons leaving below poverty line.
(2) Ratio of persons slept in hunger has increased in some 21 countries.
(3) The infant mortality rate has increased in some 14 countries.
(4) The percentage of enrolment in primary schools had been reduced in some 12 countries.
(5) Some 21 countries had recorded the fall in the 'Human Development Index'.
(6) In some 125 developing nations the average rate of increase in per capita income had remained less than 3%.
(7) In some 54 nations there became decrease in place of increase in the average per capita income.

The seldom case of these kinds were seen before 1990. The honey of economic prosperity obtained from globalization was shared fully by the developed and rich countries. The developing and under-developed countries got only the poisonous wastages of it. Thus the reality of the achievements of globalization can be understood by observing the vast gap of disparity taken place due to it within the developed and developing countries and again within the rich picture of economic disparity between rich and poor persons of the world and the persons within the country as well. Some examples are visible such as:

(1) The total income of 5% most prosperous (the richest) persons of the world is 4 times more than the total income of 5% most backward (the poorest) persons of the world.
(2) The total income of only 1% of the most prosperous persons (the richest among the rich) is equal to the total income of the 57% poor persons of the world.
(3) The total income of some 2.5 crore richest persons of USA is equal to total income of 2 Arab the most poor persons of world.

There became the huge gap in the disparity of income within the state took place due to globalization policies. In the survey report of 73 countries within the two decades (1980-90 and 1990-2000) there became—

(1) Record increase in the economic disparity took place in 42 countries out of 73.
(2) In 6 countries, out of 33 developing countries mentioned in the sample, mere became fall in the economic disparity.
(3) In 17 countries there become rise in economic disparity.

It is evident by comparing different evidences that the vehicle of globalization is running fast bypassing most of the poor persons and regions of the world having cared, and attention of some selected elite persons of the world. For example in India the rate of per capita economic growth of Gujarat remained 7.8% within 1992-97, the same remained negative (–0.2%/–0.2%) in Bihar. The development strategy should be trained by the concerned nations according to their own needs and priorities. The all nations should not be compelled to obey and follow the same strategy formulated and engineered in the direction of World Bank/IMF (SAP, etc.). The report suggest for implementing, labour-oriented development models for paving the path of development and eliminating the rate of poverty. The report also suggests for the active role (participation) of the state in the human development sector and increase in the public investment. This report also advocates the land reform programs and redistribution of the land as tool to eliminate poverty. Good governance (strict administration with proper law and order) is also the primary factor for eliminating poverty.

INDIA DIVIDED

The scene of internal economic disparity among the states is visible with some facts such as Bangalore now has more in common with the Bay Area in San Francisco, US, than with Bihar. Life on the fields of eastern U.P. resembles that in certain parts of East Africa more closely than in Western U.R itself. At the sprawling shopping pulls in Delhi's Southern or eastern outskirts a branded polo shirt costs of $ 100, whereas other parts of Delhi is infested of vast expanses of slums. Although most Indians seem to be better off today than a decade ago, some regions have improved their lot much more than others. Goa, Delhi, Gujarat, and Maharashtra notched up the fastest growth in the 1990s, whereas growth rates in the half of the 15 biggest of its actually declined. On a per head basis, the difference is even starker. Some state where growth is slower, including the two biggest Uttar Pradesh and Bihar, also have fast growing populations. The yarning gaps are only growing. For every new 'hotspot' emerging as a symbol of modern India, there are at least a dozen 'rot spots' serving as reminders of decay. The question is no longer whether India's economic fragmentation will happen. The question is, why has it happened and what can be done about it?

TABLE 4

Prosperous States	*Striving /Middling States*	*Poor States*
Gujarat, Maharashtra, Haryana, Punjab, Delhi, Goa, Meghalaya	Andhra Pradesh, Karnataka, Tamil Nadu, Kerala, Pondicherry, Sikkim, Arunachal Pradesh, Chhatisgarh, Orissa, Pradesh, Nagaland, Manipur, Mizoram, Jammu and Kashmir	Uttaranchal, Uttar Pradesh, Bihar, Jharkhand, Madhya Pradesh, Assam

It is indicative, not definitive categorization.

Source: *India Today*, May 19, 2003.

Till the mid-1980s there was slow growth rate. Consequently inequalities did not increase rapidly. The impoverishment of rural economy during most of the 1990s, the declining share of agriculture in India's GDP, the urge in services economy and above all the infusion of competition and market, forces have begun to deepen the divide. Competition promotes efficiency, not equality. It rewards good performers generously and punishes laggards, often harshly. The increasing flow of money and people largely from the rust belt of the east to the Pockets of west, south, and north will only perpetuate the divergence. Some optimist sees hopes of convergence too. They argue that the winners of the free will demonstrate to the losers the price of non-performance. Especially those winners who have come on their own in the competitive environment. For instance, Andhra Pradesh and H.P.—one has made strides in economic performance and the other in social development. But right now, such case studies are too few to be hopeful of a large scale convergence.

India still has some time to set things right. Compared to many other poor and developing countries—including China—its inequalities are less severe. The first task is to rise the spending on health and education in the long neglected Hindi-belt and some eastern states. U.P. spends just Rs. 55 a year on the health care of each person in the state, compared with Rs. 382 in Goa. Kerala brings high position in health care (equal to U.S.A.) by spending only Rs. 28 per person.

The laggards states have do doggedly pursue reforms, in governance and in business. It is not as improbable as it sounds. Any way, the most governments can do is to ensure that different regions grow to their potential, even if they still grow unequally.

In the recent ranking survey made by "India Today" group if small Indian states have piped the bigger ones to the post—the top five states (Goa, Delhi, Punjab, Kerala and H.P.) accounts for less than 8% of India's population—it is not because they had suddenly turned into the country's growth engines and became able to make their states most prosperous.

TABLE 5(A)

Poverty Level

Sl. No.	Best Three		Sl. No.	Worst Three	
	States	*% Population below Poverty line*		*States*	*% Population below Poverty line*
1.	Goa	4.40	1.	Orissa	47.15
2.	Punjab	6.16	2.	Bihar	42.60
3.	H.P.	7.63	3.	M.P.	37.43

TABLE 5(B)

Literacy

Sl. No.	Best Three		Sl. No.	Worst Three	
	States	*% of illiterate Population*		*States*	*% of illiterate Population*
1.	Kerala	9.08	1.	Bihar	50.83
2.	Goa	17.68	2.	J&K	45.54
3.	Delhi	18.18	3.	U.P.	41.89

TABLE 5(C)

Health Care Spending

Sl. No.	Best Three		Sl. No.	Worst Three	
	States	*Rs. per person a year**		*States*	*Rs. per person a year**
1.	Goa	382	1.	U.P.	48
2.	H.P.	251	2.	Bihar	61
3.	J&K	245	3.	M.P.	75

*State government spending.
Source: India Today, May 19, 2003.

TABLE 6

Ranking in Highly Populous States*

Sl. No.	*States*	*Population (in Crores)*	*Ranking*
1.	T.N.	6.21	1
2.	Gujarat	5.05	2
3.	Maharashtra	9.67	3
4.	Karnataka	5.27	4

(Contd.)

Sl. No.	*States*	*Population (in Crores)*	*Ranking*
5.	Andhra Pradesh	7.57	5
6.	Rajasthan	5.65	6
7.	W. Bengal	8.02	7
3.	M.P.	8.12	8
9.	U.P.	17.45	9
10.	Bihar	10.90	10

*Accounts for 84% of India's population.

TABLE 7

Overall Ranking of States

Sl. No.	*In order of Ranking States*
1.	Goa
2.	Delhi
3.	Punjab
4.	Kerala
5.	Himachal Pradesh
6.	Tamil Nadu
7.	Haryana
8.	Gujarat
9.	Maharashtra
10.	Karnataka
11.	J&K
12.	Andhra Pradesh
13.	Rajasthan
14.	W. Bengal
15.	M.P.
16.	Assam
17.	U.P.
18.	Orissa
19.	Bihar

TABLE 8

States Different Sectors*

Nos.	*Prosperity & Budget*	*Law & order*	*Education*	*Health*	*Infra-structure*	*Invest-ment Scenario*	*Con-sumption Market*	*Agriculture*	
1	*2*	*3*	*4*	*5*	*6*	*7*	*8*	*8*	*10*
1.	Delhi	1+1	5+3	3+4	2+2	2+2	6+2	1+1	2+9
2.	Goa	2+2	2+9	1+1	1+1	1+1	1+1	2+2	5+6
3.	Punjab	3+3	17+14	7+7	5+6	4+4	4+5	3+3	1+1
4.	Gujarat	4+4	8+6	8+11	8+9	6+9	3+4	8+9	10+5
5.	Haryana	10+5	12+12	9+12	11+13	8+7	5+3	4+4	3+2
6.	Maharashtra	6+6	9+10	5+6	9+10	7+8	8+7	6+5	17+11
7.	T. N.	8+7	3+2	6+5	7+7	10+6	13+9	11+10	6+3
8.	Karnataka	5+8	4+7	11+8	10+8	9+11	10+8	10+11	17+7

(Contd.)

1	2	3	4	5	6	7	8	8	10
9.	H.P	14+9	6+4	4+2	3+4	3+3	7+6	6+6	15+17
10.	Andhra Pradesh	7+10	13+11	15+13	12+11	12+12	12+10	17+14	8+4
11.	J&K	9+11	16+15	13+9	6+3	5+10	2+12	5+8	9+14
12.	Kerala	11+12	1+1	2+3	4+5	11+5	17+14	9+7	13+15
13.	Rajasthan	12+13	7+5	18+17	14+14	14+13	9+13	12+13	18+12
14.	W. Bengal	15+14	14+16	12+14	13+12	16+15	18+17	13+12	11+10
15.	M.P.	13+15	10+8	16+16	17+15	13+14	14+16	14+17	4+13
16.	U.P.	16+16	18+17	17+18	19+19	17+16	15+15	15+16	7+8
17.	Assam	17+17	15+18	10+10	18+17	18+18	11 + 11	16+15	19+19
18.	Bihar	19+18	19+19	19+19	15+16	19+19	19+19	19+19	16+16
19.	Orissa	18+19	11+13	14 +15	16+18	15+17	16+18	18+18	14+18
Fastest mover in the 1990s		Hima chal Pradesh	Punjab	Rajas-than	M.P	Assam & T.N.	Delhi	Andhra Pradesh	Raj-asthan

RANKING OF STATES IN DIFFERENT SECTORS

In each sector Ranking in 1991+ Ranking in 2001 respectively. (*Source*: compiled details of survey made by *India Today* Group, *India Today*, May 19, 2003)

Features of Small States (Small States *versus* Happy People). The above ranking of *India Today* is not survey-based; it is based on objective parameters. Such a ranking places higher value on the adequacy rather than the availability of facilities and utilities. So if Goa, Delhi and Himachal Pradesh rank higher than bigger states like Gujarat, Maharashtra, Karnataka or even Uttar Pradesh it is not because small states get more investment or have more infrastructure. It is because their investment environment and infrastructure facilities are more accessible to new investment. That makes small states sweethearts of the booming services economy. The traditional wealth creation still thrives largely on the industrial infrastructure of western India, small states are cashing in on the growth of IT and services companies. Cutthroat Competition Tends to Inequality, Paves Way to Poverty. There is an undesirable aspect of India's diversity. It has states like Maharashtra, Gujarat and Karnataka which have grown as fast as Asia's tiger economies (proved as to be India's tiger economies) during the past ten years, it also has Bihar, with a population size of Germany's and living standards on a par with Burundi's. If that is not bad enough, the divisions are deepening—simply because in the 1990s the guiding principle of sharing resources has shifted from entitlement to competition combined with economic liberalization, competition among the states compels to raise disparity widely. The state rankings clearly point to the widening wedge between living standards of different states. The rich are getting richer. The poor are not getting poorer absolutely, but they are not getting richer as fast as the rich. In 1991, Bihar's per capita income (Rs. 4,230 a year) was 4.2 times lower than the per capita income of Goa (Rs. 17,670 a year). By 2001, the difference had grown to 6.7 times—Rs. 4,616 for Bihar and Rs. 30,744 for Goa.

The opportunity of liberalization and privatization have sharpen the edge of cut-throat competition (not healthy competition). Rich and successful are not always good performers and poor are not always non-performers. It becomes due to the melody or deformity of the economic system that the poor are pushed in the 'vicious cycle of poverty' (the poor is poor because he is poor). The exploitation of poor by rich more and more elevate this disparity and further poverty. The advocates of new economic reform and policy of liberalization (as *India Today* Survey analysis also) prove the poor as non-performers and rich as good performers The Planning Commission of India and Finance Commission are also the agencies of the rich. Redistribution of resources from rich to poor is shrinking absolutely day-by-day under the undeclared vested conspirated economic policies directed by the different national and international financial organizations. Private investment is free to go where it wants to. Unfettered by governmental dictates, most private investment has shied away from poor states (may be poorly governed too as U.P. and Bihar) and has flowed almost entirely too rich states (may be better managed too as Gujarat, Maharashtra, etc.). Poor in Development, Rich of Consumer Market—The South-West region of India is developed and rich. But the North-East region is underdeveloped and poor. In South-West states, more investment took place and more development made its face prosperous. But in the North-East parts, industries are being sick, capital fled in other state, made its face dark and gloomy.

NORTH, THE LARGEST CONSUMER MARKET

The northern states are emerging as a bundle of contradiction. The largest number of India's poor live in these states, yet the north is the biggest consumption market of the country. It is not only the consumption market of basic necessities but of life style and luxury products as well. Five of the top ten states for the consumer markets are the northern states. Per capita ownership of two-wheelers and televisions are high only in prosperous Punjab, Haryana, and Delhi, but even in U.P. on the whole north India has become the top most consumer market.

EAST, THE MOST BACKWARD REGION

The region that is least attractive for business and living is the east. Even on Critical infrastructure indicators like percentage of households with electricity connection, ratio of road length to population and spread of bank branches, the eastern states—Bihar, West Bengal, and Orissa—fare very badly. Prospects of a possible revival of the east do not seem promising. About 75% of small scale industries registered in West Bengal and a third of those in Orissa are sick. Per capita investment expenditure of state governments is a dribble and private investors are reluctant to invest in the region. The east is undoubtedly the sick child of the Indian economy right now. That does not bode well for the north-east which can do justice to its potential only if it integrates with vibrant east.

AGONY OF DISTRESS

What result will this analysis focus? What shape will this picture take after some time at all-India level? Is India's destiny and development being scripted in the 30 state capitals across the country? These are true impacting the lives of millions of Indians. The failure of one state will undermine the success of others by pulling down the whole country. While there may always be high and low ranking states, India cannot be ranked high unless the growing gap between the lives of people is arrested and diminished by that one all important factor—good governance with proper law and order situation on the whole.

Quandary of Plenty and Poverty and is the 4th Topmost Economic Power of the World)—

> 'India is rich but the Indians are poor'. The greater number of poor persons in India and the nature of its acute poverty are visible at the instance, but India has instituted itself as the 0 topmost economic power of the world. According to the current development indicators of the world, India obtained the 0 position in topmost economic powers of the world in respect of its purchasing power, just after the US,. China and Japan. According to the traditional measurement gross national income of India is only $477.4 Arab, but it affords the purchasing capacity of $2,913 Arab. Morgan Stanley has foretold that India will reach the position of 'Apex Economic Power of the World'.

TABLE 9

Countries and their Purchasing Power

Sl. No.	*Names of Countries*	*Purchasing Power (In Arab $)*	*Gross National Income (In Arabs)*
1.	U.S.A.	9,781	
2.	China	5,027	
3.	Japan	3,246	
4.	India	2,91,3	477.4
5.	Germany	2,580	
6.	England	1,431	
7.	France	1,425	
8.	Italy	1.422	
Not in Order	Russia	995	
	Canada	825	

Source: Morgan Stanley Report, 2003.

PARADOX OF DESPAIR AND HAPPINESS

The Census of 2001 revealed many trifles. Some of the important among those is as follows:

(1) In India total number of buildings is 24.9 crore. There are 17.9 crore houses (76.8%) therein. There 17.9 crore houses are available for 19.2 crore families.
(2) In India 52% people live in such houses which have *pucca* walls and roofs.
(3) 55.8% people have electric facilities and 43.3% people spend their days with kerosene oil only.
(4) 38% people have access to pure drinking water, where as 62% are deprived of it.
(5) Worship places (temples, mosques, gurudwaras, churches etc.) are 0.24 crore (1%) in number, whereas number of schools and colleges etc. is 0.15 crore (0.60%), and number of hospitals, medical treatment centres, etc. is 0.6 crore (0.3%). It is very surprising and symbol of orthodox that the total number and percentage worship places is more than total number and percentage of schools, colleges and hospitals, etc. This is also an indication of development lessness and a result of anti-development attitude.
(6) 2.2 crore persons (12%) have no kitchen and they cook under open sky. 52.5% people depend on woods for fuel.
(7) In India the total users of cooking gas are 3.36 crore (17.5%) in which rural people are only 0.78 crore (6%) and urban people are 2.57 crore (48%).
(8) In India the male-female ratio is 933, whereas it is 1,058 in Kerala and 773 in Chandigarh.

In short, it presents the picture of paradox of poverty and prosperity. Development, Disparity and Discontent bound to be more challenging. The tempo of events will increase and the pattern of change will become more intricate involved, demanding clear thought and finer balance in the formulation of political, economic, and social values. The temptation to force facts into the straight jacket of pet theories and wishful models will have to be avoided. The problem of unemployment and under employment in India is formidable but not insurmountable. The Planning Commission wants 10 million new jobs every year and does top of the desirability of a "new pattern of growth in furtherance of the goal of employment and redistributive justice." Without full employment there can be no redistributive justice. It is only employment which puts purchasing power in the hands of many, without which even industrialization, which depends so much on the home market in India, cannot expand, and grow in full measure. The improvements of the living condition of the poor depend on the useful implementation of such a policy. The mechanical aping of the west is suicidal. M.K. Gandhi experienced it and warned us against it's evils. Gandhi said that the poor can be helped not by mass production but by the production by the masses. What he said is even more relevant today. India has been divided into two parts—rural and urban. With regard to the rural scene it is important not to overlook the crucial diversities in our impatience to arrive at sort of superficial conceptual unity.

The baffling contradictions will have to be unraveled and resolved in order to arrive at the truth. What is the connection between the new agricultural strategy, land reforms and the increasing rural tension in different parts of the country is a question which cannot be answered without reference to the experience in the last one decade (especially after reform) and the various seemingly unconnected factors which go to make up the social milieu. The subtle play of innumerable natural forces behind the changing colors and contours of the social horizon will have to be seen with a deep and discerning eye, free of political myopia. Rural India to be changing but changing unevenly. And sometimes, what appears to be a change is a change from tweedledum to tweedledee.

Food production no doubt increased, but not faster than growth of population The philosophy of dissatisfaction and contentment also undergoes a qualitative change with modernity. Pockets of rural tension (due to poverty) vary from state to state. The situation of north-east states is rigorous. In south-west states development is growing rapidly thus the rate of poverty and discontentment is declining.

RURAL DISPLEASURE

Rural displeasure is a more symptom than a cause of all these developments. Whether displeasure is creative or not, it is not the same thing as the capacity to forge effective and purposive political, economic, and social institutions that function efficiently and deliver the goods. It is stated that 'greed foments revolution'. But one must be reasonably strong, even to be noticeably greedy and not reasonably greedy to move ahead without breaking down. Under rain fed conditions, the bulk of small holdings represent subsistence farming. A new integrated technology for dry regions with cost-return ratios which are feasible even for the small farmer is yet to be developed. When this happens it will be a very major breakthrough in Indian farming. It emphasizes the social responsibility also to contribute to the promotion of development and eliminating the ratio of poverty. Social responsibility implies a progressive social philosophy.

GLOBALIZATION AND POVERTY

The experiences of globalization in Argentina, Chile, Mexico, South Korea, Indonesia, Ecuador and Uruguay prove that in spite of different advantages from globalization, due to the trade and financial liberalization, it has enhanced inequality in the distribution of income and wealth. The habits-pattern has become changed in such away that the demand of luxurious goods like—motor cars, televisions, air conditioners, refrigerators, computers, cold drinks and fast food, etc. raised and the production of such things commonly used by the poor reduced or became stagnant. There are different other adverse affects of globalization on poverty.

Global Difference in Poverty Rates and Tread-Poverty rates and trends differ across the globe. (A) (i) In East Asia and Pacific significant reductions in poverty were achieved in the 1990s, with the number of people living on less than $1 a day falling from about 420 million in 1987 to 280 million in 1998. (ii) But in Europe and Central Asia, Latin America, South Asia, and Sub-Saharan Africa the number of poor people are growing. (B) Poverty also has a gender dimension. Throughout the world women continue to be disadvantaged relative to men.

In South Asia, in about 44% of the world's poor women have only about half as many years of schooling as men limited their income-earning ability. And in many countries women's health is worse than men's.

ATTACKING POVERTY

Efforts to reduce poverty have often focused on narrowly defined goals, such as implementing 'free market reforms' or spurring 'economic growth'. But as the World Bank's World Development Report, 2000/2001: Attacking Poverty argues, governments also need to ensure that the benefits of the growth reach the poor. Growth may not be enough. Almost half of the world's people (some 2.8 billion) live on less than $2 a day, and 5th (some 1.2 billion) live on less than $1 a day. This terrible level of poverty persists despite unprecedented—but unevenly distributed—raises in global wealth in the past century. Over the past 40 years the gap between rich and poor has doubled, with income in the richest 20 countries now averaging 37 times that in the poorest 20.

(A) Earlier Approaches to Reducing Poverty: The Bank's approach to reducing poverty has evolved over the years as new theoretical models have been developed and lessons have been learned from the experience.

(i) In the 1950s and 1960s the prevailing wisdom was that large investments, in physical capital and infrastructure would spur development, and the Bank financed large projects such as dams and power plants. The failure of those projects to significantly reduce poverty convinced Bank policy makers that investing in physical capital was not enough.

(ii) World Development Report, 1980 captured the new thinking, arguing that investments in health and education were important not just in their own right but also as a way of increasing the incomes of poor people.

(iii) In the wake of the debt crisis and the global recession of the 1980s the Bank shifted emphasis once again, focusing on moving economic management and allowing market forces greater play.

(iv) Finally in the 1990s, governance and institutions moved to centre stage as development thinkers reached the conclusion that market reforms can't succeed unless the necessary institutions are in Place.

(B) New Strategy for Attacking Poverty—The Bank's new strategy builds on the experience of the past decade in proposing a broader approach to fighting poverty. The three-pronged approach focuses on increasing opportunities for poor people, facilitating their empowerment and enhancing their security.

(a) *Promoting Opportunities for Poor*--Poor people often leave without the opportunities that better-off people take for granted: jobs, credit, roads, electricity, market for their goods and access to the schools, water, and sanitation and health services that underpin the health and skills essential for work. This lack of opportunity locks poor people into a life of poverty.

To address the problem, the Bank's new strategy focuses on promoting opportunities for the poor by stimulating overall growth making markets work for poor people and building their assets by addressing in equalities in the distribution of such endowments as education for e.g. Specific recommendations include the following:

(i) Encourage effective private investment by reducing risks for private investors, ensuring the rule of law, and fighting corruption.
(ii) Expand into international markets.
(iii) Build the assets of the poor.
(iv) Address asset inequalities across gender, ethnic, racial, and social device.
(v) Improve infrastructure and increase knowledge in poor areas, etc.

(b) *Facilitating Empowerment*—State and social institutions can play a powerful role in promoting growth and reducing poverty if they function soundly and are responsive to the poor. Governments can act in a variety of ways to help create such institutions:

(i) Lay the political and legal basis for inclusive development.
(ii) Create public administrations that foster growth and equity.
(iii) Promote inclusive decentralization and community development.
(iv) Promote gender quality.
(v) Tackle social barriers.
(vi) Support poor people Social capital, etc.

(C) Enhancing Security—Vulnerability to illness, economic dislocation and natural disasters in much greater among poor people—the very people least equipped to deal with such set backs. What can governments do to help reduce this vulnerability?

(i) Formulate a modular approach to helping poor people manage risks.
(ii) Develop national programmes to prevent, prepare for and respond to macro-shocks, including both financial and natural disasters.
(iii) Design national systems of social risks management that are also pro-growth.
(iv) Prevent civil conflict.
(v) Undertake the HIV/AIDS epidemics, etc.

For all circumstances transparent, popular, and honest governance is essential.

OUTCOME OF VARIOUS POVERTY CONFERENCES OF THE WORLD

In proceeding about 21 years so many world level conferences held at different places. Some details of such conferences are as follow:

(1) 1982—At Stockholm—World Conferences on Environment (Earth Conference 1).
(2) 1992—At Rio-de-Jenerio—U.N. Environment Development Conference (Earth Conference II).

Poverty in India

K.S.S. Uduman Mohideen and K. Ramchandran

Poverty is a great curse on humanity. It is accursed not merely for the misery it inflicts, but also for the degradation that it brings. A poor person not only lives a wretched life and is unable to enjoy the barest necessaries of life, but he is also morally degraded. He cannot conduct himself as a human being. The treatment that it is meted out to him in society demoralizes him.

Indians, by and large, are fatalists. They believe in *kismat*. The poor man reconciles himself to his poverty and his rich neighbour may show him all the sympathy he can but feels that nothing can be done to relieve him of his poverty because he believes that he is condemned to poverty by his previous *karma*. In the past, therefore, the Indian society had learnt to live with poverty and there the matter ended.

But the times have changed. Philanthropists like Dadabhai Naoroji took up the cause of the poor. The socialist preaching awakened the Indian masses and the few swear by the thesis that the poor, must remain poor. Mrs. Gandhi's election slogan 'Garibi Hatao' caught the imagination of the masses, though they are at present dejected and disillusioned and they may think that this slogan was a cruel joke. It is however, gratifying that the Planning Commission in the Approach Document to the Fifth Plan, has focused the attention of the government and the people to the serious problem of poverty, The present paper attempt to analyse the level of poverty in India.

The estimates of poverty in the country are made at national and state level by the Planning Commission at an interval of approximately five years from the large sample survey data on consumer expenditure conducted by the National Sample Survey Organization (NSSO). Comparable estimates based on a consistent methodology and data set are available until 1993-94.

These estimates show a secular decline in the poverty ratio, though the number of poor remained stable for a fairly long period of two decades (1973-93) mainly due to increase in population.

TABLE 1

Estimates of Poverty

(Per cent)

Year	*All India*	*Rural*	*Urban*
1973-74	54.9	56.4	49.0
1977-78	51.3	53.1	45.2
1983	44.5	45.7	40.8
1987-88	38.9	39.1	
1993-94	37.3	32.4	
1999-2000			
30 day recall	26.10	27.09	23.62
7 day recall	2@	24.02	21.59

Source: *Economic Survey*, 2000-01, p. 194.

DEVELOPMENT PLANNING

The first five year plan attempted to stimulate balanced economic development while correcting imbalances caused by World War II and partition. Agriculture, including projects that combined irrigation and power generation, received priority. By contrast, the second five year plan emphasized industrialization. Particularly basic, heavy industries in the public sector, and improvement of the economic infrastructure. The plan also stressed social goals, such as more equal-distribution of income and extension of the benefits of economic development to the large number of disadvantaged people. The Third five year plan (FY 1961-65) aimed at a substantial rise in national and per capita income while expanding the industrial base and rectifying the neglect of agriculture in the previous plan. The third plan called for national income to grow at a rate of more than 5 per cent a year, self-sufficiency in food grains was anticipated in the mid-1960s.

Economic difficulties distrusted, the planning process in the mid-1960's. In 1962 when a brief war was fought with China on the Himalayan Frontier, agriculture output was stagnating, industrial production was considerably below expectations, and the economy was growing at about half of the planned rate. The defences expenditures increased sharply, and increased foreign aid needed to maintain the development expenditures eventually provided 28 per cent of public development spending. Midway through the third plan, it was clear that its goals could not be achieved. Food prices rose in 1963, causing rioting and looting or grain warehouse in 1964. War with Pakistan in 1965 sharply reduced foreign aid available. Successive severe draughts disrupted the economy and planning. Three annual plans guided development, while plant policies and strategies were re-evaluated. Immediate attention centered on increasing agriculture growth, stimulating exports, and searching for efficient uses of industrial assets. Agriculture was to be expanded, largely through the supply of inputs to take advantage of new high-yield seeds becoming available for food grains. The Rupee was substantially devalued in 1966, and export incentives were adjusted to promote exports. Controls affecting industry were simplified, and greater reliance was placed on the price mechanism to achieve industrial efficiency.

The 4th five year plan called for a 24 per cent increase over the third plan in real terms of public development expenditures. The public sector accounted for 60 per cent of plan expenditures, and foreign aid contributed 13 per cent of plan financing. Agriculture, including irrigation, received 23 per cent of public outlays; the rest was mostly spent on electric power, industry, and transportation. Although the plan projected national income growth at 5.7 per cent a year, the realized rate was only 3.3 per cent.

The fifth five year plan was drafted in late I973 when crude oil prices were rising rapidly; the rising prices quickly forced a series of revisions. The plan was subsequently approved in late 1976 but was terminated at the end of financial year 1977 because a new government wanted priorities and programs. The fifth plan was in effect only one year, although it provided some guidance to investments throughout the five year period.

The sixth five year plan was intended to be flexible and was based on the principle of annual "rolling" plans. It called for development expenditures of nearly Rs 1.9 trillion of which 90 per cent would be financed from domestic sources, 57 per cent would come from the public sector. Public sector development spending would be concentrated in energy (29 per cent), agriculture and irrigation (24 per cent); industry including mining (16 per cent); and social services (14 per cent). In practice, slightly more was spent on social services at the expense of sportation and energy. The plan called for GDP growth to increase by 5.1 per cent a year, a target that was surpassed by 0.3 per cent. A major objective of the plan was to increase given cows, bullock carts, and handlooms; however, subsequent studies indicated that the income of only about 10 per cent of the poor rose above the poverty level.

The seventh five year plan envisioned a greater emphasis on the allocation of resources to energy and social spending at the expense of industry and agriculture. In practice, the main increase was in transportation and communications, which took up 17 per cent of public-sector expenditure during this period. Total spending was targeted at nearly Rs. 3.9 trillion, of which 94 per cent would be financed from domestic resources, including 48 per cent from the public sector.

The planners assumed that public savings would increase and help finance government spending. In practice that increase did not occur, instead, the government relied on foreign borrowing for a greater share of resources than expected.

The schedule for the eighth five year plan was affected by changes of government and by growing uncertainly over what role planning could usefully perform in a more liberal economy. Two annual plans were in effect in financial years 1990 and 1991. The eighth plan was finally launched in April 1992 and emphasized market-based policy reform rather than quantitative targets. Total spending was planned at Rs. 8.7 trillion of which 94 per cent would be financed from domestic resources 4.5 per cent of which would come from the public sector. The eighth plan included three general goals first, it sought to cut back the public sector by selling off failing and in essential industries while emphasized the eighth plan included three general goals. First, it sought to cut-back the public sector by selling of failing and inessential industries while encouraging private investment in such sectors as power, steel, and transport. Second, it proposed that agriculture and rural development have priority. Third, it sought to renew the assault on illiteracy and improve other aspects of social infrastructure, such as the provision of fresh drinking water. Government documents issued in 1992 indicated that GDP growth was expected to increase from around 5 per cent a year during the seventh plan to 5.6 per cent a year during the eighth plan. However, in 1994 economists expected annual growth to be around 4 per cent during the period of the eighth plan.

POVERTY ALLEVIATION AND EMPLOYMENT GENERATION PROGRAMMES

Alleviation of poverty remains a major challenge before the nation. While there has been a steady decline in poverty over the last two decades the total number of poor people has perhaps remained constant because of growth in population. Acceleration of economic growth which is employment-intensive, facilitates the reduction of poverty in the long-run. However, this strategy needs to be complemented with a focus on provision of basic services for improving the quality of life of the people through state intervention in the form of targeted anti-poverty programmes. The specifically designed anti-poverty programmes for generation of both self-employment and wage employment have been redesigned and restructured in 1999-2000 in order to make these Programmes more effective. For the year 2000-01, an outlay of Rs. 9760 crore was provided as compared to Rs. 9351 crore for 1999-2000. The major poverty alleviation programmes in operation in rural and urban areas are as follows:

1. Jawahar Gram Samridhi Yojana (JGSY)

Introduced in April 1999 as a successor to Jawahar Rozgar Yojana (JRY) is implemented as a Centrally Sponsored Scheme—on a cost-sharing ratio of 75:25 between the Centre and States.

All works that can result in the creation of durable productive community assets are taken up under the programme.

2. Swarna Jayanti Gram Swarozgar Yojana (SGSY)

Introduced in April, 1999 as a result of reconstructing and combining the Integrated Rural Development Programme (IRDP) and allied Programmes along with Million Wells Scheme (MWS) into a single self-employment programme. It aims at promoting micro enterprises and helping the rural poor into self-help groups. It is implemented as a centrally sponsored scheme on cost sharing ratio of 75:25 between the Centre and States.

3. National Social Assistance Programme (NSAP)

Launched on 15 August 1995 as a 100 per cent centrally sponsored scheme with the objective of providing social assistance benefit to poor households affected by old age, death of primary breadwinner or need for maternity care. The Programme supplements the efforts of the State Governments with the objective of ensuring minimum level of well-being.

4. Employment Assurance Scheme (EAS)

Started on 2 October 1993 in 1772 backward blocks situated in drought and hill areas. Subsequently expanded to cover all blocks of the country. The primary objective of the EAS was creation of additional wage employment opportunities during the period of acute shortage of wage employment, through manual work for the rural poor living below the poverty line. Restructured in 1999-2000 to make it the single wage employment programme and implemented as a centrally sponsored scheme on a cost-sharing ratio of 75:25.

5. Pradhan Mantri Gramodaya Yojana (PMGY)

Introduced in Budget 2000-01 with an allocation of Rs. 5000 crore, focusing on village level development in five critical areas: health, primary, education, drinking water, housing and rural roads with the objective of improving the quality or life of people in the rural areas.

6. Swarna Jayanti Shahari Rozgar Yojana (SJSRY)

The Urban Self-Employment Programme and the Urban Wage Employment Programme—are the two special schemes of the Swarna Jayanthi Shahari Rozgar Yojana (SJSRY) which substituted in December 1997 various programmes operated earlier for urban poverty alleviation. SJSY is funded on a 75:25 basis between Centre and the States. During 1997-98, 1998-99 and 1999-2000, a sum of Rs. 102.51 crore, Rs. 162.28 crore and 123.07 crore respectively were spent in the States and U.Ts under different components of SJSRY.

CONCLUSION

There is no doubt that the government and people in India are now awakened to the serious problem of poverty and apparently some frantic efforts are being made to reduce its incidence. It may look cynical but it is true that poverty cannot be eradicated. The poor have always been with us and we are callously convinced that they will continue to be with us. This, however, does not mean that we sit tight over it. We have to march forward and boldly to fight poverty by all the means we can. Poverty is a great menace to political stability.

REFERENCES

Baulch Bob and Hoddinott John (2000), Economic Mobility and Poverty Dynamics in Developing Countries, *Journal of Development Studies*, Vol. 38, No. 6, pp. 1-24.

Economic Survey (2001), Ministry of Financial, Government of India.

Kurian, N.J. (2000), Widening Regional Disparities in India: Some Indicators, *Economic and Political Weekly*, February 12, 2000.

NIRD (2000), *India: Rural Development Report*, Regional Disparities in Development and Poverty, National Institute of Rural Development, Hyderabad.

Planning Commission (1998), Ninth Five Year Plan (1997-2002).

Poverty Re-Examined

VIMAL SHANKAR SINGH, SHWETA SINGH AND SUBHRA SINGH

From the point of view of a Nation-State all efforts towards attainment of prosperity boil down to the accomplishment of two major goals—(1) Elimination of Poverty, and (2) Sustainable development. The first one is, being both the prerequisite and results and also the essence of the second one. This is because almost all distortions of the human society find manifestation in the phenomenon of poverty. According to Gerd Theiskn, a German scripture scholar, we humans are the missing link between apes and true. Humanity, i.e. we are a stage towards it but not a mined it. Had, it been so we could not have lived with holocausts and starvation comfortably. According to Vedic perspective, there is no greater sorrow than the sorrow of being poor. The barbarism and malignance of poverty has far reaching repercussion. Besides being a cold-blooded murder it also deepens the human spirit of its source of sustenance leaving it paralyzed. Coming to sustainable development it can be defined as a path of development which the options of future generation are not compromised because of the steps taken by the present generation. It has now been established that the development process should be such in which growth is accompanied by equality. It is also argued that the growth profile, which aggravates inequality, cannot be sustained since persistence of inequalities would generate serious dislocation in the process of growth and structural for nation in the economy as a whole. Poverty found its genesis in the growth of materialistic as capitalism spread roots the under privileged players of the market were rendered jobless. This created inequality and unrest, which found vent in the worst sagas of humanity— "The World Wars". The World community was thus compelled to acknowledge the ancient MM that only equitable distribution of wealth and reduction of mass poverty could lead to all round development. The same is preached by all religions. Be it Daan and Yagyna of Hinduism or Zakat of Muslims all go on to strengthen the idea of redistribution in the society. According to Bible, we do not have the right to speak about the poor, instead our poor. Economic systems too realized the fact that poverty is one of the major decelerations of the developmental process and poverty elimination occupied the place of primacy in the visionary exercisers of World Welfare. Growth, employment, food security, inequality and poverty are all highly interrelated aspect of economy. Deprivation of development capability is the source of all types of poverty. Further, failure of trickle-down-effect could also contribute to persistence of poverty, even when growth is supposed to have taken place.

INDIA'S POVERTY SCENARIO

In India, the culmination of British Raj was followed by the abolition of the Kingship and Zamandari system followed by the land reforms. As a result of this 44.92 lakh-acres land out of the 73.48 lakh acres of land was redistributed among the 41.52 lakh landless cultivators. In order to feed the ever-growing population, green revolution was stressed and emphasized. Public distribution system gained momentum. The reduction of poverty as an agenda found place in almost all the five year plans. Thus they were implemented in succession with good intentions for the achievement of a great vision—"A poverty free India". More than five decades of Independence have passed and what a remains of these plans and strategies is but a travesty of grandiose visions *verses* harsh realities.

The harsh realities regarding the poverty in India are: the poverty ratio though, has declined over the years, yet the number of poor is still very high. Poverty ratio in 1973-74 was 54.9 per cent of the total population, it came down to 26.1 per cent in 1999-2000, yet the number of poor was 260 million in 1999-2000. The sorrow picture is continuing in 260 million in[1] spite of the fact that there are—a number of programs putforth and implemented by the government for the reduction of poverty in India. A high degree of poverty differential still persists among different states of the country. In the same way in spite of an good increase in the national income were on in the gross domestic savings (around 22 per cent of G.D.P.) and capital formation (around 23 per cent), but an increase in the unemployment rate (7.32 per cent in 1999-2000 from 5.99 in 1993-94) and number of unemployed (26.58 million in 1999-2000). How can we take pride of development when we still have extremely marathon challenge of eliminating over 27 per cent of rural poverty and around 23 per cent of urban poverty encompassing several crore of humanity—in the coming years. Were five or is poverty invincible? If answer to both the questions is be, then one is compelled to doubt the efficiency of the successive governments and their line of thought. The following is a critical examination of the various poverty elimination programs and their contribution towards sustainable development. Let's see the idea of redistribution still have relevance in the present scenario.[2]

"Food for all" was the primary focus of the poverty elevation. Program as food is a basic necessity of life. The result was a plethora of steps taken by the government through their policy aptly supplemented by the new technology. The success of green revolution can be proved easily by the fact that 4000 years of progress was repeated in just 41 years of production of wheat rose from 7 million tones in 1947 to 17 million tones in 1964-68. Total production of food grains too increased from 50 million tones in 1951 to 208.9 million tones in 1900-2000. Our population rose from 36 crore in 1951 to 103 crore, i.e. 3 times but food production increased by 4 times.[3]

Though not doubting the success of the green revolution, one would agree that green revolution fire reached a saturation point. It cannot feed the ever growing population of this country, unless technological development takes place. Again green revolution has encouraged uncontrolled use of chemical fertilizers, which has hampered soil fertility also adversely affecting its productivity. This goes the idea of sustainable development, marring future prospects for the fulfilment of present needs. Further, with the increase in the population, the per capita availability of the land is also going down, which will make India's food perspective more bleak in order to meet the challenge of making green revolution to evergreen revolution we will have to address all these challenges alongwith craving out for gene revolution, Eco-technology revolution and information and communication revolution, which will involve a lots of capital and at the time was to be an uphill task. V.R. Panchamukh presented an international comparison of per capita food production and calorie consumption. According to him, India's historical growth of food production was 0.58 per cent. The required growth rate for India to catch up with China and Brazil in per capita production of food in 2020 is three and a half times and five and a half times the historical rate respectively. Secondly, the historical rate of growth of per capita calorie consumption of India for the period 1992 to 1994-96 was 0.56 per cent. If India has to catch up with per capita calorie consumption of China and USA by 2020, growth rate of India's per capita calorie consumption will have to three times and four and a half times respectively. This analysis shows an uphill task before India to achieve food security.[4]

In agriculture and allied activism land is considered as one of the basic inputs of production. Land reform in India was introduced to alter the pattern of land ownership and to bring a systematic structural change in rural society for the attainment of the goal of production and justice. But close examination shows that the reforms actually did not evolved efficient production and egalitarian society. The first round of fragmentation was brought about by the land reforms itself. If the ceiling limit of the best category of land was 18 acres in July 1971 so that every land tiller is given justice, its level would certainly drop in 2001 when number of tillers have increased but not the land and would continue to come down with the increase in population. The marginal farmers of today would become big farmers for tomorrow and distributive justice will make them petty farmers of the yester year. Already in India the—size of the agriculture holding is quite uneconomic, small and fragmented. The average size of holding in India is expected to decline from 1.5 hectares in 1990-91 to 1.3 hectares in 2000-01. The marginal holdings which were 59.7 per cent in 1990-91 are 62.1 per cent by 2000-01. N.J. Kurian observed that out of 97.8 million holdings in 1985-86, 58.1 per cent was of marginal category, and the remaining category of holding include—small category (18.3%) @ semi- and medium (8.1%) and large (2.0%) holdings can be considered as uneconomic—Ionic and remaining 41.9 per cent as economic. The problem of increased sub-division actually finds its roots in the increasing pressure of population which has to be supported. This sub-division leads to further problems such as wastage of land, managerial problems, litigations, and low productivity and disguised unemployment. Thus, according to us the ceiling act of land reforms in no way holds relevance in the coming years and if followed would be a deterrent to development. To cover up the flaw of fragmentation of holdings, co-operative farm is suggested. A critical evaluation of co-operative farming too shows that it promotes inequality and unemployment. It also results in the loss of independence of farmers. With such marginal traits, co-operative farming can never encourage sustainable development. Moreover, in our view, co-operative farming on a large scale is also not feasible.

To cover up the flaw of fragmentation of holdings, co-operative farming is suggested. A critical evaluation of co-operative farming too shows that it promotes inequality and employment. It is also results in the loss of independence of farmers. With such marginal traits, co-operatives farming can never encourage sustainable development.

Further, there has always been a lot of hue and cry about prevention of immigration, which leads to the increase of liability of the, nation-state. But, influx of population from the neighbouring countries continuously farming a significant portion of the nation's morning burden. This will have to be chocked if development is to be assured. Yet another point relating to poverty is human resource development. There is no doubt that human resource play a significant role in the development of any economy. We talk of providing education and employment to all. But, there is no thought given to from where the massive resource for this purpose will come and has the country capacity to absorb such a huge battalion of unskilled work force. Human resource can be greatest asset provided it is adequately equipped. India is a place where every 6th person of the world lives ranks 132nd in the group of 174 developing and developed countries. We are trying to feed all at the expense of a few in the name of social justice. Though, we do not doubt the pious intention behind this, but would the economy be able to sustain such a justice for a long time. Are not we on the path of ruin encouraging a jobless, futureless growth of population, which leave apart being an asset is a liability.

Finally, it is said that because of trickle down effect, the fruits of development can be reaped by the poorest of the poor also. But if the poor are in extremely bad condition and providing additional income to them enormously uplifts their welfare without diminishing the total output and income of the society, the redistribution is definitely justified. But in reality it is found that transfer of income from the rich to the poor reduces the income and output of the society.[5] The loss occurs due to administrative and other costs of implementing the programs. Again, all this redistribution involves the transfer of money from a place where it could have been saved and invested to a place where it will be spent or consumed. This directional change in the flow of the economy's assets is unfavourable for the same in the long-run.

SUMMING UP

The above discussion shows that we adopted planned economic development to remove unemployment, inequality and poverty from the country. Socialism became our cherished goal. In the name of this goal we have eaten everything, Kings, landlords, green and industrial revolution, infrastructure development, investment, etc. In spite of a good in the national income, an increase in the social sector facilities we find poverty, unemployment and misery. Now-a-days economists advocate, and rightly too that no development can last long without development with human face. It is said corresponding increase in investment on health, nutrition, education, sanitation, housing, etc. But are not we following this policy vigorously since Independence? We have adopted socialist pattern of society, public sector incurred heavy losses due to charging lower prices of their commodities, public distribution system provided commodities to the poor on subsidized rates, rich taxed heavily in favour of poor, etc. Now in spite of all these steps, still we are predominantly a poor country with 26 per cent of population living below the poverty line and around 26 crore of poor, then whom to blame? It goes without saying that it is the humongous and villainous population of this country, which is the retarding factor of all economic development. A nation howsoever rich cannot possibly cater to the Herculean task of feeding its unlimited inhabitants at one hand and keep pace with developing activities on the other.

Thus, we have three policy options for the removal of poverty. First, we should policy always, have enormous pool of poor and also always have an opportunity to talk on them, or secondly, we should reduce poverty with the help of diluting the definition of poverty as suggested recently by the FAO,[6] Gopalan,[7] etc., or thirdly, we should restrict our population growth. In our view, population control can be the only cure for a poverty-stricken country with slow race of development. Prevention is better than cure. Why breed poor and then cure their poverty instead let not the poor be born. So, let us change our policy from "Reduce poor and Reduce poverty". This is the real answer to the problem of poverty and we should do everything to attain this policy.

Only population control and specially of poor can restrict, as Panchamukhi visualized, a jobless growth—growth which does not create employment opportunities; ruthless growth—growth which aggravates inequality; voiceless growth—growth which doesn't encourage empowerment of the deprived sections of the society; futureless growth—growth which increases environmental unsustainability; rootless growth—growth which destroys—ultimate edifice of the society. Let us extend our helping hands in fulfilling the great Visionary President A.P.J. Abdul Kalam's vision true of making India a developed country by 2020 not by adopting the age old theory of redistribution of income and wealth which has seized its relevance at least at present, but instead of it we showed, adopt the policy of reduction of number of poor.

NOTES AND REFERENCES

1. Quoted by Danial C. Maguire, 'Population, Poverty and Sustainable Development.' *Earth Ethics*, Vol. A.7. Nos. 3&4, Spring/Summner, 1996, p. 1.
2. Swaminathan, M.S., Food and Environment—Walking the Tightrope, Published by Forurn—For Free Enterprise, Mumbai, 2001, p. 5.
3. Panchamukhi. V.R., India Vision-2020, Presidential Address, Fourth Annual Conference of the Economic Association of Bihar, Patna, 27-29, May 2000, p. 11.
4. Kurien, N.J., Employment Potential in Rural India, *Economic and Political Weekly*, Dec. 29, 1990, p. 179
5. Gil (1976). Quoted by Dhillon, S.S. and Raikhy, P.S., 'Social Choice, Growth and Income Distribution: Theory and Evidence', The Indian Economic Association, Conference Volume, 1999, p. 453.
6. Food and Agriculture Organisation (1996): The Sixth World Food Survey (Rome).
7. Gopalan, C. (2000): Nutritive Value of Indian Foods National Institute of Nutrition, Hyderabad.

9

Absolute and Relative Poverty in India: A New Way to Re-examine Old Issues

Arvind Awasthi

I. INTRODUCTION

It is generally believed that poverty is more a direct reflection of low levels of per capita income rather than skewed income distribution. However, available empirical evidences contradict this widely held view point. It follows, therefore, that development strategies which succeed in raising the level of per capita income may not have any impact on absolute poverty if they are accompanied by a deterioration in relative income shares. It has been observed that during the post-reform period (1993-94 to 1999-2000) in India, the real per capita income has increased at a rate of little over 4% per annum, while the incidence of poverty has been falling by a little less than 1 percentage point. This implies that the disparities in the consumption expenditure on food among different expenditure classes of consumers should have declined. This proposition follows from the fact that people in higher expenditure class spend proportionally less income on food compared to those in lower expenditure class, as their per capita income increases. Further, if the people in the higher expenditure class tend to save more and spend lesser amount of increased income on non-food items, then disparities in per capita expenditure may even decline for non-food items. Thus, declining disparities in the consumption expenditure of food and non-food items is a sign of rising prosperity for people in the lower expenditure group too. This obviously will tend to reduce absolute poverty in a country. Poverty reduction, therefore, is not merely a function of rising per capita income but the extent to which increased per capita income has tended to benefit different sections of society.

II. OBJECTIVE, SCOPE AND METHODOLOGY

The purpose of this paper is to examine the pattern of disparities in food, non-food and overall consumption expenditure, along with the behaviour of the household savings-income ratios so that one could comprehend the direction of change in the relative poverty levels over a period of time.

Our analysis will obviously throw light on the behaviour of disparities in the food and non-food consumption expenditure along with the overall income distribution. If these disparities overtime have displayed a tendency to decline significantly, then it depicts that the benefits of economic development have been distributed among different classes rather than confining to upper class only. This has facilitated in lowering the absolute poverty levels in the country.

Quite evidently, the objective of this paper is to examine the pattern of relative poverty levels in India since the first quinquennial round of household consumption-expenditure, i.e. 1972-73 upto 1999-2000. This will not only reflect the extent of redistribution of income in promoting consumption of lower expenditure classes, but it will also facilitate to examine viability of inverted-U hypothesis (1955).

The examination of Kuznets hypothesis becomes all the more imperative considering the fact that much of the evidences in the recent past have been accumulated against his hypothesis. In his inverted-U hypothesis, Kuznets has suggested that economic growth (i.e. a rise in average per capita income) can initially perpetuate relative poverty but subsequently it leads to a fall in relative poverty within a country, though his findings were based on a cross-country analysis. For instance, Deiminger and Squir (1996) find no confirmation of the inverted-U Kuznets curve. The drawback with the Kuznets study is that, its generalization about relative poverty levels is based on a cross-country comparisons (in context of developed and developing countries), rather than on the basis of a time period analysis for a particular country,

It is generally observed that a study of income distribution over time is marred by the lack of proper data but still one can manage to draw inferences about pattern of relative poverty on the basis of trend of the disparities in consumption expenditure and behaviour of household savings of different expenditure classes. In India, since 1972-73 NSSO has been regularly publishing quinquennial round reports on the level and pattern of consumption expenditure. Moreover, NSSO is also regularly publishing data on sources of household income in India corresponding to different quinquennial round on consumer expenditure. The two together will facilitate to draw inferences about the behaviour of relative poverty or income disparities in India.

The scope of the study is confined to the all India level and has covered a period from 1972-73 to 1999-2000. The analysis is conducted for rural and urban areas separately, while Gini's coefficient is estimated in order to measure the extent of disparities in different types of consumption expenditure among various expenditure groups. This estimation of Gini's coefficient is indeed noteworthy and may be a useful alternative technique for all those who could not directly estimate it on the basis of conventional and standard trapezoidal rule which is not directly applicable in India on account of serious data limitations and which have been pointed out during the course of analysis.

III. ANALYSIS

III.A. Measurement of Disparities

In order to measure the extent of disparities in the consumption expenditure of different classes, Gini's coefficient are estimated for food, non-food and total consumption expenditure of different classes both for the rural as well as urban areas of the economy. In India, estimation of Gini's coefficient geometrically (i.e. by drawing Lorenz Curve and finding its area) is indeed difficult since NSSO data over time has taken different number of expenditure classes and which contain different proportion of persons. Therefore, alternatively, we have first estimated the area below Lorenz curve by integrating the standard equation of a curve which starts from the point of origin:

$$Y = AN^{*}$$

where, Y is the cumulative percentage of total expenditure corresponding to each class in proportion to the sum of the total expenditure of all classes. Similarly, N is cumulative percentage of the number of persons in proportion to the total number of persons.

The form of equation clearly represent the Lorenz curve since it starts from point of origin and is convex from below. Further, the Lorenz curve takes various values from 0 to 1, therefore, taking the limit from 0 to 1 and solving, we get the area of the portion between Lorenz curve and x-axis, as A/1 + a. The values of A and a are estimated by regressing the above mentioned equation.

Once the area below Lorenz curve is estimated, the value of Gini's coefficient is calculated as usually done in statistics, i.e.

$$\rho = \frac{0.5 - \text{area below Lorenz curve}}{0.5}$$

It is in place to mention that the data provided by the NSSO for the year 1999-2000 regarding percentage distribution of persons among different expenditure classes is quite evenly distributed. It has provided us an opportunity to test the accuracy of our alternative method by estimating area below Lorenz curve, since the area below Lorenz curve can also be estimated on the basis of trapezoidal rule for the year 1999-2000, which hitherto cannot be used for other years covered by the study, since NSSO data for other years is not evenly distributed with regard to the percentage distribution of persons. The estimates of area under Lorenz curve as well as that of Gini's coefficients representing disparities regarding food, non-food and overall consumption expenditure on the basis of standard trapezoidal rule and on the basis of our methodology for the year 1999-2000 are shown in Table 1.

TABLE 1

Gini's Coefficient and Area Under Lorenz Curve in Case of Food, Non-Food and Overall Consumption Expenditure on the Basis of Trapezoidal Rule and Our Methodology for the Year 1999-2000

(in percentage terms)

Trapezoidal	*Rule*			*Our Methodology*		
	Food Exp.	*Non-Food Exp.*	*Total Consum. Exp.*	*Food Exp.*	*Non-Food Exp.*	*Total Consum. Exp.*
Area Under Lorenz Curve (Rural)	39.76	33.65	37.28	39.71	33.59	37.26
Area Under Lorenz Curve (Urban)	38.02	28.43	33.04	38.12	28.16	33.05
Gini's Coefficient (Rural)	20.48	32.70	25.40	20.58	32.83	25.50
Gini's Coefficient (Urban)	23.97	43.14	33.93	23.76	43.69	33.91

Source: Estimated on the basis of NSSQ report entitled: 'Level and Pattern of Consumer Expenditure', 6th Quinquennial Survey, 1999-2000, Dept. of Statistics, Government of India, New Delhi.

It is clearly evident from the table that the two estimates almost match each other so that the difference between them is of around 1% or even less than that. Thus, our methodology gives precise, consistent and realistic estimates of Gini's Coefficient and area below Lorenz curve. In the absence of even distribution of persons among different expenditure groups, where trapezoidal rule cannot be applied, our methodology can be effectively used to determine area below Lorenz curve and hence Gini's coefficient to determine disparities with regard to any variable like consumption expenditure, income, wealth, etc.

III.B. Analysis of Absolute and Relative Poverty in Rural India

The trend in absolute rural poverty and the extent of disparities in the food, non-food and overall consumption expenditure among different expenditure classes on the basis of our methodology are presented in Table 2.

TABLE 2

Absolute Poverty Ratios and Gini's Coefficient Representing Disparities in Food, Non-Food and Overall Consumption Expenditure in Rural India During the Last Six Quinquennial Rounds

(in percentage terms)

Quinquennial Rounds	*Absolute Food*	*Food Expenditure*	*Non-Food Expenditure*	*Total Consumption Expenditure*
1st Round 1972-73/ 1973-74	56.4	22.16	41.09	26.80
2nd Round 1977-78	53.1	25.86	51.29	31.32
3rd Round 1983	45.7	20.42	41.01	28.05
4th Round 1987-88	39.1	21.93	41.24	30.36
5th Round 1993-94	37.3	20.51	39.76	27.46
6th Round 1997-2000	27.1	20.58	32.83	25.50

Source: Estimated on the basis of last six Quinquennial rounds reports on Level and Pattern of Consumption Expenditure in India, NSSO, Dept. of Statistics, Government of India, New Delhi.

Table 3 reveals the growth rate of real per capita net domestic product in rural areas for different sub-periods.

TABLE 3

Growth Rate of Rural Per Capita Net Domestic Product in Real Terms

(in Percentage terms)

Period	*1970-71 to 1980-81*	*1980-81 to 1993-94*	*1993-94 to 1999-2000*
Growth Rate	0.32	2.98	3.36

Source: National Accounts Statistics of India, 1950-51 to 2000-01, *EPW*, Research Foundation, Mumbai and Net Domestic Product by Economic Activity in Rural/Urban Areas, CSO, Government of India.

Both these tables show interesting facts. The real per capita NDP during 1970s, increased at a rate of around 0.32% per annum while the rural poverty dipped marginally from approximately 56% to 53% only. During the same period, disparities in food, non-food and overall consumption expenditure increased significantly, especially the disparities in non-food expenditure.

Obviously, the benefits of economic development has favoured the rural rich and the marginal decline in rural poverty, that has occurred, is owing to some possible drift of benefits of the increased per capita income to lower expenditure classes of society. Thus, on account of increased disparities in household consumption expenditure among different classes and that savings are largely constituted by the people in higher expenditure class, therefore, during 1970s, income disparities too have aggravated. Thus, our analysis fully corroborates the first part of Kuznets hypothesis that initially economic development will aggravate the inequalities in income distribution. Moreover, it also highlights the fact that initial decline in absolute poverty will only be marginal, especially in developing countries and which will possibly occur on account of insignificant drift of benefits of economic development towards the lower expenditure classes. The case of rural India is a testimony to it. Thus, mere rise in overall per capita income is not sufficient to reduce poverty. Rather, its distribution is more important for absolute poverty to decline.

The estimated growth rate of per capita rural NDP in real terms for the period 1980-81 to 1993-94 is approximately 3.0% per annum. It is in place to mention that this is a fairly long period, which we have to consider for estimating the growth rate of rural per capita NDP, as the data for rural and urban NDP was not available for other intervening years. The significant improvement in the per capita NDP growth rate from 0.3% per annum to around 3.0% per annum as well as considerable decline in disparities regarding food, non-food and overall consumption expenditure of different classes in rural areas has facilitated to reduce absolute rural poverty significantly. The absolute poverty which was 53% in 1977-78 has come down to 37% in 1993-94. There has been a gradual decline in absolute poverty between 1977-78 to 1993-94 but the decline in the disparities in consumption expenditure on food items of different classes is not so, during the same period (refer Table 2). In such a situation, one may argue as to how the redistribution of income had facilitated in reducing poverty when the consumption expenditure of different classes on the basic wage good (i.e. food) has not converged gradually. It has declined between 1977-78 and 1983, but thereafter, it has increased marginally. This is also contrary to Engel's law which suggests that with the rise in income, proportion of income spent on food declines, i.e. richer community tends to spend lesser proportion of income on food than the poor community. Since this did not happen, one may wonder whether redistribution has really helped in curtailing the absolute rural poverty. It is indeed noteworthy that between 1983 to 1987-88, there has been a major shift in consumption of food basket especially for rural rich. The shift is from the traditional items of cereals to more nutritious food items, such as milk, milk products, meat, etc. This shift is clearly evident from Table 4, which shows that although the MPCE (monthly per capita expenditure) on cereals has declined by 6 percentage points, but overall food expenditure has declined only marginally between 38th (1983) and 43rd (1987-88) NSS rounds. Prior to this, such a significant shift was not visible. It is in place to point out that though MPCE on cereals during the 27th (1972-73) and 32nd (1977-78) NSS rounds has declined by about 8 percentage points, but it has simultaneously led to a decline in overall food expenditure by about similar percentage points. This depicts absence of any compositional shift in the food expenditure of different classes, especially the rural rich during 1972-73 to 1977-78. However, such a change in food basket is clearly visible during 1983 to 1987-88. It is on account of this visible change in the food consumption basket which occurred during 1983 to 1987-88 that the distribution of increased per capita NDP even to the lowest classes is not at all evident in terms of decline in the disparities in consumption expenditure on food among different classes but its impact in curtailing absolute poverty from approximately 46% to 39% can well be explained in terms of the major shift occurring in the composition of food basket, especially for rural rich in India.

The shift in composition of food basket continued even thereafter, but the extent of change is not significant (refer Table 4). As a consequence, there is a marginal decline in the disparities of food consumption expenditure among different classes during the period 1987-88 to 1993-94.

TABLE 4

Percentage Distribution of Monthly Per Capita Expenditure (MPCE) on Different Food Items over NSS Rounds in Rural India

Items	*Average MPCE as Percentage of Total MPCE*					
	27th	*32nd*	*38th*	*43rd*	*50th*	*55th*
Cereals	40.6	32.8	32.3	26.3	24.2	22.2
Gram	0.6	0.4	0.3	0.2	0.2	0.1
Cereal Substitutes	0.5	0.3	0.2	0.1	0.1	0.1
Pulses & Products	4.3	3.8	3.5	4.0	3.8	3.8
Milk & Milk Products	7.3	7.7	7.5	8.6	9.5	8.8
Edible Oils	3.5	3.6	4.0	5.0	4.4	3.7
Meat, Egg, Fish	2.5	2.7	3.0	3.3	3.3	3.3
Vegetables	3.6	3.8	4.7	5.2	6.0	6.2
Fruits & Nuts	1.1	1.1	1.4	1.6	1.7	1.7
Sugar	3.8	2.6	2.8	2.9	3.1	2.4
Salt & Spices	2.8	3.0	2.5	2.9	2.7	3.0
Beverages	2.4	2.5	3.3	3.9	4.2	4.2
Food	72.9	64.3	65.6	64.0	63.2	59.4

Source: Level and Pattern of Consumer Expenditure, 6th Quinquennial Survey, 1999-2000, NSSO, Dept. of Statistics, Government of India, New Delhi.

Further, it is also evident from our analysis that between 1977-78 to 1993-94, the disparities in the non-food consumption expenditure has declined from about 50% to 40%. The decline is fairly substantial but one should not interpret it as an indicator of declining income disparities too. There are three important reasons for it:

(i) Non-food expenditure in NSSO estimates represents a smaller fraction of total expenditure as compared to the food expenditure. Therefore, even smaller increases in non-food expenditure in money terms reflect large changes in percentage terms in it. On account of this, though the disparities in non-food expenditure has fallen from 51% to 40%, yet the overall disparities in consumption expenditure has declined from just about 31% to 27% during 1977-78 to 1993-94.

(ii) The household savings-income ratio has increased from 16.86% to

23.08% (refer Table 5), during 1977-78 to 1993-94. This increase in household savings appear to be far more than the decline experienced in disparities in consumption expenditure of different classes, a point which we have further discussed at a little later stage of our analysis in this section.

(iii) NSS estimates have been criticized for underestimation of consumption expenditure especially of the higher expenditure classes (Dandekar and Rath, 1971). Our analysis too has revealed it (refer Table 5). This underestimation has been both in the food and non-food segments. The difference in the NSS and NAS estimates is fairly low regarding food expenditure, while it is relatively high in case of non-food expenditure (refer Table 5), especially the expenditure on miscellaneous items. What is indeed noteworthy is that the underestimation with regard to non-food expenditure, especially the expenditure on miscellaneous category, as reported by NSS, has a tendency to increase.

The data on different sources of household income for the last 3 quinquennial rounds (refer Table 6) clearly reveal a major jump in the number of households reporting income from interest and dividend during the period 1987-88 to 1993-94. Our analysis for the subsequent period will throw enough light on the fact that these households are especially those whose monthly per capita expenditure is highest. Thus, over-time there has been substantial increase in savings by the households in the higher expenditure groups.

All these evidences are sufficient enough to suggest that income disparities may have either increased or remained somewhat stable during 1977-78 to 1993-94 but at least it has not converged.

Thus, our analysis of fairly long period from 1977-78 to 1993-94 clearly reflects that the benefits of economic development, as expressed in terms of a significant increase in the per capita NDP has percolated even to the poorest section of society which has caused disparities in the consumption expenditure of different classes to narrow down. It reaffirms our earlier finding that mere increase in the per capita income is not enough to curtail absolute poverty, rather the distribution of increased per capita income among different classes of society is more significant in reducing poverty. Moreover, in the light of available evidences, it is too difficult to accept the second part of Kuznets hypothesis, that rising per capita income will eventually lead to a fall in income disparities. Rather income disparities during this phase have remained stable or increased marginally. Thus, Kuznets inverted-U curve appears to be more reasonable and logical for the disparities in the consumption expenditure, than for income distribution, at least in the rural areas.

During the terminal period (1993-94 to 1999-2000) of our analysis, the growth rate of real per capita NDP in rural areas has further gone upto 3.36% per annum but the disparities in consumption expenditure on food has not declined. Rather, it has marginally increased. Moreover, during this period,

TABLE 5

A Comparative Estimates of NSSO and NAS Regarding Monthly Per Capita Consumption Expenditure (expressed in Rs.) of Different Items and Household Savings-Income Ratio (expressed in percentage terms)

	1972-73		*1977-78*		*1983*		*1987-88*		*1993-94*		*1999-00*	
	NSS	*NAS*	*NSS*	*NAS*	*NSS*	*NA.S*	*NSS*	*NAS*	*NSS*	*NAS*	*NSS*	*NAS*
Food	33.90	38.67	47.40	59.60	79.39	99.30	110.55	139.06	273.0	2.71.0	323 12	496.27
Non-Food	14.11	28.78	27.83	48.20	45.53	85.78	70.50	132.33	131.21	259.20	266.03	542.70
Pan, Tobacco	1.44	2.23	3.00	2.80	3.52	6.50	5.40	8.25	9.44	14.12	14.01	38.48
Intoxicants	3.14	3.18	0 18	0 20	10.35	8.94	11.04	12.78	10.79	28.54	38.40	44 71
Clothing	0.24	38	0.53	0.02	1.28	1.22	1.84	2.00	2.93	3.75	0.07	6.11
Footwear	2.71	2.11	4.01	3.79	8.75	7.93	13.00	12.12	23.20	19.73	44.85	35.74
Miscellaneous	0.01	20 88	14.25	34.78	21.63	61.13	38.09	97.18	78.84	193.00	161.43	41760
Total	48.00	67.45	75.29	107.87	124.92	185.08	181.06	271.39	404.21	530.21	589.17	1038.97
HH Saving Income Ratio	12.40		16.86		15.58		21.17		23.08		24 33	

Sources: (i) Level and Pattern of Consumer Expenditure, 1 to 6 quinquennial Survey, 1972-73, 77-78, 1983, 1987-88, 1993-94 and 1999-2000, NSSO, Dept. of Statistics, Government of India, New Delhi.
(ii) National Accounts Statistics of India, 1950-51 to 2000-01, *EPW Research Foundation*, Mumbai.

TABLE 6

Proportion of Households Reporting Receipt of Income from Different Sources During the Last Three Quinquennial Rounds in Rural India

NSS Round	Per 1000 No. of households reporting income during last 365 days							
	Cultivation	*Farming & other Agricul. Enterpr.*	*Wage Salaried Empl.*	*Non-agricultural enterp.*	*Pension*	*Remit-ances*	*Interest & Devedend*	*Other Source*
43rd Round (1987-88)	624	197	567	181	23	32	11	95
50th Round (1993-94)	605	195	565	183	25	79	25	90
55th Round (1999-2000)	571	145	558	184	28	86	24	92

Source: Sources of Household Income in India, NSS Report No. 463, NSSO, Dept. of Statistics, Government of India, New Delhi.

there are no evidences of any further shift in the composition of food basket, as the decline in the percentage amount of consumption expenditure on cereals has resulted in a overall decline in the percentage amount food expenditure (refer Table 5). Despite this, the official estimates of the government has claimed that during this period, absolute poverty in rural areas has gone down from about 37 per cent to 27 per cent. Such a claim lacks support from other official document, namely Employment-Unemployment Survey (1999-2000). Sundaram (2002) has revealed this discrepancy. The Employment-Unemployment survey has revealed that at All-India level rural poverty ratio has gone down from 39% to 36% during 1993-94 to 1999-2000. Sundaram (2002) therefore, rightly observed that, 'in all cases, even at the All-India level, the order of decline (wherever it has materialized) in the poverty prevalence rates, revealed by the employment-unemployment survey, has been significantly smaller than that revealed by the 55th round consumer expenditure survey'. Moreover, even if one considers the results of absolute poverty, as estimated in other consumption expenditure surveys, between 50th and 55th rounds based on thin samples, then one will find that the poverty rates have gone up rather than going down during 1993-94 to 1999-2000. Prof. Sen (2001) too is of a similar viewpoint. During the 1990s, Prof. Sen felt that poverty reduction has stalled and poverty rates may have even risen. In the light of all these evidences, one can only say that absolute poverty in rural areas has either not declined or even if it has, its magnitude is insignificant.

All these observations clearly signify that absolute poverty has either declined marginally or has remained more or less stable during 1993-94 to 1999-2000. Further, the disparities in the non-food consumption expenditure has declined as revealed by Gini's coefficient, whose value has gone down from around 40% to 33%. This has resulted in the decline in disparities in the overall consumption expenditure of different classes. To some extent, decline in disparities in non-food consumption expenditure could be explained by the rise in the household-savings income ratio, whose increase has most likely occurred because of the further expansion of savings of the households belonging to the higher expenditure groups. Though we do not have any direct evidence to supplement our observation but whatever indirect evidences that are available, they reveal that in 1999-2000 the major recipients of interest and dividend are those households whose monthly per capita expenditure is highest (refer Table A-1) i.e. these households received enough amount of payment through interest and dividend that it constituted a good source of their income. This apart, to a great extent decline in disparities in non-food consumption expenditure has occurred on account of too much under-reporting of non-food consumption expenditure by NSSO, especially of the households belonging to the middle and higher expenditure groups due to which discrepancy between NSS and NAS estimates regarding consumption expenditure in general and non-food expenditure in particular has substantially increased over time.

In the light of these facts, it is too difficult to accept any convergence in income disparities. Thus, Kuznets inverted-U hypothesis is only partially correct, since with economic development, income disparities have initially increased but thereafter it has remained more or less stable. Our analysis has also demonstrated that mere low levels of per capita income is not the cause of poverty and neither the sustained rise in it can reduce absolute poverty, until it is accompanied by an adequate redistribution of income.

III.C. Analysis of Absolute and Relative Poverty in Urban India

During the process of development, there is substantial migration of workers from rural to urban areas in search of employment. Large scale migration of workers significantly influences urban population and which also affects absolute and relative poverty levels in the urban areas of the country. In such a situation, pattern of change in absolute and relative poverty in urban areas may not be same as in rural areas. Our detailed analysis on poverty for urban household sector in India will facilitate to throw light on it, as well as on Kuznets inverted-U hypothesis. Moreover, the analysis will also examine the behaviour of absolute poverty to changes in per capita income, and trace the pattern of change regarding disparities in consumption expenditure on food, non-food and total expenditure components along with the overall distribution of income.

TABLE 7

Growth Rate of Urban Per Capita Net Domestic Product in Real Terms

(in percentage terms)

	1970-71 to 1980-81	*1980-81 to 1993-94*	*1993-94 to 1999-00*
Growth Rate	–0.21	3.28	5.84

Source: Estimated from National Accounts Statistics of India, 1950-51 to 2000-01, *EPW Research Foundation*, Mumbai and Net Domestic Product by Economic Activity in Rural/Urban Areas, CSO, Government of India.

It is indeed noticeable that during 1970s, the real per capita NDP in urban areas has declined from Rs. 1294 to Rs. 1267. This is in contrast to what has been observed in the rural areas. One important reason for decline is that in the urban areas, population growth rate (3.75% per annum) was more than double the population growth rate in rural areas (1.46% per annum), which is possibly on account of large scale migration of workers to urban areas, as mentioned earlier. Moreover, an overall price increase of around 10% per annum in urban areas is also responsible for depressing the real per capita NDP in urban areas.

It is important to note that despite the decline in real per capita NDP during the period of 1970s (refer Table 7), absolute poverty in urban areas declined from 49% to 45.2%, while disparities in food, non-food and total consumption expenditure increased during the major period of 1970s (refer Table 8). The only plausible explanation for this contrasting pattern at the macro-level is the significant differential increase in the price of cereals, food and non-food items. For instance, price of cereals between 1972-73 to 1977-78 increased at a rate of just 5.6% per annum while the price of overall food items increased at around 8.4% per annum. A fairly higher increase of price of non-cereal food items forced people in the lower expenditure class to consume cereals rather than other food items, which are more nutritious and which are a part of the consumption basket of the rich people. This has caused disparities in the food expenditure to widen. Moreover, the disparities in the nonfood consumption expenditure rose more sharply than the food consumption expenditure which is mainly on account of the fact that the price of non-food items showed an increase at a rate of 10.8% per annum between 1972-73 and 1977-78. It is owing to such a steep rise in the prices of non-food items that the overall prices index too displayed a rise at a rate of over 9% per annum. This, coupled with the fact that urban population increased at a rate of 3.75% per annum caused the real per capita NDP to decline. However, since the price of basic wage goods, like rice, wheat, etc. increased much slowly, therefore, consumption expenditure on cereals is not much affected as the consumption expenditure on other food and non-food items. Considering the fact that absolute poverty is mainly a function of the consumption expenditure on cereals in particular and food in general, its decline is not unusual despite the fall in real per capita NDP in urban areas during 1972-73 to 1977-78. Thus, the apparent contradiction between declining absolute poverty and real per capita NDP in urban areas is well explained by significant differential movements in the price indices of cereals, food, and non-food items. This differential movement is also responsible for escalating disparities in food, non-food and overall consumption expenditure. Our analysis thus, has clearly revealed that mere low per capita income is not the cause of high absolute poverty, rather it is influenced by other factors too. Moreover, rising disparities in consumption expenditure during the initial phase of economic development is at least an indicator of increasing income disparities or relative poverty too. Thus, the first part of Kuznets hypothesis is also corroborated by the available evidences from urban areas. This is in line with our findings for rural household sector of India.

The slow down in the urban population growth rate during the decade of 1980s and thereafter, along with a substantial acceleration in the net domestic product helped to make a marked improvement in the per capita NDP after 1981.

The improvement in nominal per capita net domestic product is so much significant that despite the prices of cereals, food and non-food items increased by over 12% between 1977-78 to 1983, the real per capita net domestic product increased on an average by about 3.28% after 1981 and until 1993-94. The benefits of economic development between 1977-78 to 1983 is certainly experienced by all sections of the society, but is definitely biased towards urban rich. Our observation is based on the fact that though absolute poverty declined from 45.2% to 40.8% during 1977-78 to 1983, but the relative poverty has increased further as is evident from the rising disparities in the food, non-food and overall consumption expenditure (refer Table 8).

TABLE 8

Absolute Poverty Ratios and Gini's Coefficients Representing Disparities in Food, Non-Food and Overall Consumption Expenditure in Urban India During Last Six Quinquennial Rounds

(in percentage terms)

Quinquennial Round	*Absolute Poverty*	*Gini's Coefficient (ρ)*		
		Food Expenditure	*Non-Food Expenditure*	*Total Consumption*
1st Round (1972-73 to 1973-74)	49.0	16.70	28.17	25.84
2nd Round (1977-78)	45.2	20.55	40.05	31.86
3rd Round (1983)	40.8	24.08	48.24	33.96
4th Round (1987-88)	38.2	24.32	46.19	33.73
5th Round (1993-94)	32.4	23.56	46.13	33.55
6th Round (1999-2000)	23.6	23.76	43.69	33.91

Source: Estimated on the basis of past six quinquennial rounds reports on level and pattern of consumption expenditure in India, NSSO, Dept. of Statistics, Government of India, New Delhi.

Absolute poverty would have declined still further and disparities in consumption expenditure may not have increased, had the price of basic food items as well as of nonfood items would not have been of a tall order.

The price of basic food items (i.e. cereals) increased at an average rate of about 13.6% per annum while that of non-food items increased at a rate of 12.6% per annum. Such a high rise in the prices of basic wage goods seems to have left little income in the hands of people in the lower expenditure group to spend on other food and non-food items, thereby enhancing the level of disparities in the food, non-food and overall consumption expenditure. Moreover, sharp increase in the price of basic wage goods has deprived many people in the lowest expenditure group to have enough quantities of these food items to be able to lift them above poverty line.

Therefore, it is sufficient to suggest that mere increase in per capita NDP is not enough to make a substantial dent on the absolute poverty. Rather, redistribution of income and the extent to which price of basic food items increases during the process of economic development are reasonably important variables governing the level of poverty in a country. Furthermore, the disparities in all types of food, non-food and overall consumption expenditure have increased between 1977-78 to 1983, therefore, it is quite reasonable to infer that relative poverty during this phase in urban areas has increased, i.e. the first part of Prof. Kuznets hypothesis, that rising disparities with increasing per capita incomes, continues to hold good.

The average real per capita NDP during 1980s and the beginning of 1990s increased at an average rate of 3.28% per annum but the decline in absolute poverty between 1983 and 1987-88 has been of a lowest order, while the relative disparities in food consumption expenditure increased marginally during this period. The slow decline in absolute poverty and increased disparities in food consumption expenditure is on account of the obvious and known fact that the year 1987-88 was a year of severe drought where area, production and productivity under foodgrains fell sharply which resulted in food prices to escalate significantly. Moreover, the decline in disparities in non-food consumption expenditure has caused the overall disparities in consumption expenditure to converge marginally. The convergence is primarily on account of too much divergence in the National Sample Survey (NSS) and National Accounts Statistics (NAS) estimates regarding non-food consumption expenditure with regard to miscellaneous items especially. This fact is already highlighted in Table 5.

It is also noticeable from the table that the divergence between the NAS and NSS estimates has a tendency to widen gradually overtime. The divergence seems to have occurred on grounds of under-reporting of non-food consumption expenditure, especially of people in the higher expenditure class by the NSSO. In this context, an observation made by Dandekar and Rath (1971) is worth-mentioning. 'It is also known that the upper middle and the richer households both in rural and urban areas have become inaccessible to the NSS investigators who are after all class III government servants. It thus seems perfectly possible that the consumer expenditure of the upper middle and the richer section has been progressively underestimated, as evidences shows'.

This observation coupled with rising households savings-income ratio are sufficient evidences to suggest that overall disparities in income distribution during 1983 and 1987-88 have not converged. Thus, Kuznets hypothesis, that with rising per capita NDP, relative poverty or income disparities will converge, is not observed in India, at least upto 1987-88.

The benefits of increased real per capita NDP in urban areas has further drifted towards the people in lower expenditure class, which has caused marginal decline in the disparities regarding food, non-food and overall consumption expenditure. The relative improvement in the consumption expenditure of people in the lower expenditure group has caused absolute poverty ratio to dip by almost 6 per cent (i.e. from 38.2% to 32.4%) during 1987-88 to 1993-94.

It is indeed noteworthy that during 1987-88 to 1993-94, there has been a substantial increase in the number of people reporting income from interest and dividend (refer Table 9) which has facilitated to raise household savings to income ratio from 21.17% to 23.08% during 1987-88 to 1993-94. The major saving holders belong to the group whose monthly per capita expenditure is highest. This is evident from the break-up of the number of people in different expenditure classes reporting income from interest and dividend for the year

TABLE 9

Trends in Proportions of Households Reporting Receipt of

Household Type	*Year*	*Per 1000 No. of Households Reporting Income During Last 365 days from*							
		Cultivation	*Fishing & other Agricul. Enterpr.*	*Wage/ Salaried empl.*	*Non-agri. enterp.*	*Pension*	*Remittances*	*Interest & Dividend*	*Other Sources*
All Household Types	1987-88	85	49	626	343	42	81	44	107
	1993-94	80	50	626	347	50	88	76	107
	1999-2000	70	40	600	351	63	68	74	74

Source: NSS Report No. 463: Sources of Household Income in India, 1999-2000.

1999-2000 (refer Table A-1). This break up is not available for the year 1993-94, however, it equally applies to the year 1993-94 since there is virtually no change in the number of people reporting income from interest and dividend during the period 1993-94 to 1999-2000 (refer Table 9). These evidences are enough to indicate that the marginal decline in the disparities in food, non-food and overall consumption expenditure has occurred on account of a substantial increase in the number of people in the highest monthly per capita expenditure group as major saving holders. This, therefore, implies that relative poverty or income disparities have not abridged during the period 1987-88 to 1993-94. The analysis of the terminal period will further facilitate to substantiate our inference, where one will find that as the number of households constituting major portion of savings in urban areas almost stagnated and the disparities in consumption expenditure will rise. Thus, decline in disparities in consumption expenditure is not a sign of declining income disparities. Rather, it has to be viewed in the light of the behaviour of household savings as well as those who constitute it.

During the terminal period of our study (1993-94 to 1999-2000), the real per capita NDP increased at a much faster rate than those during the preceding periods. The average real growth rate of per capita NDP is 5.84% per annum, which is the maximum growth rate so far observed in any other sub-period, either in rural or urban areas.

Despite a higher growth rate of real per capita NDP, the disparities in food expenditure or in overall consumption expenditure has not declined. Rather, it has increased marginally, which shows that benefits of economic development has not drifted further to raise the food expenditure of the lower expenditure classes. In the absence of any further redistribution of income, it is too naive to expect such a significant decline in absolute poverty, since mere increase in per capita income is not enough to curtail poverty, rather its redistribution is equally important in making a significant dent on absolute poverty. Thus, the official estimates of a substantial decline in urban poverty ratio from 32.4% to 23.6% during the terminal period of our analysis is not consistent with our inference. Moreover, official estimates are even inconsistent with its own preceding survey estimates (based on thin sample, refer Table 10) as well as the estimates based on the consumption expenditure data published in the employment-unemployment survey, which is another official document of the Government of India. Even Prof. Sen's (2000) skepticism about decline in absolute poverty during 1993-94 to 1999-2000 is quite justified.

It is also evident from our analysis that relative poverty among different expenditure classes has not converged since household savings-income ratio has increased along with the disparities in the overall consumption expenditure.

Thus, even in the terminal period of our analysis, Kuznets observation of a decline in the relative poverty with increase in real per capita income is not corroborated.

TABLE 10

Percentage of People below Poverty Line in India Since 1999-2000

	46th (TS) 1990-91	*48th (TS) 1992*	*50th (LS) 1993-94*	*51st (TS) 1994-95*	*52nd (TS) 1995-96*	*53rd (TS) 1997*	*54th (TS) 1998*	*55th (LS) 1999-00*
Rural	35.04	41.70	37.27	38.03	38.29	38.46	45.25	27.1
Urban	35.29	37.80	32.36	34.24	30.05	33.97	35.48	23.6
Combined	35.11	40.70	36.07	26.98	36.08	37.23	43.01	26.1

Note: TS = Thin Sample; LS = Large Sample
Source: Dutt and Sundaram, Indian Economy, 47th Edition, 2003.

IV. CONCLUSION AND POLICY IMPLICATIONS

There is no single source from which one can directly get consistent data for India regarding income distribution over a period of time so that one can draw inferences about relative poverty or income disparities and its pattern over time which is of utmost importance for policy formulation. Despite this drawback, we are able to track the pattern of changes in relative poverty and compared it with the movements in per capita income and absolute poverty. Our analysis is indeed useful to verify two widely held viewpoints, especially at a time when empirical evidences have begun to accumulate against them, and require further support in their favour in order to convincingly contradict both the widely held viewpoints. These two widely held viewpoints are:

(i) Poverty is more a direct reflection of low levels of per capita income rather than skewed income distribution.
(ii) Relative poverty or income disparities increased initially with increase in real per capita income but subsequently it diminishes as per capita income grows further. This is Prof. Kuznets famous inverted-U hypothesis.

In the absence of consistent availability of data on income distribution over time, we have indirectly analyzed relative poverty in rural and urban areas of India on the basis of consumption expenditure distribution and the behaviour of household savings over a time period stretching from 1972-73 to 1999-2000.

The analysis was not straight forward, especially with regard to estimation of disparities in consumption expenditure among different classes but our innovative method of estimating Gini's coefficient has facilitated our task. The broad conclusions and policy implications that have emerged from our analysis are as follows:

1. It is clearly demonstrated during the course of our analysis that mere

increase in per capita income is not enough to reduce poverty rather redistribution of per capita income and rate of change in the price of cereals are crucial variables, which govern the level of absolute poverty in India. This also contradicts the general belief that poverty is more a direct reflection of low levels of per capita income rather than skewed income distribution.

2. In India, it is indeed difficult to estimate disparities in the consumption expenditure of different groups geometrically on the basis of Lorenz curve, since it is not directly possible to calculate the area between the Lorenz curve and x-axis for the different years during 1972-73 to 1993-94. This is mainly on account of uneven percentage distribution of persons among different expenditure classes. Therefore, an alternative method is devised to determine the area below Lorenz curve. This method has given fairly accurate estimates which are substantiated by results for the year 1999-2000, the year for which percentage distribution of persons among different expenditure classes is evenly given. Areas below Lorenz curve, regarding overall consumption expenditure in rural and urban areas on the basis of our methodology are respectively 37.25 and 33.05, while on the basis of trapezoidal rule, these areas are respectively 37.28 and 33.04, which are almost identical.

   Thus, in the absence of even percentage distribution of persons among different expenditure classes, our methodology can be used to determine areas below Lorenz curve, since trapezoidal rule becomes inapplicable to determine area below Lorenz curve in such a situation.

3. Prof. Kuznets inverted-U hypothesis regarding real per capita income and relative poverty is not supported by the available evidences from rural and urban areas of the Indian economy. Our inference is not the only one, but there are many other evidences like, by one provided by Deininger and Squire (1996), which has been accumulated over the years against the inverted-U hypothesis. This has serious implications for future growth since conventional wisdom that higher inequality promotes growth finds no clinching evidences in its favour during the recent past. Rather, Smith (2001) has effectively demonstrated that higher initial income inequality is an impediment for a higher economic growth. He, therefore, concluded that, "when (poor) individuals cannot borrow against future income, the initial distribution of income affects physical and human capital accumulation and economic growth". The need in India is to design policies which must lessen relative poverty or income inequalities. Privatization and Liberalization cannot help to achieve it in developing countries like India.

4. The estimates of consumption expenditure provided by National Account Statistics is much higher than those given by National

Sample Survey Organization. The substantial underestimation of consumption expenditure on the part of NSSO has occurred because of a fairly low estimate of miscellaneous items in the category of non-food expenditure. There is an urgent need on the part of NSSO to amend it since it significantly affects relative disparities in non-food consumption expenditure, which has serious policy implications.

5. It has been observed that during 1993-94 to 1999-2000, real per capita NDP growth rate has been maximum both in rural and urban areas, but relative disparities in food consumption expenditure too has increased. Moreover, household savings-income ratio has expanded further which is mainly on account of enhanced savings, especially by those whose monthly per capita expenditure is highest. It is reflected by the fact that the one the important source of income is through interest and dividend. This coupled with substantial under-reporting of non-food consumption expenditure of households in the higher expenditure classes leave little room for doubt about income distribution becoming more skewed since liberalization. This has raised serious apprehension about the official claim of a significant reduction in absolute poverty both in rural and urban areas. Our apprehensions are well supported by the evidences about poverty reduction, based on other government documents like employment-unemployment surveys, and preceding official surveys on consumption expenditure, based on thin sample. No rational policy framework can be designed in developing countries especially where reliable and correct poverty estimates are not available. Time has come when higher authorities should properly monitor the entire survey, rather than taking it as a routine work. They must comprehend the significance of their exercise as future course of policy depends a lot on their estimates.

REFERENCES

Ahluwalia and Chenery, 1984, 'Measuring Development', published in '*Leading Issues in Economic Development*', 4th Edition, ed. Meier, Gerald, M., pp. 15-19, Oxford University Press, Delhi.

Ahluwaiia, Montek S. and H.B. Chenery, 1979, 'The Economic Framework in Redistribution with Growth', Oxford University Press, New York.

Ahluwaiia, Montek S., 1986, 'Rural Poverty, Agricultural Production, and Prices: A Re-Examination', published in '*Agricultural Change and Rural Poverty*', ed. John W. Mellor and Gunvant M. Desai, Oxford University Press, Delhi, pp. 59-75.

Atkinson, A., 1975, The Economics of Inequality', Oxford University Press, London.

Chenery, H.B. *et. al.*, 1966, 'Redistribution with Growth', Oxford University Press, London.

Dandekar, V.M. and Rath, N., 1971, 'Poverty in India', *Economic and Political Weekly*, Jan. 2 and Jan. 9, 1971 (Special Articles), pp. 25-45 and pp. 143-46.

Deininger, K. and Squire, L., 1998, 'New Ways of Looking at Old Issues: Inequality and Growth', *Journal of Development Economics*, 57, pp. 259-87.

Deininger, K.S. Squire, L., 1996, 'A New Data Set Measuring Income Inequality', *World Bank Economic Review*, 10, 565-91.

Dutt, Gaurav and Ravallion Martin, 2002, 'Is India's Economic Growth Leaving the Poor Behind ?', *Journal of Economic Perspectives*, Vol. 16, No. 3, Summer 2002, pp. 89-108.

Economic Survey, 2002-03, Ministry of Finance and Company Affairs, Economic Division, Government of India, New Delhi.

Kuznets, S., 1995, 'Economic Growth and Income Inequality', *The American Economic Review*, 45:1, pp. 1-28.

Lange, Oskar, 1959, 'Introduction to Econometrics', Pergamon Press, New York.

National Accounts Statistics of India, 1950-51 to 2000-091: New Linked Series with 1993-94 as the Base year, *Economic and Political Weekly Research Foundation (EPWRF)*, Mumbai.

Nijhawan, Inder P., 1983, 'Income Distribution and Poverty', published in *India's Economic Problems: An Analytical Approach*, ed. Uppal, J.S., 3rd Edition, Tata-McGraw Hill, New Delhi, pp. 236-254.

NSSO (1993-94, 1999-2000), 'Employment and Unemployment Situation in India', Reports No. 409 and 458, NSSO, Dept. of Statistics, Govt. of India, New Delhi.

NSSO (1999-2000), 'Sources of Household Income in India', Report No. 463, Dept. of Statistics, Govt. of India, New Delhi.

NSSO, 'Level and Pattern of Consumer Expenditure', 1st, 2nd, 3rd, 4th, 5th, 6th Quinquennial Surveys during years 1972-73, 77-78, 1983, 1987-88, 1993-94, and 1999-2000, National Sample Survey Organization, Dept. of Statistics, Government of India, New Delhi.

Sen, Abhijit, 2001, 'Estimates of Consumer Expenditure and its Distribution: Statistical Priorities After the NSS 55th Round', *Economic and Political Weekly*, Dec. 16, 35, pp. 4499-4518.

Smith, D., 2001, 'International Evidence on How Income Inequality and Credit Market Imperfection Affect Private Saving Rates', *Journal of Development Economics*, 64, pp. 100-127.

Sundaram, K. and Suresh D. Tendulkar, 2001a, 'NAS-NSS Estimates of Private Consumption for Poverty Estimation: A Disaggregated Comparison for 1993-94', *Economic and Political Weekly*, January 13, 36:2, pp. 119-29.

Sundaram, K., 2001, 'Employment and Poverty in 1990s: Further Results from NSS 55th Round Employment-Unemployment (E-U) Survey, 1999-2000', *Economic and Political Weekly*, August 11, 36:32, pp. 3039-3049.

Thorbecke Erik and Charumilind Chitatong, 2002, 'Economic Inequality and Its Socio-Economic Impact', *World Development*, 30:9, pp. 1477-95.

Todaro, Michael, P., 1985, 'Economic Development in the Third World', 3rd Edition, Orient Longman, New Delhi.

World Bank, 2001, World Development Report, 2000/01: Attacking Poverty, Oxford University Press, New York.

TABLE A-1

Number per 1000 of Households Reporting Receipts of Income from Different Sources During the Period of Last 365 days by MPCE Class

MPCE Class (Rs.)	*Cultivation*	*Fishing/ Other Agri. Enter.*	*Wage/ Salaried Employ.*	*Non-Agri. Enter.*	*Pension*	*Rent*	*Remi-tances*	*Interest & Dividend*	*Others*	*All*
1	*2*	*3*	*4*	*5*	*6*	*7*	*8*	*9*	*10*	*11*
Less than 225	37	27	56	30	29	27	34	8	59	Rural 44
225-255	40	29	55	33	17	31	28	1	51	42
255-300	81	67	107	85	39	47	64	15	85	87
300-340	90	78	105	79	41	57	76	20	90	90
340-380	93	79	103	97	43	73	75	31	92	93
380-420	94	84	97	92	52	47	85	43	91	92
420-470	103	98	100	98	77	84	84	65	101	100
470-525	98	96	89	103	77	53	102	74	90	96
525-615	116	121	96	121	111	134	115	131	105	111
615-775	120	145	92	116	183	148	145	213	111	113
775-950	62	81	46	72	129	112	74	134	66	.61
950 and above	66	94	55	75	202	186	118	265	58	71
All classes	1000	1000	1000	1000	1000	1000	1000	1000	1000	1000
Avg. MPCE (Rs.)	490	.536	450	504	691	640	539	753	475	486

Less than 300	42	55	35	42	12	6	36	2	65	Urban
										38
300-350	45	44	35	43	14	21	27	3	48	37
350-425	96	99	72	94	26	36	53	13	82	75
425-500	108	104	83	99	46	73	70	27	94	86
500-575	92	102	86	99	62	69	65	38	81	86
575-665	106	109	89	98	81	89	73	53	86	91
665-775	99	102	96	98	85	104	94	88	96	96
775-915	96	84	106	104	99	120	106	98	82	103
915-1120	104	109	115	103	140	144	136	134	102	113
1120-1500	114	98	137	109	171	166	134	181	113	130
1500-1925	49	45	72	50	126	82	76	140	60	67
1925 & above	50	49	74	61	137	90	129	222	90	77
All classes	1000	1000	1000	1000	1000	1000	1000	1000	1000	1000
Avg. MPCE (Rs.)	763	731	857	810	1119	981	982	1346	839	855

Source: Sources of Household Income in India, 1999-2000, NSS Report No. 463, NSSO, Department of Statistics, Government of India, New Delhi.

SECTION III

POVERTY AND ITS MEASUREMENT

Measurement and Indicators of Poverty in India

S. BORBORA AND R. MAHANTA

I. INTRODUCTION

Poverty can be defined as a social phenomenon in which a section of society is unable to fulfil even the basic necessities of life. When a substantial segment of society is deprived of the minimum level of living and continuous at a bare subsistence level that society is said to be plagued with mass poverty. The deprivation of a significant section of the society of minimum basic needs in the face of luxurious life for the elite classes, makes poverty more glaring. It is also believed that poverty anywhere is a threat to prosperity everywhere. In India most of the states are suffering from mass poverty which is a threat to the prosperity of India.

Conceptually, the notion of poverty is a complex phenomenon in its content and scope. It is both widespread and intensive, and intrinsically related to socio-cultural, socio-political and socio-economic factors which indicate tile contemporary ideologies and policies followed by a society. As such, there is no absolute meaning attached to the word poverty; nor is there a generally satisfactory definition and concept of poverty for adoption by researchers and policy-makers. Ever since poverty has become an subject of study with policy implication, attempts have been made to: (i) identify the poor, and (ii) measure their poverty to establish an acceptable and generalized 'poverty line'. The concept of poverty line was introduced by Charles Booth, an English Sociologist. Booth defined those who lived at or below the 'poverty line' as having an average income (at 1889 prices) of 21 to 22 Shillings per weak for a very small family or up to 25 to 26 Shillings for one of a larger family. In economics, majority of analysis of poverty identify poor as those who are not able (involuntarily) to maintain a defined level of consumption or income applicable in these instances. It has now become common to use some physical index of consumption (such as a per diem intake of calories) identify the door.

The basic idea behind the concept of poverty is the criterion whereby we identify the poor. Evolution of this criterion culminates in establishing a 'poverty line' does only the part of the job. Though it is correct that the poor are those whose income lies below poverty line. However, Sen observes that, generally, poverty line does only part of the job. The concept of absolute poverty is based on absolute norms for living (measured in terms of consumption expenditure), laid down according to specific minimum standard and all such individuals or groups whose consumption expenditure is below this standard, are classified as poor. The proportion of such individuals and groups in the population indicates the extent of poverty. Under the relative concept of poverty, a family (or an individual) is deemed to be poor if its level of income/consumption expenditure falls below the predetermined level. Then the income distribution of the population in different fractile groups is estimated and a comparison is made between the level of living of people at bottom layer and at the top layers of population to assess the relative levels of poverty. The relative concept is more suitable for developed countries while the absolute concept is more relevant for the developing countries. In developing countries, for the purpose of measurement of poverty, consumption expenditure may be considered more appropriate than income. In addition, the concepts of poverty has two connotations namely, individual poverty and collective poverty. By individualized poverty is meant those individuals who are not able to incur even the minimum expenditure on the most essential items for survival viz. food, clothing and housing. This can also be eliminated by the government through suitably increasing expenditure on human welfare needs such as education, health, etc., and also by discouraging expenditure on various social customs.

After defining the different concepts of poverty, the factors responsible for poverty may be grouped into four heads, viz. economic, demographic, sociological and other:

1. The economic factors include:
   - (i) Land;
   - (ii) Irrigation facility;
   - (iii) Employment Potential;
   - (iv) Availability of loan;
   - (v) Saving capacity; and
   - (vi) Investment potential.
2. Demographic factors include:
   - (i) Size of family,
   - (ii) Age-composition of family members, and
   - (iii) Level of Literacy.

3. Sociological factors include:
   (i) Caste;
   (ii) Joint family; and
   (iii) Rigidity of social systems.
4. Other factors are:
   (i) Awareness about developmental programmes;
   (ii) Level of participation in village politics; and
   (iii) Ability to provide local leadership.

II. MEASUREMENT OF POVERTY

In India, the approach based on the minimum requirement of food, clothing and shelter which reflects purchasing power is generally used for measurement of poverty. The Planning Commission obtaining the data from the National Sample Survey and the recommendations of the Task Force on Projection of Minimum Needs and Effective Consumption Demand (1979), defined the poverty line on the basis of caloric norms of 2400 per capita per day in rural areas and 2100 per capita per day in urban areas in the base year 1973-74. The poverty line was so defined was Rs. 49.10 for rural areas and Rs. 56.60 for urban areas

From the following Tables 1 and 2, we can see the population below the poverty line determined by Planning Commission and The Expert Group Methodology.

TABLE 1

Population Below the Poverty Line (as per the Planning Commission, GOI)

(Population in Millions)

Sl. No.	*Sector*	*1983-84*	*1984-85*	*1987-88*	*1989-90*	*1993-94*
1.	Rural	221.5	222.2	196.0	168.6	141.1
2.	Urban	49.5	50.5	41.7	42.2	27.1
	Total	271.0	272.7	237.7	210.8	168.2
Poverty Ratio (%)						
1.	Rural	40.4	39.9	33.4	28.4	21.7
2.	Urban	28.1	27.7	20.1	19.3	11.6
	Total	37.4	36.9	29.9	25.3	16.9

Source: CSO, Press Report.

The Tables 1 and 2 shows a lots of difference in the number of population below poverty line and percentage of poverty ratio between the Planning Commission, GOI and Expert Group. In 1983-84 as per there were 271.0 million people (percentage of Poverty ratio is 37.4) below the poverty line as per Planning Commission whereas according to Expert Group methodology 322.9

million people below the poverty line and percentage of poverty ratio is 44.5. In the same way we can see that in 1993-94 as per Planning Commission 166.2 million people were below the poverty line whereas according to Expert Group methodology it was 320.3 millions people. Projection of National poverty ratios in percentage are given in Table 3. It is seen that projected national poverty ratio is less than 5 per cent in the year 2011-12 which is quite satisfactory for a populous developing country.

TABLE 2

Population Below the Poverty Line (As per the Expert Group Methodology)

(Population in Millions)

Sl. No.	*Sector*	*1973-74*	*1983-84*	*1987-88*	*1993-94*	*1999-2000*
1.	Rural	261.3	252.0	231.9	244.0	193.2
2.	Urban	60.0	70.9	75.2	76.3	67.0
	Total	321.3	322.9	307.1	320.3	260.2
Poverty Ratio (%)						
1.	Rural	56.4	45.7	39.1	37.3	27.1
2.	Urban	49.0	40.8	38.2	32.4	23.6
	Total	54.9	44.5	38.9	36.0	26.1

Sources: Planning Commission, Ninth Five Year Plan 1997-2002, Volume 1, "Number and Percentage of Population Below Poverty Line by States", *The Hindu*, 26 Feb. 2001.

TABLE 3

Projection of National Poverty Ratios

(in percentage)

Region	*1996-97*	*2001-02*	*2006-07*	*2011-12*
Rural	30.55	18.61	9.64	4.31
Urban	25.58	1.6.46	9.28	4.49
Total	29.18	17.98	9.53	4.37

Source: Planning Commission, Ninth Five Year Plan, 1997-2002, Vol. 1.

The following Table 4 shows the number and percentage of population below poverty.

The total number and the percentage of population below poverty line have been shown in Table 4 for 1983-84, 1993-94 and 1999-2000 respectively. Its seen that the total number of people below poverty line has decreased in rural areas from 2529.6 lakhs in 1983-84 to 1932.43 in lakhs in 1999-2000. The combined (taking both rural and urban areas) number and percentage of people below poverty line is also decreases sharply from 3221.0 lakhs in 1983-84 to 2602.50 lakhs in 1999-2000 and from 37.6 per cent to 26.10 per cent respectively.

TABLE 4

Sl. No.	States/ UTs	1883-84 Rural		1883-84 Urban		1883-84 Combined		1993-94 Rural		1993-94 Urban		1993-94 Combined	
		No. of Persons (lakhs)	% of persons	No. of Persons (lakhs)	% of persons	No. of Persons (lakhs)	% of persons	No. of Persons (lakhs)	% of persons	No. of Persons (lakhs)	% of persons	No. of Persons (lakhs)	% of persons
1	2	3	4	5	6	7	8	9	10	11	12	13	14
1.	Andhra Pradesh	112.2	26.0	57.1	40.8	168.2	29.7	79.41	15.92	74.47	38.33	153.97	22.19
2.	Arunachal Pradesh	—	—	—	—	—	—	3.62	45.01	0.11	7 73	3.73	39.35
3.	Assam	57.1	29.9	6.0	26.3	63.1	29.5	94.33	45.01	2.03	7.73	96.36	40.86
4.	Bihar	405.2	62.7	51.0	51.3	465.2	61.2	450.86	58.21	42.49	34.50	493.35	54.96
5.	Goa	—	—	—	—	—	—	0.38	5.34	1.53	27.03	1.19	14.92
6.	Gujarat	50.0	20.3	36.5	31.4	86.5	23.8	62.13	22.18	43.02	27.S9	105.19	24.14
7.	Haryana	19.1	17.8	9.9	30.1	29.0	20.6	36.56	28.02	7.31	16.38	43.88	25.05
8.	Himachal Pradesh	5.9	14.2	0.5	13.3	6.4	14.1	15.40	30.34	0.46	9.18	15.86	28.44
9.	Jammu & Kashmir	110	22.1	5.1	36.7	16.2	25.3	19.05	30.34	1.86	9.18	20.92	25.17
10.	Karnataka	103.6	37.5	54.3	45.1	157.9	39.8	95.99	29.88	60.46	40.14	156.46	33.16
11.	Kerala	73.3	33.9	24.9	47.2	98.1	36.5	55.95	25.76	20.46	24.55	76.41	25.43
12.	Madhya Pradesh	237.2	54.3 I	61.8	51.3	299.0	53.7	216.19	40.64	82.33	48.38	298.52	42.52
13.	Maharashtra	175.0	41.0	83.6	34.4	258.6	38.6	193.33	37.93	111.90	35.15	305.22	36.86
14.	Manipur	1.8	16.2	0.8	18.8	2.6	16.9	6.33	45.01	0.47	7.73	6.80	33.78
15.	Meghalaya	—	—	—	—	—	—	7.09	45.01	0.29	7.73	7.38	37.92
16.	Mizoram	—	—	—	—	—	—	1.64	45.01	0.30	7.73	1.94	25.66
17.	Nagaland	—	—	—	—	—	—	4.85	45.01	0.20	7.73	5.05	37.92
18.	Orissa	167.3	69.1	15.7	43.2	183.0	65.7	140.90	49.72	19.70	41.64	160.60	48.56
19.	Punjab	13.7	10.8	15.0	29.0	28.7	16.1	17.76	11.95	7.35	11.35	25.11	11.77

(Contd.)

TABLE 4 (*Contd.*)

1	2	3	4	5	6	7	8	9	10	11	12	13	14
20.	Rajasthan	91.1	31.5	32.2	39.0	123.2	33.1	94.68	26.46	33.82	30.49	128.50	27.41
21.	Sikkim	—	—	—	—	—	—	1.81	45.01	0.03	7.73	1.84	41.43
22.	Tamil Nadu	162.8	48.3	81.6	47.5	244.4	48.1	21.70	32.48	80.40	39.77	202.10	35.03
23.	Tripura	—	—	—	—	—	—	11.41	45.01	0.38	7.73	11.79	39.01
24.	Uttar Pradesh	487.8	51.2	126.3	55.3	614.1	52.0	496.17	42.28	108.28	35.39	604.46	40.85
25.	West Bengal	215.5	51.0	62.3	39.8	277.8	47.9	209.90	40.80	44.66	22.41	254.56	35.66
26.	Delhi	0.3	6.2	10.2	15.5	0.5	4.9	0.19	1.90	15.32	16.03	15.51	14.69
UTs													
27.	A&N Islands	—	—	—	—	—	—	0.73	32.48	0.08	39.77	1.06	34.47
28.	Chandigarh	—	—	—	—	—	—	0.07	11.35	2.38	11.35	0.80	11.35
29.	D&N Haveli	—	—	—	—	—	—	0.72	51.95	0.06	39.93	0.77	50.84
30.	Lakshadweep	—	—	—	—	—	—	0.06	25.76	0.08	2455	0.14	2504
31.	Pondicherry	—	—	—	—	—	—	0.93	32.48	2.38	39.77	3.31	37.40

Source: Central Statistical Organisation (CSO), Selected Socio-Economic Statistics India, 1993 and 1996-97.

TABLE 4A

Sl. No.	States/ UTs	1999-2000 Rural		1999-2000 Urban		1999-2000 Combined	
		No. of Persons (Lakhs)	% of Persons	No. of Persons (Lakhs)	% of Persons	No. of Persons (Lakhs)	% of Persons
1.	Andhra Pradesh	58.13	11.05	60.88	26.63	119.0	15.77
2.	Arunachal Pradesh	3.80	40.04	0.18	.47	3.98	3.4
3.	Assam	92.17	0.04	2.38	7.47	4.55	-36.09
4.	Bihar	376.51	4.30	9.13	2.91	425.64	42.60
5.	Goa	0.11	1.35	0.59	7.52	0.70	4.40
6.	Gujarat	39.80	13.17	28.09	15.59	67.89	14.07
7.	Haryana	11.94	8.27	5.39	9.99	8.74	
8.	Himanchal Pradesh	4.89	7094	0.29	4.63	5.12	7.63
9.	Jammu & Kashmir	2.97	3.97	0.49	1.98	3.46	3.48
10.	Karnataka	59.91	17.38	44.49	25.25	104.40	20.04
11.	Kerala	20.97	9.38	20.07	2 7	41.04	12.72
12.	Andhra Pradesh	217.32	7.06	1.22	6.44	98.54	-37.43-
13.	Maharashtra	125.12	23.72	102.87	26.81	227.99	25.02
14.	Manipur	6.53	40.04	0.66	7.47	7.19	28.54
15.	Meghalaya	.89	0.04	34	47	8.2 3	33.87
16.	Mizoram	1.40	0.04	.45	.47	85	-19.47
17.	Nagaland	1 5.21	40.04	0.28	7.47	5.49	32.67
18.	Orissa	143.69	11.40	42.83	169.09	47.15	
19.	Punjab	10.20	6.35	4.29	5.75	14.49	6.16
20.	Rajasthan	55.06	3.74	26.78	19.85	81.83	15.28
21.	Sikkim	2.00	40.04	0.04	7.47	2.05	36.55
22.	Tamil Nadu	80.51	20.55	49.97	22.11	130.48	21.22
23.	Tripura	12.53	40.04	0.49	7.47	13.02	34.44
24.	Uttar Pradesh	412.01	31.22	117.88	30.89	529.89	31.15
25.	West Bengal	180.11	31.85	33.38	14.86	213.49	27.02
26.	Delhi	0.07	.40	11.42	.42	1.49	8.23
UTs							
27.	A&N Islands	0.58	20.55	0.24	22.11	0.82	20.99
28.	Chandigarh	0.06	5.75	0.45	5.75	0.51	5.75
29.	D&N Haveli	.30	17.57	0.03	13.52	0.33	17.14
30.	Lakshadweep	0.03	9.38	0.08	20.27	20.27	15.60
31.	Pondicherry	0.64	W.55	1.77	22.11	2.41	21.67
32.	Daman & Diu	0.01	1.35	0.05	7.52	0.06	4.44
	All India	1932.43	27.09	670.07	23.62	2602.50	26.10

Source: "Number and Percentage of Population below poverty line by States," *The Hindu*, Feb. 2001.

TABLE 5

Distribution of Households by Availability of Two Square Meals a Day—India

(in Percentage)

Sl. No.	Members of the HHs getting two square meals a day	Rural		Urban	
		50th Round (1993-94)	55th Round (1999-2000)	50th Round (1993-94)	55th Round (1999-2000)
1.	Throughout the year	94.5	96.2	9-8.1	98.6
2.	Only some months of the year	4.2	2.6	1.1	0.60
3.	Not Even some months	0.90	0.70	0.50	0.30
4.	Not Reported	0.40	0.50	0.30	0.40
5.	All	100.0	100.0	100.0	100.0
6.	Proportion of HHs reported inadequacy of food (items 2+3)	5.1	3.3	1.60	0.90

Source: NSSO, Reported Adequacy of Food Intake in India, 55th Round, 1999-2000, Report No. 466(55/10/7), August 2001.

Rural Households by Availability of Two Square Meals a day—India

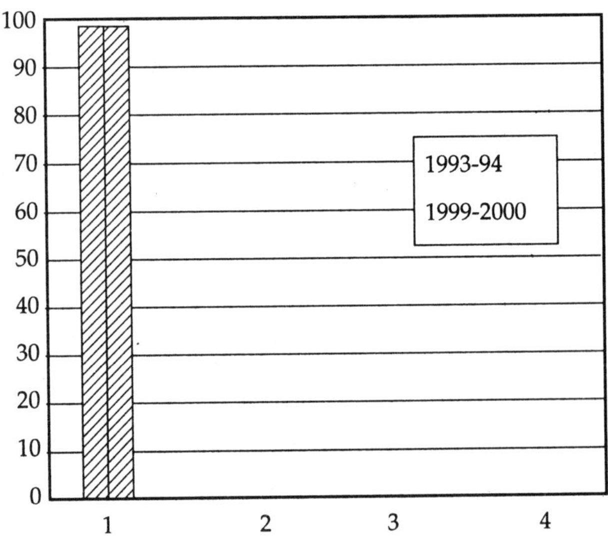

1. Throughout the year
2. Only some months of the year
3. Not even some months
4. Not reported

Distribution of households by availability of two square meals a day in India is shown in the above table. It is revealed that according to 55th Round in 1999-2000, 96.2 per cent members of the households getting two square meals a day in rural areas whereas it is 98.6 per cent in 1999-2000. In case of the percentage of members of households getting two square meals a day in only some months of the year and not even some months is very less in comparison to earlier category.

III. INDICATORS OF POVERTY

The literature of indicators of employment finds that per capita income, literacy rate, life expectancy rate, infant mortality rate and access to safe drinking water are some of the main indicators. In this section, we had made a cross-sectional analysis to identify tile indicators that have bearing in the position of poverty in India. This has been undertaken with reference to two periods of time, viz. 1991 and 2001. The task has been very difficult because proper data are not available with respect to many of the influencing variables for the respective states. In view of this limitation, we have analysed the effects of (1) Per capita state domestic income at current prices (XI), (2) Literacy rate (X2), (3) Life expectancy at birth (X3), (4) Infant mortality rate (X5), (5) Access to safe drinking water in households (X5) on poverty for the year 1991 and 2001. The percentage of access to safe drinking water in households for the two year, viz. 1991 and 2001 are same because of non-availability of data for 2001 separately. Tables 6 and 7 show the correlation coefficient matrices for 1991 and 2001 respectively.

TABLE 6

Correlation Coefficient Matrix of Percentage Shares of Poverty and other Variables 1991

	X1	*X2*	*X3*	*X4*	*X5*	*X6*
X1	1.00	—	—			
X2	.39	1.00	—			
X3	.52	.80*	1.00	—		
X4	.48	.57*	.82*	1.00	—	
X5	.65*	.31	.04	.09	1.00	—
X6	.74*	.46	.66*	.67*	.40	1.00

*Significance at 5% level.

The correlation matrix-1991 (Table 6) shows that though there are positive correlation between literacy rate (X2) and access to safe drinking water in households (X5) with percentage of population below poverty line (X6), but they are not significant. On the other hand, correlation between percentage of population below poverty line with respect to per capita net state domestic income at current prices (XI), Life expectancy at birth (X4) and Infant mortality rate (X5) are positive and significant at 5% level of significance. This shows that these three indicators viz. per capita net state domestic product, life expectancy at birth and infant mortality rate are prominent indicator of poverty. The same result is also obtained from the Table 7 for the year 2001. Here we can find that these three indicators has positive correlation with percentage of population below poverty line and they are significant also at 5% level of significance.

TABLE 7

Correlation Coefficient Matrix of Percentage Shares of Poverty and other Variables 2001

X1	*X2*	*X3*	*X4*	*X5*	*X6*
X1	1.00	—			
X2	.43	1.00	—		
X3	.56*	82	1.00	—	
X4	.47	.59*	.81*	1.00	—
X5	.57*	.22	.05	.16	1.00
X6					

*Significance at 5% level.

IV. POVERTY ALLEVIATION PROGRAMME

Poverty alleviation has been one of the guiding principles of the process economic development in India. The role of economic growth in providing more employment avenues to the population has been clearly recognized. The growth-oriented approach has been reinforced by focusing on specific sectors, which provide greater opportunities to the people to participate in the growth process. The various dimensions of poverty relating to health, education and other basic services have been progressively internalized in the planning process. Central and State governments have considerably enhanced allocations for the provision of education, health, sanitation and other facilities which promote capacity-building and well-being of the poor. Investments in agriculture, area development programmes and afforestation provide avenues for employment and income.

Special programmes have been taken up for the welfare of Scheduled Castes (SCs) and Scheduled Tribes (STs), minorities, the disabled and other vulnerable groups. Anti-poverty programmes that seek to transfer assets and skills to people for self-employment, coupled with public works programmes that enable people to cope with transient poverty, are the third strand of the larger anti-poverty strategy. The Targeted Public Distribution System (TPDS) protects the poor from the adverse effects of rise in prices and ensures food and nutrition security at affordable prices. The success of the anti-poverty strategy can be gauged from the decline in poverty levels from 35.97 per cent in 1993-94 to 26.10 in 1999-2000. Kerala, Haryana, Bihar, Himachal Pradesh, Karnataka, and Rajasthan experienced a sharp reduction in poverty levels (a drop of more than 12 percentage points between 1993-94 and 1999-2000). Uttar

Pradesh, West Bengal and Tamil Nadu also registered significant reduction in poverty (8-12 percentage points). However, Orissa and Madhya Pradesh have shown virtually no reduction in poverty levels. In fact, these are the states where the absolute number of poor has actually gone tip between 1993-94 and 1999-2000. Central Government had implemented various anti-poverty programmes in the ninth plan. The Integrated Rural Development Programme (IRDP), introduced in selected blocks in 1978-79 and universalized from 2 October 1980 has provided assistance to rural poor in the form—of subsidy and bank credit for productive employment opportunities through successive plan periods. Subsequently, Training of Rural Youth for Self-Employment (TRYSEM), Development of Women and Children in Rural Areas (DWCRA), Supply of Improved Tool Kits to Rural Artisans (SITRA) and Ganga Kalyan Yojana (GKY) were introduced as sub-programmes of IRDP to take care of the specific needs of the rural Population. On 1 April 1999, the IRDP and allied programmes, including the Million Wells Scheme (MWS), were merged into a single programme known as Swaranjayanti 'Gram Swarozgar Yojana (SGSY) the rural poor into self-help groups, capacity building, planning of activity clusters, infrastructure support, technology credit and marketing linkages. The National Rural Employment Programme (NREP) and Rural Landless Employment Guarantee Programme (RLEGP) were merged in April 1989 under the Jawahar Rozgar Yojana (JRY). The JRY was meant to generate meaningful employment opportunities for the unemployed and underemployed in rural areas through tile creation of economic infrastructure and community and social assets. Initially, the JRY also included the Indira Awas Yojana (IAY) and the MWS. Both these schemes were made into independent schemes in 1996. Under JRY, 73,764.83 lakh mandays of employment were generated till 1998-99. Sampoorna Gramin Rozgar Yojana (SGRY) scheme was implemented in September 2001 aim of the scheme continues to be generation of wage employment, creation of durable economic infrastructure in rural areas and provision of food and nutrition security to the poor.

The Approach Paper to the Tenth Plan has set-up a target for reduction of poverty and creation of high quality gainful employment during the plan period. The projected GDP growth rate of 8 per cent for the period 2002-07, if achieved, would lead to reduction o incidence of poverty by 5 percentage points by 2007. Compared to expected to decline by 15 percentage points by 2011-12. Effective implementation of anti-poverty programmes would be central to achieving the plan reductions in poverty. The challenge before the State is to provide employment opportunities which provide enhanced incomes. This becomes more important in view of the fact that the substantial additions to labour force are expected to take place during the next five years.

Enlargement of self and wage-employment programmes and their effective delivery becomes an imperative in such a scenario. The following table shows the financial and physical performance under various Poverty Alleviation Programmes during Eighth an Ninth Plan.

TABLE 8

Financial and Physical Performance under Poverty Alleviation Programmes
IRDP/SGSY, JRY/JCSY and EAS during Eighth and Ninth Plan Yearwise

(Rs. Crores)

Sl. No.	Years	IRDP/SGSY			JRY/JGSY			EAS		
		Total Allocation (Centre-State)	Total Expenditure	Lakh Families Swarozgar	Total Allocation (Centre-State)	Total Expenditure	Employment in Lakh Mandays	Total Allocation (Centre-State)	Total Expenditure	Employment Lakh Mandays
Eighth Plan										
1.	1992-93	662.22	693.88	20.69	3169.05	2709-59	7821.02	0.00		
2.	1993-94	1093.43	956.65	25.39	4059.42	3878.71	10258.4	0.00	83.75	494.74
3.	1994-95	1008.3	22.15	4376.92	4268.33	9517.07	0.00	1235.45	2729.56	
4.	1995-96	1077.16	20.89	4848.70	4466.91	8958.25	0.00	1720.61	3465.56	
5.	1996-97	1097.21	1131.68	19.24	2236.79	2163.98	4006.32	0.00	2160.41	4030.02
	Total	5048.29	4867.68	108.36	18690.88	17487.52	40561-06	0.00	5200.22	10719.6
Ninth Plan										
1.	1997-98	1133.51	1109.54	17.07	2499.21	2439.38	3955.89	2404.97	29.04.97	4717.74
2.	1998-99	1162.28	1162.28	16.77	2597.03	2525.48	3766.41	2485.15	2882.18	4279.36
3.	1999-2000	1472.34	959.86	9.34	2205.58	2032.45	2683.08	2431.46	2182.61	2786.17
4.	2000-01	1332.5	1116.27	10.3	2192.96	1929.23	2683.17	2082.27	1861.11	2183.92
5.	2001-02	774.5	555.15	6.25	2493.01	699.07	860.79	1730.92	530.92	666.27
	Total	16169.13	11687.93	9625.61		13949.34	11190.28	14633.5		

Note: 2001-02, SGSY, upto January 2002, 2001-02—JGSY—upto October 2001; 2001-02—EAS—upto September 2001.
Source: Ministry of Rural Development.

V. CONCLUSION

Poverty alone with its various manifestations like Malnutrition, over crowding, slum housing conditions, life expectancy, infant-mortality has persisted even though alleviation of poverty has always been an avowed objectives since independence. There are very few countries like India who had a long experience in struggling with poverty and still tile problem persist. After implementation of various antipoverty scheme in India, still the problem of poverty is existing as a curse to Indian society. Most of the plans could not able to reach their target. All the more, people are not aware of all the employment generation scheme introduced in various plan programme. In order to resolve these problem, we have to adopt some programmatic approach. First we have to attack the main indicators, e.g. per capita net state domestic product, Life expectancy at birth and infant mortality rate, which will help in minimizing the number and percentage of population below poverty line. The poor people should be involved for the success of any anti-poverty programme. They should be informed-and educated about such type of scheme. They should be provided with better health facility and access to proper nutrition. However, after having all the above discussion, we can come to a point that government had given more emphasis to alleviate poverty after seventies and to an extent succeeded in reducing poverty from 37.6 per cent in 1983-84 to 26.10 per cent in 1999-2000, although there is long way to go to fulfil the objective of reducing poverty further.

REFERENCES

Chaubey, P.K., Poverty Measurement—Issues, Approaches and Indices, New Age International Publishers, New Delhi, 1995.

Economic Survey, Govt. of India, 2002-03.

Gaur, K.D., Extent and Measurement of Poverty in India, Mittal Publications, New Delhi.

Sen, A., Three Notes on the Concept of Poverty, World Development Programme Research Working Papers, Geneva: International Labour Office, 1979.

Sen, A., Poverty and Families, OUP, New Delhi, 1999.

Singh, J.L. and Gaur, K.D. (ed), Need for New Strategies to Eradicate Poverty, Manak Publications Pvt. Ltd., New Delhi, 1999.

Yogesh, A., The Poverty Question-Search for Solutions, Rawat Publications, Jaipur, 2002.

Vyas, V.S. and Bhargava, P. (ed.), Poverty Reduction in Developing Countries—Experiences from Asia and Africa, Rawat Publications, Jaipur, 1999.

11

Dimensions of Poverty in India: Measurement and Determinants

P.K. PAL

According to World Development Report (2000/2001) poverty implies lack of adequate food and shelter, deprivations that keep them away from a decent standard of living—implying better housing, sanitation, access to safe drinking water and so on. It is a multidimensional concept. The main dimensions are: (i) lack of income and assets to attain basic necessities, food, shelter, clothing, and acceptable levels of health and education, (ii) sense of voicelessness and powerlessness in the institutions of state and society, (iii) vulnerability to adverse shocks, linked to an inability to cope with them.

In this paper an attempt has been made to examine the different dimensions of poverty in India during 1973/74 to 1999/2000. The changing scenario of international incidence of poverty is discussed in Section I. Section II contains the measurement of poverty in India. Section III discusses the changing scenario of inter-state differentials (rural-urban differentials) of poverty in India. The determining factors (causes) of poverty are discussed in section IV. Section V contains poverty alleviation measures in India. Concluding remarks are presented in Section VI. Poverty data taken from the Planning Commission and Census data for 1991 and 2001 are used in the analysis.

I. CHANGING SCENARIO OF INTERNATIONAL INCIDENCE OF POVERTY

Poverty is an international problem. It is much acute in developing economies than developed economics. We now examine the incidence of poverty in developing economies. Developing economies have different

TABLE 1

Poverty by Region: 1987-98

Region	People living on less than $1 a day (millions)					Percentage of population living on less than $1 a day				
	1987	*1990*	*1993*	*1996*	*1998*	*1987*	*1990*	*1993*	*1996*	*1998*
East Asia and Pacific	417.5	452.4	413.9	265.1	278.3	26.6	27.6	25.2	14.9	15.3
Europe and Central Asia	1.1	7.1	18.9	23.8	24.0	0.2	1.6	4.0	5.1	5.1
Latin America and the Caribbean	63.7	73.8	70.8	76.0	78.2	15.3	16.8	15.3	15.6	15.6
Middle East and North Africa	9.3	5.7	5.0	5.0	5.5	4.3	2.4	1.9	1.8	1.9
South Asia	474.4	495.1	505.1	513.7	522.0	44.9	44.0	42.4	42.3	40.0
Sub-Saharan Africa	217.2	242.3	273.3	289.0	290.9	46.6	47.7	49.7	48.5	46.3
All	1183.2	1276.4	1304.3	1190.0	1198.9	28.3	29.0	28.1	24.5	24.0

Source: World Development Report, 2000/2001, p. 23.

regions. East Asia and Pacific, Europe and Central Asia, Latin America and the Caribbean, Middle East and North Africa, South Africa and sub-Saharan Africa. In developing economies the incidence of poverty has varied over time across the regions. Estimates reveal (Table 1) that the share of the population in developing economies living on less than $1 a day has declined from 28% in 1987 to 24% in 1998. There are large regional variations in the incidence of poverty. Declining poverty level is observed in the regions of East Asia (27.6% to 15.3%), Latin America and the Caribbean (16.8% to 15.6%), Middle East and North Africa (2.4% to 1.9%), South Asia (4.4% to 40%) and Sub-Saharan Africa (47.7% to 46.3%). It is observed that though the poverty level has reduced in Latin America, South Asia and Sub-Saharan Africa, the number of people living on less than $1 a day has risen: Latin America (63.7 million to 78.2 million), South Asia (474.4 million to 522 million and Sub-Saharan Africa (217.2 million to 291 million). In 1998 South Asia and Sub-Saharan Africa have accounted for around 70% of the population living on less than $1 a day, up 19% points from 1987. This is caused by the geographical distribution of poverty.

There are equally large variations in poverty performance across countries within each region. In Europe and Central Asia the proportion of the population living on less than $2 a day (at 1966 ppp) ranges from less than 5% in Belarus, Estonia, Hungary, Lithunia, Poland and Ukraine to 19% in Russia, 49% in the Kyrghz Republic and 68% in Tajikistan. Among seven African countries during 1990s four countries namely Burkina Faso, Nigeria, Zambia and Zimbabwe have experienced an increase in poverty while three countries namely Ghana, Mauritania and Uganda have a declining trend. Available national poverty estimates for Latin America show that between 1989 and 1996 the incidence of poverty has fallen in Brazil, Chile, the Dominican Republic and Honduras, and risen in Mexico and Venezuela.

TABLE 2

Effect of Economic Crises on Incidence of Poverty in Selected Countries

Country and type of crisis	*Before crisis*	*Year of crisis*	*After crisis*
Argentina, hyperinflation and currency	25.2 (1987)	47.3 (1989)	33.7 (1990)
Argentina, contagion	16.8 (1993)	24.8 (1995)	26.0 (1997)
Indonesia, contagion and financial	11.3 (1996)	18.9 (1998)	11.7 (1999)
Jordan, currency and terms of trade	3.0 (1986-87)	(1989)	14.9 (1992)
Mexico, currency and financial	36.0 (1994)	(1995)	43.0 (1996)
Russian Federation, financial	21.9 (1996)	32.7 (1998)	—
Thailand, currency and financial	11.4 (1996)	12.9 (1998)	—

Source: World Development Report, 2000/2001, p. 163.

In East Asia the incidence of poverty in the 1990s has been influenced by the impact of the recent economic crisis. In most of the countries poverty has risen as a result of the financial crisis of the late 1990s. Estimates reveal (Table 2) that in Indonesia poverty has increased from 11.3% in 1996 to 18.9% in 1998 (the year of crisis). Since then it appears to have declined considerably, though it is still substantially higher than precise levels as the economy recovered. In Russia the incidence of poverty has increased from 21.9% in 1996 to 32.7% in 1998 (the year of crisis). In every crisis in Latin America and the Caribbean the incidence of poverty has increased and several years later remained higher than it has been before the crisis.

In South Asia poverty reduction has also varied in the 1990s. In Bangladesh poverty has reduced from 42.7% in 1991-92 to 35.6% in 1995-96 despite the worst flood situation. But Pakistan and Sri Lanka have made little or no progress in poverty reduction in the 1990s. In India though poverty has reduced from 36% in 1993-94 to 26.1% in 1999-2000, still there is an on going debate on the accuracy of the statistics (WDR, 2000/2001).

II. MEASUREMENT OF POVERTY IN INDIA

Poverty is defined by the head count ratio which is expressed as the percentage of the people living below the poverty line. In India there are different methods to measure poverty: (i) Official estimates by the CSO, (ii) NSS estimates by the NSSO, (iii) Expert Group estimates by the Planning Commission. These methods are quite different. Official estimates are made after certain adjustments in aggregate private household consumption expenditure as estimated by the NAS and the distribution of households by consumption expenditure levels provided by the NSS. The NSS estimates of poverty seem appropriate since the NSS provides household expenditure data (as opposed to private expenditure data provided by the NAS) as well as commodity composition, not only for expenditure class groups but also for all states and for rural and urban areas separately. On the other hand, Expert Group constituted by the Planning Commission in 1993 has estimated alternative poverty head counts based on the NSS consumer expenditure distributions and with modifications incorporating the state-level price differentials. The expert did not adjust for the discrepancy in the NAS and NSS figures on consumer expenditure.

The levels of poverty have been and relative declines sharper in the official estimates compared to the expert group estimates. Estimates reveal that while the official estimates have shown a dramatic decline in poverty in urban areas, the expert group has presented a more sustained picture of decline in rural poverty relative to urban, i.e., urban poverty is not declining drastically as given the official estimates (UNFPA, 1997).

Let us now discuss the measurement of poverty in India by the Expert Group method below:

The Planning Commission in India has estimated the incidence of poverty on the basis of the Task Force Method. The Task Force was constituted under the chairmanship of Dr. Y.K. Alagh since the early 1970s. As a measure of poverty, head-count ratio measured by the percentage of people below the poverty line was taken. The Task Force has formulated a quantitative index of poverty by taking the basic minimum needs of the poorer people and the effective consumption demand of the non-poor people. Then it has defined the poverty line as monthly per capital consumption expenditure level, which meets the average per capita daily caloric requirement of 2400 kcl in rural areas and 2100 kcl in urban areas with the associated quantum of non-food expenditure. Using the 28th Round (1973-74) NSS data on household consumer expenditure both in quantitative and value terms the poverty line is defined as monthly per capita consumption expenditure of Rs. 49.09 in rural areas and Rs. 56.64 in urban areas. In later years the poverty lines were estimated by updating the 1973-74 poverty line initially by Wholesale Price Index (WPI). But the use of WPI was controversial because consumers buy goods at retail and not at wholesale prices.

In 1989 the Planning Commission has constituted the Expert Group on Estimation of Proportion and Number of Poor under the chairmanship of Prof. D.T. Lakdawala. The method is known as the Expert Group Method. The Expert Group has recommended that the Task Force poverty line is adopted as the base line. It has disaggregated national poverty line to state-specific lines. The national rural poverty line is disaggregated into state-specific poverty lines by using state-specific price indices of 1973-74 and interstate price differential. The state-specific price indices are constructed by averaging the state-specific food and non-food price indices of Consumer Price Index of Agricultural Labourers, while the inter-state price differential is done by using Fisher's Index. These state-specific rural poverty lines are updated in later years by state-specific price indices, which are constructed as weighed average of food, fuel and light, clothing and footwear, and miscellaneous of CPIAL.

Like the national rural poverty line, the national urban poverty line is disaggregated into state-specific poverty lines by using state-specific price indices of 1973-74 and interstate differential. The state-specific price indices are obtained from the Consumer Price Index (CPI) of industrial workers and the inter-state price differential is estimated by using Fisher's Index. The state-specific of CPI of industrial workers are done by averaging the CPI of food, fuel and light, housing, clothing, bedding and footwear and miscellaneous with their respective weights in the consumption basket of the poor. Later on, this Expert Group Method is modified by the Planning Commission by dropping the Consumer Price Index of Urban Non-Manual Employees and the method is known as "Modified Expert Group Method". This is because of the fact the rate of increase of the Consumer Price Index of Urban Non-Manual Employees has been faster which in turn causes a rise in the money value of the poverty line and hence the incidence of urban poverty.

The Expert Group has estimated state-specific poverty lines and hence the poverty rations, but not specifically the national level poverty lines. The national poverty lines are worked out as an interpolated value from the national level expenditure distribution obtained from the NSS data on consumer expenditure. The national level poverty ratio is estimated as an average of state-wise poverty ratios. Based on availability of state level prices the Expert Group has estimated the poverty lines and poverty ratios in rural and urban areas of 18 states and UTs. These are: Andhra Pradesh, Assam, Bihar, Gujarat, Haryana, H.P., J&K, Karnataka, Kerala, M.P., Maharashtra, Orissa, Punjab, Rajasthan, T.N., U.P., W.B. and Delhi. Unsung neighbouring state's poverty line, the poverty ratios for other state and UTs are estimated.

III. CHANGING SCENARIO OF REGIONAL DIMENSIONS OF POVERTY: RURAL AND URBAN INDIA

Already we have said that the Expert Group have estimated the poverty lines, in rural and urban areas of 18 states and UTs. Based on the poverty line, poverty level (percentage of people the below poverty line) is estimated in rural, urban and combined (rural and urban) areas at different points of time. 1973-74, 1977-78, 1993-94 and 1999-2000. Instead of 18 states and UTs we have considered 32 states and UTs in India. Estimates reveal (Table 3) that at the all India level, poverty level was as high as 54.88 in 1973-74 which came down to 38.86 in 1987-88 and to just 26.10 in 1999-2000. Thus the extent of poverty has been reduced by more than 50%. The rate of declining of poverty has been increasing: 1.7% during 1973-77, 3.4% during 1983-87 and 5.3% during 1993-1999 per year.

TABLE 3

Percentage of People Below the Poverty Line: Total

Sl. No.	*States/U.Ts.*	*1973-74*	*1977-78*	*1983-84*	*1987-88*	*1993-94*	*1999-2000*
1.	Andhra Pradesh	48.86	39.31	28.91	25.86	22.19	15.77
2.	Arunachal Pradesh	51.93	58.32	40.88	36.22	39.35	33.47
3.	Assam	51.21	57.15	40.47	36.21	40.86	36.09
4.	Bihar	61.91	61.55	62.22	52.13	S4.96	42.60
5.	Goa	44.26	37.23	18.90	24.52	14.92	4.40
6.	Gujarat	48.15	41.23	32.79	31.54	24.21	14.07
7.	Haryana	35.36	29.55	21.37	16.64	25.05	8.74
8.	Himachal Pradesh	26.39	32.45	16.40	15.45	28.44	7.63
9.	Jammu & Kashmir	40.83	38.97	24.24	23.82	25.17	3.48
10.	Karnataka	54.47	48.78	38.24	37.53	33.16	20.04
11.	Kerala	59.79	52.22	40.42	31.79	25.43	12.72
12.	Madhya Pradesh	61.78	61.78	49.78	43.07	42.52	37.43
13.	Maharashtra	53.24	55.88	43.44	40.41	36.86	35.02
14.	Manipur	49.96	53.72	37.02	31.35	33.78	38.54

(Contd.)

1	2	3	4	5	6	7	8
15.	Meghalaya	50.20	55.19	38.81	33.92	37.92	33.87
16.	Mizoram	50.32	54.38	36.00	27.52	25.66	19.47
17.	Nagaland	50.81	56.04	39.25	34.43	37.92	32.67
18.	Orissa	66.18	70.07	65.29	55.58	48.56	47.15
19.	Punjab	28.15	19.27	16.18	13.20	11.77	6.16
20.	Rajasthan	46.14	37.42	34.46	35.15	27.41	15.28
21.	Sikkim	50.86	55.89	39.71	36.06	41.43	36.55
22.	Tamil Nadu	54.94	54.79	51.66	43.39	35.03	21.12
23.	Tripura	51.00	56.88	40.03	35.23	39.01	34.42
24.	Uttar Pradesh	57.07	49.05	47.07	41.46	40.85	31.15
25.	West Bengal	63.43	60.52	54.85	44.72	35.66	27.02
26.	Andaman & Nicobar	55.56	55.42	52.13	43.89	34.47	20.99
27.	Chandigarh	27.96	27.32	23.79	44.67	11.35	5.75
28.	Dadra & Nagar Haveli	46.55	37.20	15.67	67.11	50.84	17.14
29.	Daman & Diu	0.00	0.00	0.00	0.00	15.80	4.44
30.	Delhi	49.61	33.23	26.22	12.41	14.69	8.23
31.	Lakshadweep	59.68	52.79	42.36	34.95	25.04	15.60
32.	Pondicherry	53.82	53.25	50.06	41.46	37.40	21.67
	All India	54.88	51.32	44.48	38.86	35.97	26.10

Source: Planning Commission, Government of India.

Wide variations in the poverty level are observed among the states in India over time. At different points of time, relative rankings of the Indian states have changed. Among the 32 states and UTs in India the top-most ranking was acquired by H. P. (26.39 in 1973-74), Punjab (19.27 in 1977-78, 16.18 in 1983-84), Delhi (12.41 in 1987-88), Chandigarh (11.35 in 1993-94) and J & K (3.48 in 1999-2000) while the lowest ranking was acquired by Orissa (66.18 in 1973-74, 70-07 in 1977-78, 65.29 in 1983-84), Dadra & Nagar Haveli (67.11 in 1987-88), Bihar(54.96 in 1993-94) and Orissa (47.15 in 1999-2000).Thus Orissa and Bihar are the poorest states (i.e., existence of high poverty) while the northern states like H. P., Punjab, Delhi, Chandigarh, etc. are the richest states due to low poverty level.

Poverty level has declined in almost all the states in India with some exceptional cases over time. But the rate of declining has varied among the state over time. Highest declining growth rates are observed in Goa, Haryana, H. P., J&K, Kerala, Punjab, Dadra and Pondicherry. During the reform periods (1993/94-1999/2000), poverty has remarkably reduced in the states of Goa, Gujarat, Haryana, H.P., J&K, Karnataka, Kerala, Punjab, Rajasthan, T.N., Chandigarh, Dadra & Nagar Haveli, Daman & Diu, Delhi, Lashadweep and Pondicherry. Thus poverty is relatively low in the northern states compared to other states in India due to proper implementation of poverty alleviation programmes.

Rural Poverty

Like total poverty rural poverty has also reduced in India and in its constituent states overtime. Estimates reveal (Table 4) that at the all India level in has reduced from 56.44 in 1973-74 to 1973-74 to 39.09 in 1987-88 and to 27.09 in 1999-2000. Thus poverty has been reduced by more than 50% during the period under study. Declining annual growth rate of poverty has been rising

TABLE 4

Percentage of People Below the Poverty Line: Rural Areas

Sl. No.	*States/U.Ts.*	*1973-74*	*1977-78*	*1983-84*	*1987-88*	*1993-94*	*1999-2000*
1.	Andhra Pradesh	48.41	38.11	26.53	20.92	15.92	11.05
2.	Arunachal Pradesh	52.68	59.82	42.60	39.35	45.01	40.04
3.	Assam	52.68	59.82	24.60	39.35	45.01	40.04
4.	Bihar	62.99	63.25	64.37	52.63	58.21	44.30
5.	Goa	46.85	37.64	14.82	17.64	5.34	1.35
6.	Gujarat	46.35	41.76	29.80	28.67	22.18	13.17
7.	Haryana	34.23	27.73	20.56	16.22	28.02	8.27
8.	Himachal Pradesh	27.42	33.49	17.00	16.28	30.34	7.94
9.	Jammu & Kashmir	45.51	42.86	26.04	25.70	30.34	3.97
10.	Karnataka	55.14	48.18	36.33	32.82	29.88	17.38
11.	Kerala	59.19	51.48	39.03	29.10	25.76	9.38
12.	Madhya Pradesh	62.66	62.52	48.90	41.92	40.64	37.06
13.	Maharashtra	57.71	62.97	45.23	40.78	37.93	23.72
14.	Manipur	52.67	59.82	42.60	39.35	45.01	40.04
15.	Meghalaya	52.67	59.82	42.60	39.35	45.01	40.04
16.	Mizoram	52.67	59.82	42.60	39.35	45.01	40.04
17.	Nagaland	52.67	59.82	42.60	39.35	45.01	40.04
18.	Orissa	67.28	72.38	67.53	57.64	49.72	48.01
19.	Punjab	28.21	16.37	13.20	12.60	11.95	6.35
20.	Rajasthan	44.76	35.89	33.50	33.21	26.46	13.74
21.	Sikkim	52.67	59.82	42.60	39.35	45.01	40.04
22.	Tamil Nadu	57.23	57.68	53.99	45.80	32.48	20.55
23.	Tripura	52.67	59.82	42.60	39.35	45.01	40.04
24.	Uttar Pradesh	56.53	47.60	46.45	14.10	42.28	31.22
25.	West Bengal	73.16	68.34	63.05	48.30	40.80	31.85
26.	Andaman & Nicobar	57.43	57.68	53.99	45.80	32.48	20.55
27.	Chandigarh	27.96	27.32	23.79	14.67	11.35	5.75
28.	Dadra & Nagar Haveli	46.85	37.64	14.81	67.11	51.95	17.57
29.	Daman & Diu	0.00	0.00	0.00	0.00	5!34	1.35
30.	Delhi	24.44	30.91	7.66	1.29	1.90	0.40
31.	Lakshadweep	59.19	51.48	39.03	29.10	25.76	9.38
32.	Pondicherry	57.43	57.68	53.99	45.80	32.48	20.55
	All India	56.44	53.07	45.65	39.09	37.27	27.09

Source: Same as Table 3.

from 1.5% during 1973-77 to 3.9% during 1983-87 and to 5.3% during 1993-2000. So during the reform periods the declining rate is very high due to implementation of rural poverty alleviation programmes for employment generation through non-farm activities.

Disparity in poverty level among the states are also observed over time. That is, at different time periods the relative ranking of the states have changed. Poverty is low in the states of Delhi (24.44 in 1973-74), Punjab (16.37 in 1977-78) and Delhi (7.66 in 1983-84, 1.3 in 1987-88, 1.9 in 1993-94 and 0.4 in 1999-2000) while it is high in the states W.B. (73.16 in 1973-74), Orissa (72.39 in 1977-78 and 67.53 in 1983-84), Dadra & Nagar Haveli (67.11 in 1987-88), Bihar (58.2 in 1993-94) and Orissa (48.01 in 1999-2000). Thus Bihar and Orissa are the poorest states in India.

Annual trend growth rate of rural poverty has varied across the states in India. In almost all the states there exists a declining trend growth rate. But in some cases the rate is positive during 1970's and 1980's. Positive growth rate is observed in the states of Bihar, Maharashtra, Manipur, Meghalaya, Mizoram, Nagaland, Sikkim, Tripura and Delhi. Interestingly we note that the states like Haryana, J&K, H.P., Manipur, Meghalaya, Mizoram, Nagaland, Sikkim, Tripura, U.P. and Delhi have positive growth rate during 1987-93 but negative growth rate during 1993-99. Thus compared to other states the northern and north-eastern states have remarkably reduced their rural poverty during the reform the reform period.

Urban Poverty

Like rural poverty level, urban poverty level has also reduced in India and in its constituent states over time. It has reduced from 49.01 to 38.20 in 1987-88 and to 23.62 in 1999-2000 (Table 5). Its annual declining growth rate has increased from 2% during 1973-77 to 2.8% during 1987-93 and to 5.2% during 1993-99. The acceleration in the decline of urban poverty is due to high-income growth achieved during the reform periods, which seems to have percolated to the bottom through the trickle down effect.

Wide variations in urban poverty are also observed across the states. The relative ranking of the states have also changed. Poverty level is low in H.P. for the first four points of time, Assam in 1993-94 and J&K in 1999-2000. While it is highest in Kerala in 1973-74, M.P. in 1977-78 and 1983-84, Bihar in 1987-88, M.P. in 1993-94 and Orissa in 1999-2000. During the reform period (1993/94-1999-2000) it has been substantially reduced in the states of Goa, Gujarat, Haryana, H.P., J&K, Punjab, T.N., W.B., Andaman & Nicobar, Chandigarh, Dadra & Nagar Haveli, Delhi and Pondicherry. But it has marginally increased only in Orissa (41.64 to 42.83) during the reform period.

Rural and urban poverty show that rural poverty is more than urban one in India and in its constituent states during the period under study. But in 1999-2000 urban poverty in more than rural one in the states of Andhra Pradesh, Goa, Haryana, Karnataka, Kerala, M.P., Maharashtra, Rajasthan, T.N., Andaman & Nicobar, Daman & Diu, Delhi, Lakshadweep and Pondicherry.

TABLE 5

Percentage of People Below the Poverty Line: Urban Areas

Sl. No.	States/U.Ts.	1973-74	1977-78	1983-84	1987-88	1993-94	1999-2000
1	2	3	4	5	6	7	8
1.	Andhra Pradesh	50.61	43.55	36.30	40.11	38.33	26.63
2.	Arunachal Pradesh	36.92	32.71	21.73	9.94	7.73	7.47
3.	Assam	36.92	32.71	21.73	9.94	7.73	7.47
4.	Bihar	52.96	48.76	47.33	48.73	34.50	32.91
5.	Goa	37.69	36.31	27.00	35.48	27.03	7.52
6.	Gujarat	52.57	40.02	39.14	37.26	27.89	15.59
7.	Haryana	40.18	36.57	24.15	17.99	16.38	9.99
8.	Himachal Pradesh	13.17	19.44	9.43	6.29	9.18	4.63
9.	Jammu & Kashmir	21.32	23.71	17.76	17.47	9.18	1.98
10.	Karnataka	52.53	50.36	42.82	48.42	40.14	25.25
11.	Kerala	62.74	55.36	45.68	40.33	24.55	20.27
12.	Madhya Pradesh	57.65	58.66	53.06	47.09	48.38	38.44
13.	Maharashtra	43.87	40.09	40.26	39.78	35.15	26.81
14.	Manipur	36.92	32.71	21.73	9.94	7.73	7.47
15.	Meghalaya	36.92	32.71	21.73	9.94	7.73	7.47
16.	Mizoram	36.92	32.71	21.73	9.94	7.73	7.47
17.	Nagaland	36.92	32.71	21.73	9.94	7.73	7.47
18.	Orissa	55.62	50.92	49.15	41.63	41.64	42.83
19.	Punjab	27.96	27.32	23.79	14.67	11.35	5.75
20.	Rajasthan	52.13	43.53	37.94	41.92	30.49	19.85
21.	Sikkim	36.92	32.71	21.73	9.94	7.73	7.47
22.	Tamil Nadu	49.40	48.69	46.96	38.64	39.77	22.11
23.	Tripura	36.92	32.71.	21.73	9.94	7.73	7.47
24.	Uttar Pradesh	60.09	56.23	49.82	42.96	35.39	30.89
25.	West Bengal	34.67	38.20	32.32	35.08	22.41	14.86
26.	Andaman & Nicobar	49.40	48.69	46.96	38.64	39.77	22.11
27.	Chandigarh	27.96	27.32	23.79	14.67	11.32	5.75
28.	Dadra & Nagar Haveli	37.69	36.31	27.00	0.00	39.93	13.52
29.	Daman & Diu	0.00	0.00	0.00	0.00	27.03	7.52
30.	Delhi	52.23	33.51	27.89	13.56	16.03	9.42
31.	Lakshadweep	62.74	55.62	45.68	40.33	24.55	20.27
32.	Pondicherry	49.40	48.69	46.96	38.64	39.77	22.11
	All India	49.01	45.24	40.79	38.20	32.36	23.62

Source: Same as Table 3.

It thus follows from the above discussion that Indian states have exhibited a divergent level of poverty in rural, urban and combined areas, Poverty level is low in some states while it is relatively high in some other states. All this clearly indicates the existence of inter-state disparity in poverty level. Such inter-state disparity in poverty level is clearly revealed by the Poverty Disparity Index (PDI) as:

$$PDI = 100 \left[\sum_{i=1}^{n} (p_i - P)^2/(n-1) \right]^{1/2} / \bar{p}$$

where p: poverty level in the state i, i = 1, . . . n.
P: poverty level in India as a whole.
n: Number of states and UTs in India.

Estimates reveal that PDI has risen overtime in rural, urban and combined areas. In rural areas the index has increased from 23.19% in 1973-74 to 40.96% in 1987-88 and to 67.93% in 1999-2000. The respective figures are: 27.75%, 55.98% and 67.65% in urban areas; 19.84%, 36.82% and 57.56% in combined areas. This indicates that inter-state disparity has widened more in urban areas than in rural areas during the period under study. That is to say, although the percentage of people below the poverty level has shown a steadily declining trend, yet the rising values of the index shows that instead of convergence, the Indian states have experienced rather a divergence in respect of the incidence of poverty in rural, urban and combined areas. Thus the richer states have shown a tendency to become relatively more richer while the poorer ones to become relatively more poorer.

As per UNDP's Human Development Report (1997) there are three dimensions for human well-being: (a) Longevity—the ability to live long and healthy human well-being, (b) Education-the ability to read, write and acquire knowledge, (c) Command over resources-the ability to enjoy a decent standard of living and have a socially life. So there are three of deprivation: (i) Longevity deprivation, (ii) education deprivation, and (iii) economic deprivation. Based on these deprivations, Human Poverty Index (HPI) has been constructed. As per the estimates of the National Human Development Report (2001), the HPI in India has declined from 47.33 in 1981 to 39.36 in 1991. This is also true both in rural (53.28 to 44.81) and urban (27.21 to 22.00) areas. Thus the HPI in rural areas is significantly higher than that in urban one. Also, the decline in the HPI in rural areas is slightly higher than that in urban one. The rural-urban ratio of the percentage of people below the poverty line has increased from 1.12 in 1983-84 to 1.15 in 1993-94, whereas the rural-urban ratio of HPI is a little more than two both in 1981 and 1991. Thus there is a gap for the availability of these amenities which are better in urban areas while these are scarce in rural areas of India. (Pal, 2002).

IV. DETERMINING FACTORS

Poverty is caused by economic and non-economic factors. We have considered nine (9) factors: population growth for the years of 1991 and 2001, rural literacy rate (male and female) for the years of 1991 and 2001, rural non-farm employment (male and female) for years of 1993-94 and 1999-2000, per capita NSDP (at 1980-81 prices) for the years of 1993-94 and 1997-98, urbanization for the years of 1991 and 2001, Index of agricultural prosperity (food grains output per hec.) for the years of 1995-96 and 1999-2000, degree of commercialization (non-food grains area as a percentage of total gross-cropped area) for the year of 1996-97, average daily real agricultural wages (male and female, Rs./day) for the year of 1993-94 and Human Development Index (HDI) for the year of 1993. We have statistically examined the role of these determining factors in explaining inter-state variations of rural poverty in India for the years of 1993-94 and 1999-2000. We have taken 16 large states in India: Andhra Pradesh, Assam, Bihar, Gujarat, Haryana, Himachal Pradesh, Karnataka, Kerala, Madhya Pradesh, Maharashtra, Orissa, Punjab, Rajasthan, Tamil Nadu, Uttar Pradesh and West Bengal.

States are ranked according to those variables and rank correlation coefficient (r) between rural poverty and each of those variables are estimated for the years of 1993-94 and 1999-2000. The coefficients are, in turn, statistically tersted. The testing procedure is as follows:

Let r and $\hat{r}$ be the population and sample rank correlation coefficient respectively. Then for r = o, the sampling distribution of $\hat{r}$ may be approximated by Normal Distribution (Koutsoyiannis, 1979):

$$\hat{r} - N\,[0.1/(n-1)^{1/2}]$$

The testing hypotheses are:

$$H_0 : r = O$$
$$H_a : r \neq O$$

The test statistic is here:

$$Z = \hat{r}\,(n-1)^{1/2}$$

The estimated Z is then computed with the tabulated value of Z at the chosen level of significance. For example, at 10% level of significance, Z = ± 1.645. Then the null hypothesis H_0 is rejected ir Z > 1.645, i.e., the hypothesis of the presence of rank correlation is accepted. Otherwise, H_0 is accepted.

Estimates of rank correlation coefficient are presented in Table 6. Estimates reveal that all the variables: rural literacy rate, population growth, rural non-farm employment, per capita NSDP, urbanization, agricultural prosperity, degree of commercialization, average daily real agricultural wages and Human Development Index have turned out to be significant. But these variables are not uniformly significant over time in India. Thus these variables are instrumental for reducing rural poverty in India.

In our multiple regression analysis, we have considered the following hypotheses: Rural Poverty (RP) is indirectly related to (a) the rural non-farm employment (NFE) (male and female), (b) rural literacy rate (LR) (male and female), (c) per capita NSDP (PCNSDP), (d) urbanization (UR), (e) agricultural prosperity (AP), (f) degree of commercialization (COM), (g) average daily real agricultural wages (AG) (male and female). On the other hand; rural poverty (RP) is directly related to the population growth (PG).

TABLE 6

Rank Correlation Coefficient between Rural Poverty and other Relevant Variables in India: 1993/94 and 1999/2000

Variables	*Rank Correlation Coefficient*	
	1993-94	*1999-2000*
Rural Male Literacy Rates	–0.205 (–0.794)	–0.314 (–1.216)
Rural Female Literacy Rate	–0.326 (–1.263)	–0.491 (–1.902)
Population Growth	0.136 (0.527)	0.200 (0.775)
Rural Male Non-Farm Employment	–0.482 (–1.868)	–0.609* (–2.358)
Rural Female Non-Farm Employment	–0.376 (–1.458)	–0.126 (–0.490)
Per Capita NSDP (at 1980-81 price)	–0.608 (–2.355)	–0.643* (–2.490)
Urbanisation	–0.499 (–1.933)	–0.358 (–1.386)
Agricultural Prosperity	–0.046 (–0.178)	–0.246 (–0.953)
Degree of Commercialisation	–0.758* (–2.936)	–0.425 (–1.646)
Average Daily Real Agri. Male Wages (Rs./day)	–0.552* (–2.138)	–0.635 (–2.459)
Average Daily Real Agri. Female Wages (Rs./day)	–0.458* (–1.774)	–0.555* (–2.149)
Human Development Index (HDI)	–0.564* (–2.184)	–0.593 (–2.297)

Notes: * Significant at 10% level of significance.
Figures in ( ) indicates z-values.
Source: NSSO Data, Planning Commission Data, Census Data and Economic Survey Data.

Based on the above hypotheses, we have estimated the multiple regression in India using state-wise data for the two years of 1993-94 and 1999-2000. The estimated multiple regression equations are the following:

1993-94 : RP = – 28.595 + 2.520* MLR – 1.753* FLR + 0.049 PG
(–0.410) (2.227) (–40.754) (0.003)
– 0.805 MNFE + 0.524 FNFE – 0.004 PCNSDP – 0.126 UR
(–0.966) (1.567) (–0.458) (–1.307)
– 0.278 AP – 0.546 COM – 0.107 MAG + 1.881 FAG
(–0.288) (–1.064) (–0.021) (0.239)
$R^2 = 0.95$, Adjusted $R^2 = 0.75$

1999-2000 : RP= 9.500 + 1.858 MLR – 1.536 FLR + 1.101 PG – 0.434 MNFE
(0.175) (1.696) (–1.508) (0.003) (–0.982)

0.920* FNFE – 0.0002. PCNSDP – 0.008 UR – 1.109 AP
(2.961) (–0.054) (–0.289) (–1.535)
–0.502* COM – 0.942 MAG – 0.606 FAG
(–2.248) (–0.282) (–0.137)

$R^2 = 0.92$, Adjusted $R^2 = 0.71$
Note: Significant at 5% level of significance.
Figures in ( ) indicates t-values.

From the above two equations we observe that the explanatory variables are highly significant for explaining rural poverty in India. Estimates reveal that:

(i) The coefficient of rural literacy rate is positive for male (MLR) and negative for female (FLR) in both 1993-94 and 1999-2000. But it is highly significant only for female in 1993-94.
(ii) The coefficient of population growth is positive but not significant in both the years. This implies that declining population growth is directly associated with declining rural poverty in India.
(iii) The coefficient of non-farm employment is negative for male (MNFE) and positive for female (FNFE) in both the years. But it is highly significant only for female in 1999-2000. Thus non-farm employment plays a significant role in the reduction of rural poverty in India.
(iv) The coefficient of per capita income is negative but not statistically significant. Higher the per capita income of a state, lower the level of rural poverty.
(v) The coefficient of urbanization (UR) is negative in both the years. Thus states having high urbanization have low rural poverty level during the period under study.
(vi) The coefficient of the index agricultural prosperity (AP) is negative. Increasing agricultural productivity (i.e., productivity of a land) reduces rural poverty in India.
(vii) The coefficient of the degree of commercialization is negative in both the years. But it is highly statistically significant in 1999-2000.
(viii) The coefficient of average daily real agricultural wages is negative excepting for female (FAW) in 1993-94.

V. POVERTY ALLEVIATION MEASURES IN INDIA

During the 1970s. the Govt. of India has introduced several antipoverty programmes. In the 5th Plan "Garibi Hatao" slogan was first launched. Since then several anti-poverty programmes have been undertaken: MFAL (1971), HADP (1972), CADP (1974), SIPP (1975), FFWP (1977), IRDP (1978),TRYSEM (1979), NREP (1981), DWCRA (1982), RLEGP (1983), JRY (1998), JGSY (1999), SGRY (2002), etc. These programmes are under the following categories:

(a) wage employment programmes, (b) self-employment programmes, and (c) public distribution system and nutrition programmes. The main objective of these programmes is to directly help the poor to improve their economic, physical (nutrition and health) and social conditions. The Government has funded for these programmes under the heads of 'rural and urban development'. Expenditure Budget, Vol. 2 (Government of India, 2003) shows that expenditure on the heads of rural and urban developments for poverty alleviation has increased during the reform periods excepting in 1996-97, 1999-2000 and 2003-04. Expenditure on rural development has increased from Rs. 7397 crores in 1994-95 to Rs. 18400 crores in 2002-03 and then declined to Rs. 14094 crores in 2003-04. The respective figures for urban development are: Rs. 654 crores, Rs. 3187 crores and Rs. 2662 crores. Thus in the budget (2003) Government has reduced their expenditure for poverty alleviation programmes. Though expenditure on all social services and poverty alleviation has increased, the percentage to GDP (at current market prices) has fallen from 2% in 1994-95 to 1.8% in 1996-97 and then risen to 2.7% in 2002-03. In 2003-04, the figure has reduced to 2.5%. Thus in the current financial year, the Government has allocated less funds towards poverty alleviation programmes.

VI. CONCLUDING REMARKS

International incidence of poverty in developing economics has varied across the regions. Poverty has declined in the regions of East Asia, Latin America, Middle East and North Africa, South Asia and Sub-Saharan Africa. Wide variations in poverty across countries within each region are also observed. In most of the East Asian countries poverty has risen as a result of the financial crisis of the late 1990s while most of the African countries have experienced an increase in poverty.

In the context of measurement of poverty in India, poverty is estimated by using different methods. But there is an on going debate on the accuracy of the statistics.

Poverty has declined in India and in its constituent states during the period under study. But the rate of declining has varied among the states over time in rural, urban and combined areas. Inter-state disparity in poverty has widened more in urban areas than in rural areas.

Poverty in India is determined by several factors. Among the factors population growth, rural literacy rate, rural non-farm employment, per capita NSDP, urbanization, agricultural prosperity, degree of commercialization and average daily real agricultural wages turned out to be significant. But all these factors are not uniformly significant overtime in India. Thus these factors are instrumental for reducing rural poverty in India.

The Government of India has undertaken different antipoverty measures at several times for reducing poverty. But all these measures have not been implemented properly. Expenditure on poverty alleviation programmes has been reduced in both rural (Rs. 18400 crores in 2002-03 to Rs. 14094 crores in

2003-04) and urban (Rs. 3187 crores in 2002-03 to Rs. 2662 crores in 2003-04) areas (Ref. Expenditure Budget (2003), Vol. 2, Govt. of India).

To eradicate poverty from out country we may prescribe the following policies:

(i) For reducing rural poverty, agricultural growth is important. During the reform period the growth rate of food grains and non-food grains production has been lower. We must increase the agricultural growth through crop-diversification in agriculture so that rural poverty may be removed.

(ii) In rural area there is a need for rural industrialisation. For employment generation agro-based industry may be set-up locally so that local people can be employed.

(iii) For implementation of the anti-poverty programmes there is a need for involving panchayats and NGOs, self-help groups and local people participation.

(iv) Regional economic disparities must be reduced. The Government should increase the development expenditure particularly social sector expenditure in poorer states like Bihar, Orissa, M.P., U.P., etc. so that poverty may be eradicated.

(v) Proper implementation of the anti-poverty programmes must be undertaken, otherwise, poverty will not be eradicated.

REFERENCES

Ahluwalia, M.S. (1978): "Rural Poverty and Agricultural Performance in India," *Journal of Development Studies.*

Datt., G. (1988): "Poverty in India and Indian States: An Update", *Indian Journal of Labour Economics*, Vol. 41, No. 2.

—— (1999): "Has Poverty Declined since Economic Reforms?" *EPW*, Vol. 34, No. 50.

Datta, K.L. (2002): "On Measurement of Poverty in India, Occasional Paper, State Institute of Panchayats and Rural Development, Government of West Bengal, 2002.

Expenditure Budget (2003), Vol. 2, Government of India.

Koutsoyiannis, A. (1979): Theory of Econometrics, 2nd Edition.

Mohendra Dev, S. (1988): "Regional Disparities in Agricultural Labour Productivity and Rural Poverty in India", *IJAE*, Vol. 23, No. 2.

—— (2000): "Economic Reforms, Poverty, Income Distribution and Employment", *EPW*, Vol. XXXV, No. 10.

National Human Development Report (2002): Planning Commission, Government of India.

Nayyar, Rohini (1991): Rural Poverty in India: An Analysis of Inter-state Difference, OUP, Mumbai.

Parikh, K.S. and T.N. Srinivasan (1990): "Poverty Alleviation Policies in India: Food Consumption Subsidies, Food Production Subsidies and Employment Generation," Mimeo, Indira Gandhi Institute for Development Research, Mumbai.

Pal, P.K. (2003): "Poverty and Deprivation in India: An Inter-state Analysis", Presented at the National Seminar on current issues in the Indian Economy, Organised by the Department of Economics, Rabindra Bharati University, during 21-22 March, 2003.

Rao, C.H.H. (1996): "Economic Reforms, Agricultural Growth and Rural Poverty", *The Indian Economic Journal*, No. 43, No. 4.

—— (1988): "Agricultural Growth, Sustainability and Poverty Alleviation in India: Recent Trends and Major Issues of Reform", *EPW*, Vol. 33, Nos. 29 and 30.

Radhakrishna, R. (2001): "Agricultural Growth, Employment and Poverty", delivered at the 43rd Annual Conference of the Indian Society of Labour Economics, Bangalore, Dec. 18-20, 2001.

Sen, Abhijit (1996): "Economic Reforms, Employment and Poverty: Trends and Options", *EPW*, Vol. 31, Nos. 35, 36 and 37.

Srinivasan, T.N. and Bardhan, P.K. (eds.) (1988): Rural Poverty in South Asia, OUP, Delhi.

—— (1974): Poverty and Income Distribution in India, Statistical Publishing Society, Calcutta.

Suryahadi, A., Sudarno, S., Yusuf, S. and Lant, P. (1999): "The Evolution of Poverty during the Crisis in Indonesia, 1996 to 1999," World Bank.

Tendulkar, S.D.; Sundaram, K.; Jain, L.R. (1996): "Macro-economic Policies and Poverty in India: 1966-67 to 1993-94", Paper Presented for ILO, New Delhi.

UNFPA for United Nations System in India (1997): India: Towards Population and Development Goals, OUP, Delhi.

Vaidyanathan, A. (2001): "Poverty and Development Policy", *EPW*, Vol. XXXVI, No. 21.

Visaria, Pravin (1979): "Poverty and Development in India: An Analysis of Rural Evidence", World Bank Staff Working Paper.

World Bank (1997): India: Achievements and Challenges in Reducing Poverty,

—— (2001): World Development Report (2000/2001): Attacking Poverty, OUP.

12

Poverty Measurement Studies in India

P. JEGADISH GANDHI

INTRODUCTION

"The poor are always with us, said Jesus Christ, 2000 years ago. In fact in his teaching and that of other religious leaders like the Buddha and Mahavira, there is a certain commendation of poverty. Jesus in his Sermon on the Mount blessed the poor in spirit, and on another occasion spoke of it being more difficult for a rich man to enter the Kingdom of heaven than for a camel to pass through a needle's eye. Both Guatama and Vardhaman gave up their rich, well-to-do princely ways of like and embraced poverty as a means of attaining enlightment and through the ages the beggar's bowl has received a certain sacredness and sanctity that has become part of our culture and civilization. Through our history, Indian great religious leaders and reformers like Sankaracharya, Vivekananda, Ramakrishna and Ramana embraced poverty voluntarily as the only means of developing their spiritual insights and diffusing the great religious truths as they saw and perceived them. In our own times Gandhiji donned the life of the poor peasant as a means of understanding his problems, serving him, and joining with him to fight for the liberation of himself and the country. This brief attempt to encapsulate centuries of human history and India's own special tradition brings out two important facets of poverty. First that it is as old as man himself and second voluntarily adopted, it has an ennobling quality. The poverty under reference here encompasses a style of living which is simple, meeting all the minimal physical requirements of living, and which has either no access to or shuns property and assets in any form, and all the luxuries, ostentation and conspicuous items of consumption that goes with riches and affluence."

In this paper an attempt has been made to highlight the definitional demarcation niceties of 'poverty', its definite quantitative derivatives especially in the post-reform period and its impactional experiences.

NATURE OF POVERTY

Poverty is a universal phenomenon but its peculiarity and permeability differ from country to country. "Who are the poor? What is their number and proportion in the total population? Where are the poor located? What do they do for a living and how do they survive? These are questions asked in all types of societies today. The pathology of poverty shows the inherent deficiency of the socio-economic system. "Poverty is real and illusive. It is relative and absolute. It is life-giving, life-denying, life-harassing and paradoxically, life-sustaining." No other country has paid so much attention to poverty studies as India. Several studies have been made by various economists—from Dadabhai Naoroji down to Dandekar and Rath, Ojha, E.P.W. De Costa, Amartya Sen, Minhas, Montek S. Ahluwalia, Raj Krishna, Pranab Bardhan, L.C. Jain, Suresh Tendulkar, Bhatty and Dutta—besides the Planning Commission and the World Bank.

POVERTY LINE

Economists have tended to concentrate on absolute poverty. Here, a minimum level of consumption expenditure is determined on the basis of calorie requirement. This minimum expenditure level is the "poverty line", drawn in relation to what is considered the minimum nutritional requirement for physical subsistence. 'Poverty line' suggests a clear demarcation between the poor and the non-poor. When an individual is said to be living below the poverty line, it means the person's standard of living falls below a minimum acceptable level. But this, in turn, raises two questions—what is meant by 'standard of living' and how does one calculate the minimum acceptable level? Standard of living is by nature a multi-dimensional concept. The commodities consumed by the individual and the activities engaged in, all form part of this standard of living. Given this, the first step in specifying poverty line is the specification of a minimum acceptable level along each of the dimensions. But this in itself is a problem. Bhatty (1974) uses data collected from a sample survey carried on by the National Council of Applied Economic Research. Some studies use an estimate (a per capita consumption of Rs. 20 per month at 1960-61 prices—excluding expenditure on health and education) formulated by an Expert Committee of the Planning Commission in 1962, Bardhan uses the levels recommended by the Pay Commission-1957, based on the work of Akroyd, Dandekar and Rath (1971) use an estimated minimum calorie intake level of 2250 per day. To secure this minimum calorie requirements, one would need, according to them, a consumption expenditure of Rs. 324 (at 1968-69 prices) per annum in rural areas and Rs. 486 in urban areas. Bhatty computed Sen's index of poverty, besides the head-count ratio separately for cultivators, agricultural labourers and non-agricultural workers and by States in India, using alternative poverty lines. Ahluwalia (1984) and Dutta (1986) made time-series studies on the same subject using Sen's index. In short, some of the studies on poverty are confined to the rural sector, while a few look at both the urban and rural sectors. Similarly, most of the studies look at all-India and State-level data, while some are confined to the all-India data only.

PLANNING COMMISSION ESTIMATES

The Planning Commission has defined the poverty line on the basis of recommended nutritional requirements of 2435 rounded as 2400 calories per person per day for rural areas and 2095 rounded as 2100 calories for urban areas. In rupees the poverty line is the mid-point of the expenditure class in which the calorie needs are satisfied. On this basis, the cut-off points turn out to be Rs. 107 and Rs. 122 for rural and urban areas respectively at 1984-85 prices. For a household of five members, the poverty line has been fixed at an annual income of Rs. 6400 in rural areas and Rs. 7200 in urban areas. The Planning Commission has been estimating the incidence of poverty at the national and state level using the methodology contained in the report of the Expert Group on Estimation of Proportion and Number of Poor (Lakdawala Committee) and applying it to consumption expenditure data from the large sample surveys on consumer expenditure conducted by the National Sample Survey Organisation (NSSO) at an interval of approximately five years.

The available large sample survey data on consumer expenditure are for the 55th Round covering the period July 1999 to June 2000 (Table 1). In the earlier Surveys, the NSSO estimated monthly consumption expenditure on the basis of responses using a 30-day recall period for all food and non-food items. In the 55th Round, the consumption expenditure on clothing, footwear, medical (institutional) and durable goods were collected using a 365-day recall was used as earlier. The data on consumption expenditure on food items were collected using two different reference periods of last 30-days and last 7-days from the same households. The poverty ratios indicated are estimated on the basis of 30-day recall period for 1973-74 to 1999-2000. Poverty at the national level is estimated as the weighted average of State-wise poverty levels.

But there are inherent deficiencies in the seven-day consumption computation method. No doubt, people will replay their items of spending during the last seven days in a month. It is to be noted that the marginal utility of money for the poor will be high during this period. If at all there is any reported spending, it is out of the borrowed money in anticipation of *ex ante* income in the first week of the following month.

'PULL-UP' PROCESS

The proportion of People Below the Poverty Line (PBPL) in India is not a stable entity. Its geometry is always changing. From mid-50's to 1970-71, a downward drift was noticeable. In the turbulent 70's with a number of shocks to the economy, besides the usual vagaries of weather, this downward drift in the proportion of PBPL was arrested. In fact, the decade ended with the proportion of PBPL fell to 37 per cent in 1983-84 (about one-third of India's total population, i.e. 247 million) a clear 10 per cent fall from the corresponding proportion of 47 per cent in 1970-71, which was the lowest level of poverty ever reached prior to 1983-84 (B.S. Minhas, 1985). But as per Raja Krishna's (1984) estimate, the number of such people is linearly increasing by 8.7 million per annum. If this trend continues, the number of PBPL will be more than the total population of the country at the time of Independence in 1947.

TABLE 1

Estimates of Incidence of Poverty in India

Year	*Poverty ratio (%)*			*Number of poor (million)*		
	Rural	*Urban*	*Combined*	*Rural*	*Urban*	*Combined*
1973-74	56.4	49.0	54.9	261.3	60.0	321.3
1977-78	53.1	45.2	51.3	264.3	64.6	328.9
1983	45.7	40.8	44.5	252.0	70.9	322.9
1987-88	39.1	38.2	38.9	231.9	75.2	307.1
1993-94	37.3	32.4	36.0	244.0	76.3	320.3
1999-00	27.1	23.6	26.1	193.2	67.1	260.3
2007*	21.1	15.1	19.3	170.5	49.6	220.1

* Poverty Projection for 2007.
Source: Tenth Five Year Plan, Vol. I, Planning Commission.

According to official statistics, the PBPL was 54.9 per cent in 1973-74 and it came down to 36.0 per cent in 1993-94. Further the ratio declined to 26.1 per cent in 1999-2000, which meant nearly 10 per cent of the PBPL has been helped to rise above the poverty due to various anti-poverty strategic programmes. When there is a substantial concentration of population at the poverty line, as in India, small changes in the level of consumption can shift a large number of people above or below it. This snakes-and-ladders game points to the need to identity a new group, that is, *People on the Poverty Line* (POPL). In the present case, it is debatable whether this 10 per cent actually crossed the poverty line or is bargaining to live on the borderline. More objectively, it is assumed that these people are still *on the poverty line* due to the strong inflationary forces.

The poverty line itself is, in real terms, an absolute figure derived from 1973-74 NSS results. In 1993-94, the national poverty line at current prices was Rs. 2708, about 34 per cent of per capita income of that year. In 1999-2000, the national poverty line was Rs. 4350, as compared to a per capita income of Rs. 15,887. The national poverty line is now only 27 per cent of the per capita income of that year. In fact, this ratio will keep falling with an improvement in per capita income. According to P.R. Brahmananda's estimate that in 1960-

61, the national poverty line of that year would have been about 75-80 per cent of the per capita of that year. With increasing per capita income, since the poverty line is a constant figure, the latter should go down as a ratio to per capita income. However, with the per capita income growth rate rising because of the declining population growth rate and the higher rate of increase in per capita income, there should be a natural tendency for the proportion of people below the poverty line to continue to fall.

RECENT TRENDS

According to the 2008 World Bank Report the number of poor people increased by 39.8 million in absolute numbers during the 15 years (1991-2005) coinciding with the reform period. The increase is 9.6 per cent in relative terms, when we raise the level of income from US $ 1 per day to US $ 1.25 per day. In reality, 42.2 per cent or 4 out of 10 Indians, were poor in 2005 at an income of about Rs. 50 per day. This is the most damaging observation on the quality of Indian governance. In fact, the number of poor in India, at 455.8 million in 2005, is strikingly higher than that in sub-Saharan Africa, where it was 384.2 million in the same year. The total lack of a humanistic social policy to improve the lot of the poverty-stricken majority of this country, as seen from the *laissez-faire* attitude adopted towards them, is shocking. Therefore, in order to avoid such conflicting and misleading claims the poverty line must be redefined for a realistic evaluation of the number of poor in our country.

NEW METHODOLOGY

In this connection, the methodology used by Australia may be worth studying. The country takes into account even non-income indicators to calculate poverty and updates its poverty line every quarter. Adopting a similar approach, Mohan Guruswamy and Ronald Joseph Abraham of the Centre for Policy Alternatives, Delhi in a February 2006 report, "Redefining Poverty: A New Poverty line for a New India" presented a case for fixing the poverty line at about Rs. 840 per capita per month after factoring in costs for nutrition (Rs. 573), health (Rs. 30), clothing (Rs. 17), energy consumption (Rs. 5), and miscellaneous expenditure (Rs. 164). Even this figure of Rs. 840, they said, would not fully reveal the true state of poverty in India because a person spending more than Rs. 840 a month does not necessarily have access to all the fundamental needs of life such education, health, nutritious food, clean water, clothing, sanitation, transport, housing, and access to national resources.

HARD REALITIES

The reality is that the Indian economy is in a shameful state. The paradox is that the country's natural resources have been and continue to be plundered by a chosen few, while millions go without a proper meal. According to the September 30, 2007 Status Report of the Ministry of Programme

Implementation, out of 897 projects, 276 suffered cost over-runs with an anticipated cost of Rs. 1,42,227 crore, against the original estimate of Rs. 95,913 crore, a colossal 48 per cent increase. This shows that for more than 30 per cent of the projects, the accountability factor is of a very low order. How can one account for such huge differences unless the money is drained away on useless work or simply laundered? In this futile and grossly wasteful exercise, it is the really poor who suffer most, because, they are the voiceless. A new Asian Development Bank report on estimating the number of poor says that poverty reduction can differ by at least 7 per cent depending on the policies implemented.

INCLUSIVE GROWTH PROCESS

Apart from an indicative target of an 8 per cent average GDP growth rate, specific monitorable targets for key indicators have been finalized for the Tenth Plan (2002-07) and beyond. One of these pertains to the reduction in poverty ratio by five percentage points by 2007 and by 15 percentage points by 2012. The poverty reduction target set by the Planning Commission for the Tenth Five Year Plan aims at achieving a poverty ratio of 19.3 per cent for the country as a whole by 2007, 21.1 per cent for the rural, and 15.1 per cent for the urban areas.

Planning Commission Deputy Chairman Montek Singh Ahluwalia regretted that poverty reduction was not achieved to the desired extent during the years of planned development pointing out that the growth process should have been more inclusive—"growth has not been even among all sections. The benefits of growth has trickled down differently among different sections and classes of people". It was this problem of uneven trickle down effect that led to a world of extreme disparity—some being very rich while others wallowed in absolute poverty and deprivation. Growth could be promoted in such a manner that it benefited the poor and other vulnerable sections. For that to happen, poverty has to be viewed in a broader context, not just as poverty based on low income but one which took acute deprivation in consideration while poverty continued to persist in today's world of rising expectations, fuelled by growth in education, better health opportunities and general awareness, the economic growth process could be made more inclusive by imparting a greater thrust to agriculture. For this, the growth rate of the farm sector had to leapfrog from 1.5 to four per cent.

CONCLUSION

Poverty reduction in India is not a number game, its dynamics lies in the redressal of the deprived basic needs of the poor. The strategic step in the onslaught on poverty is to see that it is no longer self-perpetuating. Unless a comprehensive protective coverage of the socio-economic content is evolved, may be in terms of better income-incremental opportunities or increasing the employability of the people on the poverty line, all the efforts taken in this sector will prove to be Sisyphean. To quote A.P.J. Abdul Kalam, former President of India: "While aggregated indicators are important, it does not make sense to achieve a 'developed' status without a major and continuing upliftment of all Indians who exist today and of the many more millions who would be added in the years to come. They should all have a secure and enjoyable 'present' and also be in a position to look forward to a better 'future'. Such a developed India is what we are looking for."

REFERENCES

Adiseshiah, S. Malcolm: "The 'Triple' action alone could remove Poverty", *Yojana,* February 16-28, 1983.

——: "The Indian Economy in four decades", *Indian Economic Issues,* Part I, Pointer Publishers, Jaipur, 1989.

Bage, Lennant : "Enabling Ruralfolk to overcome poverty," *The Hindu,* May 9, 2005.

Brahmananda, P.R. : "The Poverty Controversy" *Business Line,* November 1, 2000.

Chandrasekhar, C.P and Jayati Ghosh: "The Calorie Consumption Puzzle", *Business Line,* February 11, 2003.

Jacobs, Garry: "Employment Guaranteed," *The New Indian Express,* January 6, 2005.

Dandekar and Rath. : "Poverty in India. Dimensions and Trends," *Economic and Political Weekly,* 2 January, 1971.

Dreze, Jean : "Employment as a Social responsibility, *The Hindu,* November 22, 2004.

Dutta, B. : "On Poverty in India", *Indian Economic Review,* Vol. XXI, No. 2, 1986.

Gandhi, Jegadish P. : "The Pathology of Poverty in India", *Southern Economist,* 15 May, 1977.

——: "Root out poverty from the rural base", *Indian Express,* 12 December, 1977.

——: "Is poverty eradicable in India?" *Topics and Opinion,* 15 December, 1977.

——: *Indian Economy: Some Issues,* Chapter I, Institute for Social Sciences and Research, Vellore, 1982.

——: "Eradication of Poverty in India", a Paper presented at the UGC Seminar B.T. College, Madanapalle, 22 March, 1984.

——: (Ed.) *Indian Economic Issues,* Part I, Chapter 5, Pointer Publishers, Jaipur, 1989.

——: "Poverty Profile; The Snakes and Ladders Game", *The Hindu,* 9 January, 1990.

——: "People on the Poverty line: A Periscopic View", *The International Journal of New Ideas,* Vol. 1, No. 2, 1992, London.

——: "Claims on Poverty—Drawing the Line Right", *Business Line,* February 16, 1996.

——: Reduction in Poverty: Is it real?, *Economic Growth and Social Change,* March 1996.

——: "The Poverty Puzzle," *People's Reporter,* Sept. 25–Oct. 10, 2000.

——: "Poverty Reduction; Not a Number Game", *Business Line,* November 30, 2000.

——: Book Review article: "Rural Poverty Report 2001—The Challenge of Ending Rural Poverty" by International Fund for Agricultural Development, Oxford University Press, New Delhi, *Business Line,* June 10, 2002.

——: "Poverty Measurement Studies in India: A Game of Norms and Numbers", *86th Annual Conference Volume,* Indian Economic Association, Kolhapur, December 29-31, 2003.

——: "Poverty Studies in India: A Critique" in *Poverty and Sustainable Development. Third World Perspectives* (Ed) R.K. Singh, Abhijeet Publications, Delhi, 2005, Vol. II.

——: *The Socio Economic Thoughts of A.P.J. Abdul Kalam,* Vellore Institute of Development Studies, 2004.

—— (Ed): *Dr. Kalam's PURA Model and Societal Transformation,* Deep & Deep Publications, New Delhi, 2005.

Faizur Rahman, A. : "Bailout Economics: A Stimulus that Neglects the Real India," *The New Indian Express*, December 12, 2008.

Guhan, S. : "A Premier on Poverty", *Financial Express*, 18 December, 1981.

Lakshman, Narayanan: "Food For Work: Promise and Challenges", *The Hindu*, November 17, 2004,

Kanbur, Ravi S.M.: "Measurement and Alleviation of Poverty: With an application to the effects of macro-economic adjustment', IMF *Staff Papers*, Vol. 34, No. 1, March, 1987.

Kumar, K. Shubh : "The Income Approach to Measuring Poverty: A Note on Human Welfare Below the Line". *Agricultural Change and Rural Poverty. Poverty: An Ordinal Approach for Measurement* (mimo), 1974.

Prabhakaran Nair, K.P.: "Whither India?: The Real India is getting Poorer by the Day", *The New Indian Express*, September 22, 2008.

Rao, Bhanoji : "NREG Bill: Fine-Tuning will make is Work Better", *Business Line*, January 4, 2005.

Reddy, Sanjay and Heuty, Antoine, "A Forceful Message, but will it end poverty," A commentary on Jeffrey Sachs, *The End of Poverty* (2005), *The Hindu*, April 22, 2005.

Sen, Amartya : *Poverty and Famine: An Essay on Entitlement and Deprivation*, Oxford University Press, Delhi (Second Impression), 1984.

——: "India's Poor needed a radical Package", *The Hindu*, January 9, 2005.

Shanmugasundram, Vedagiri: A General Theory of change from Poverty to Plenty", Presidential Address, 69th Annual Conference of the Indian Economic Association, Surat, 27 December, 1979.

Srinivasan, T.N. : "Guarantee in Employment: a Palliative?", *The Hindu*, January 3, 2005.

Thone, Dominique : "A Poverty Measure", *The Indian Economic Journal*, Vol. 30, No. 4, April-June, 1983.

GOI : *Economic Survey*, 2002-03, 2004-05.

World Bank Report, 2008.

SECTION IV

POVERTY ALLEVIATION AND SUSTAINABLE DEVELOPMENT

13

Causes, Trends and Alleviation of Poverty in India

S.K. DHAGE

INTRODUCTION

The concept of poverty is multidimensional (viz. Income poverty and non-income poverty). It covers not only levels of income and consumption, but also health and education, vulnerability and risk; and marginalization and exclusion of the poor from mainstream society. The performance of India in terms of income and non-income indicators has not been satisfactory. This is not to deny that progress has certainly been made in reduction in both income and non-income poverty. The pace of reduction in poverty has been, however, slow as compared to many other countries particularly in South East and East Asia.

Actually it was the Fourth Five Year Plan which, for the first time, laid emphasis on the "Common man" and the "Less privileged" section of society. For the benefit of the less privileged classes, it adopted several programmes such as S.F.D.A. of M.F.A.L. (for small and marginal farmers respectively), etc. In the Fifth Plan the objective of "removal of poverty" was given more emphasis. Poverty is wide-spread in India.

WHAT IS POVERTY?

In simple words, poverty is a social phenomenon in which a section of the society is unable to fulfil even its basic necessities of life. However, when a substantial segment of a society is deprived of the minimum level of living and continues at a bare substance level, that society is called to be plagued with mass poverty. A group of experts argues that poverty can be assessed on the ground when one fails to get a certain minimum consumption standard.

But others have asserted that it is difficult to agree on the amount of income that ensures the minimum consumption standard at one point of time. According to Planning Commission a standard of private consumption expenditure of Rs. 20 per capita per month is a bare minimum on the basis of 1960-61 prices. But, the individual researchers like B. S. Minhas and A.V. Vaidyanathan who studied rural poverty accounted the poverty line while others, P.K. Bardhan, Dandekar, and Ahluwalia have determined their own poverty lines. In the mean time, Planning Commission in Sixth Five Year Plan (1980-85) has followed an alternative definition of poverty as per Task Force on Projections of Minimum Needs and Effective Consumption Demand. In its report, Task Force has defined having a daily calorie intake of 2400 per person in rural areas and 2100 in urban areas. Further, the cut-off points turn out to be Rs. 76 for rural areas and Rs. 88 for urban areas on the basis of 1979-80 prices.

TRENDS IN POVERTY IN INDIA

The trends in poverty in India in various years are shown in the following Table 1. Similarly, Table 2 provides official estimates from 1973-74 to 1999-2000. Based on the 30-day recall methodology, the NSSO (National Sample Survey Organization) data reveals that the poverty at the all-India level was 26.1 per cent (over 26 crores of population) as against 36 per cent as recorded by the 1993-94 NSS data. However, the poverty ratio in 1999-2000 was much higher than the target of 16 per cent set for the end of the Ninth Plan period.

TABLE 1

Trends in Poverty, All India

	Datt's estimates		*S.P. Gupta's estimates*		
	Rural	*Urban*	*Rural*	*Uraban*	*Total*
1973-74	55.72	47.96	—	—	—
1977-78	50.60	40.50	—	—	—
1983	45.31	35.65	45.65	40.79	4.48
1886-87	38.81	34.29	—	—	—
1987-88	39.23	36.20	39.09	38.20	38.86
1988-89	39.06	36.60	—	—	—
1989-90	34.30	33.40	33.70	36.00	34.28
1990-91	36.43	32.76	35.04	35.29	35.11
1991	37.42	33.23	—	—	—
1992	43.47	33.73	41.70	37.80	40.70
1993-94	36.66	30.51	37.27	32.36	35.07
1994-95	41.02	33.50	38.03	34.24	36.98
1995-96	37.15	28.04	38.29	30.05	36.08
1997	35.78	29.99	38.46	33.97	37.23
1998 (six months)	—	—	45.25	34.58	43.01

Source: Development, Poverty and Fiscal Policy (Decentralization of Institution), 2002, M. Govinda Rao, Oxford University Press, New Delhi.

TABLE 2

Official Estimates of Poverty, All India

Year	*Total*	*Rural*	*Urban*
1973-74	54.9	56.4	49.0
1977 78	51.3	53.1	45.2
1983	44.5	45.7	40.8
1887-88	38.9	39.1	38.2
1993-94	36.0	37.3	32.4
1999-2000			
30-day recall	26.1	27.1	23.6
7-day recall	23.3	24.0	21.6

Source: Development, Poverty and Fiscal Policy (Decentralization of Institution), 2002, Rao M. Govinda, Oxford University Press, New Delhi.

POVERTY RATIO OF DIFFERENT STATES OF INDIA

We can find an idea of the poverty ratio of different states of India of 1973-74 and 1999-2000 from the following Table 3 and the Chart 1.

TABLE 3

Poverty Ratio in 1973-74 and 1999-2000

Sl. No.	*States*	*1973-74*			*1999-2000*		
		Rural	*Urban*	*Combined*	*Rural*	*Urban*	*Combined*
1	*2*	*3*	*4*	*5*	*6*	*7*	*8*
1.	Jammu & Kashmir	45.51	21.32	40.83	3.97	1.98	3.48
2.	Goa	46.85	37.69	44.26	1.35	7.52	4.40
3.	Chandigarh	27.96	27.96	27.96	5.75	5.75	5.75
4.	Punjab	28.21	27.96	28.15	6.35	5.75	6.16
5.	Himachal Pradesh	27.42	13.17	26.39	7.94	4.63	7.63
6.	Delhi	24.44	52.23	49.61	0.40	9.42	8.23
7.	Haryana	34.23	40.18	35.36	8.27	9.99	8.74
8.	Kerala	59.19	62.74	59.79	9.38	20.27	12.72
9.	Gujarat	46.35	52.57	48.15	13.17	15.59	14.07
10.	Rajasthan	44.76	52.13	46.14	13.74	19.85	15.28
11.	Lakshadweep	59.19	62.74	59.68	9.38	20.63	15.6 '
12.	Andhra Pradesh	48.41	50.61	48.86	11.05	26.63	15.77
13.	Dadra & Nagar Haveli	46.85	37.69	46.55	17.57	13.52	17.14
14.	Mizoram	52.67	36.92	50.32	40.04	7.47	19.47
15.	Karnataka	55.14	52.53	54.47	17.38	25.25	20.04
16.	Andaman & Nicobar Islands	57.43	49.40	55.56	20.55	22.11	20.99
17.	Tamil Nadu	57.43	49.40	54.94	20.55	22.11	21.12

(Contd.)

1	2	3	4	5	6	7	8
18.	Pondicherry	57.43	49.40	53.82	20.55	22.11	21.67
19.	Maharashtra	57.71	43.87	53.24	23.72	26.81	25.02
20.	All India	56.44	49.01	54.88	27.09	23.62	26.10
21.	West Bengal	73.16	34.67	63.43	31.85	14.86	27.02
22.	Manipur	52.67	36.92	49.96	40.04	7.47	28.54
23.	Uttar Pradesh	56.53	60.09	57.07	31.22	30.89	31.15
24.	Nagaland	52.67	36.92	50.81	40.04	7.47	32.67
25.	Arunachal Pradesh	52.67	36.92	51.93	40.04	7.47	33.47
26.	Meghalaya	52.67	36.92	50.20	40.04	7.47	33.87
27.	Tripura	52.67	36.92	51.00	40.04	7.47	34.44
28.	Assam	52.67	36.92	51.21	40.04	7.47	36.09
29.	Sikkim	52.67	36.92	50.86	40.04	7.47	36.55
30.	Madhya Pradesh	62.66	57.65	61.78	37.06	38.44	37.43
31.	Bihar	62.99	52.96	61.91	44.30	32.91	42.6
32.	Orissa	67.28	55.62	66.18	48.01	42.83	47.15

Source: Planning Commission, Five Year Plan (2002-07), Vol. III, Govt. of India, New Delhi.

Note for 1993-94

1. Poverty ratio of Assam is used for Sikkim, Arunachal Pradesh, Meghalaya, Mizoram, Manipur, Nagaland and Tripura.
2. Poverty ratio of Tamil Nadu is used for Pondicherry and Andaman and Nicobar Islands.
3. Poverty ratio of Kerala is used for Lakshadweep.
4. Poverty ratio of Goa is used for Dadra and Nagar Haveli.
5. Urban Poverty ratio of Punjab is used for both rural and urban poverty of Chandigarh.
6. Poverty line of Maharashtra and expenditure distribution of Goa is used to estimate poverty ratio of Goa.

Note for 1999-2000

1. Poverty ratio of Assam is used for Sikkim, Arunachal Pradesh, Meghalaya, Manipur, Nagaland and Tripura.
2. Poverty line of Maharashtra and expenditure of Goa is used to estimate poverty ratio of Goa.
3. Poverty line of Himachal Pradesh and expenditure distribution of Jammu and Kashmir is used to estimate poverty ratio of Jammu and Kashmir.
4. Poverty ratio of Tamil Nadu is used for Pondicherry and Andaman and Nicobar Islands.
5. Urban poverty ratio of Punjab is used for both rural and urban poverty of Chandigarh.
6. Poverty line of Maharashtra and expenditure distribution of Dadra

CHART 1

Percentage of Population in Poverty in States during 1999-2000 in Comparison to 1973-74 (Bottom Five and Top Five States)

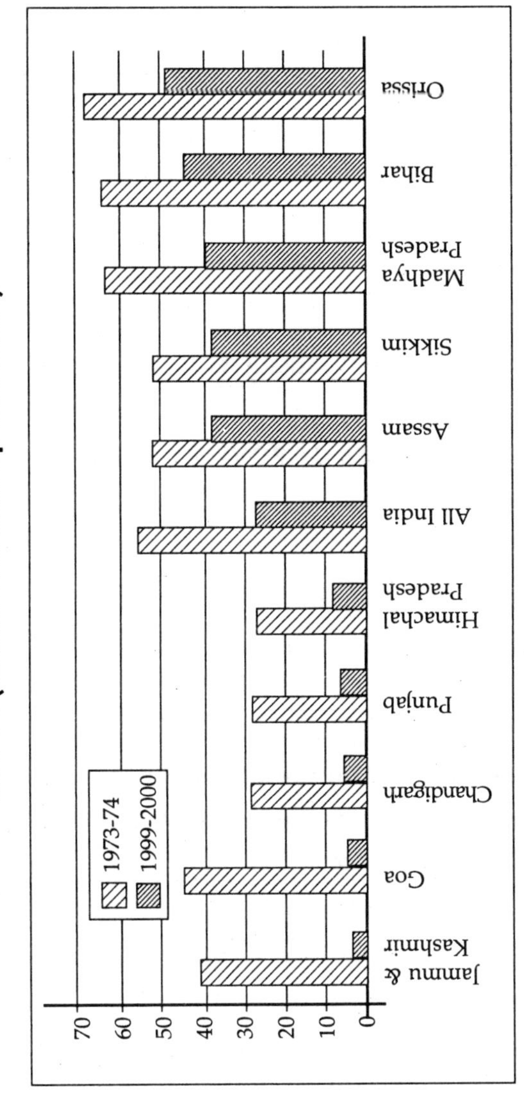

Source: Planning Commission, Five Year Plan (2002-07), Vol. III, Govt. of India, New Delhi.

and Nagar Haveli is used to estimate poverty ratio of Dadra and Nagar Haveli.

7. Poverty ratio of Goa is used for Daman & Diu.
8. Poverty ratio of Kerala is used for Lakshadweep.
9. Urban poverty ratio of Rajasthan may be treated as tentative.

The Table 3 shows the rural and urban poverty ratios of different states in India. West Bengal had more than 70 per cent rural poor. While Orissa, Bihar and Madhya Pradesh also had more than 60 per cent of rural population in Poverty in 1973-74. Among the states with lower levels of rural poverty in period 1973-74 where Haryana, Punjab and Himachal Pradesh where rural poverty was 34, 28 and 27 per cent respectively.

According to the latest estimates, Orissa now has the maximum rural poverty, followed by Bihar. The north-eastern states have also recorded improvement in urban poverty ratios, which have declined from 36.92 per cent to 7.47 per cent.

CAUSES OF POVERTY IN INDIA

The following are the important factors responsible for the problem of poverty in India.

(1) Rapid Growth of Population

The population of Indian during the decade 1981-91 has increased by 2.1 per cent per annum in a compound manner. This adversely affects the growth of per capita income and per capita consumption.

(2) Unemployment and Underemployment

The existence of mass unemployment and underemployment is an important cause of rampant poverty in the country. Most of the small and marginal farmers and landless agricultural labourers suffer from disguised unemployment in India. There are socio-economic factors responsible for poverty in India. Poverty in India is a deep-seated and long-term problem of our country.

(3) Low Agricultural Productivity

The level of productivity in agriculture in India is low due to sub-divided and fragmented holdings, lack of capital, use of traditional methods of cultivation, illiteracy, etc.

(4) Low Rate of Economic Development

The rate of economic development has been below the required level in India. Therefore, there persists a gap between levels of availability and requirements of goods and service. And the net result is poverty.

(5) Inequality

Inequality in the distribution of income and wealth has also been an important factor of mass poverty in India. As we know that production and distribution are inter-linked in a more fundamental sense, the pattern of income distribution determines the pattern of production. Unless the pattern of income distribution is altered, the objective of increasing the production of wage goods sufficiently to remove poverty will be distorted. And for this purpose an attack on the maldistribution of assets, both in the rural and urban sectors is a *sine qua non*.

(6) Price Rise

The continuous and steep price has added to the miseries of the poor. It has benefited a few people in the society and the persons in power income group find it difficult to get their minimum needs.

POVERTY ALLEVIATION PROGRAMMES

To control poverty the government of India has taken the following important measures.

(1) Marginal Farmers and Agricultural Labour Development/ Agency (MFALDA)

On the recommendations of Rural Credit Review Committee (1969), Marginal Farmers and Agricultural Labour Agencies were set-up along with the SFDA. The fundamental objective of the MFALDA programme is to assist the marginal cultivators in making the maximum productive use of their small holdings by undertaking horticulture, animal husbandry, dairy, etc.

(2) Minimum Needs Programmes

Keeping in view the basic notion of 'Garibi Hatao' and growth with justice, the minimum needs programme was introduced in Five Year Plan. It envisaged the provision of free and subsidized services through public agencies to improve the consumption levels of those living below the poverty line and raise productive efficiency of both rural and urban workers. Its basic components are as of elementary, health, water supply, roads, electrification, improvement of slums and nutrition, etc.

(3) Rural Landless Employment Guarantee Programme

Rural Landless Employment Guarantee Programme (RLEGP) was launched on 15 August 1983 to generate additional employment in rural areas particularly for the rural landless workers. The programme has basic objectives (i) to improve and expand employment opportunities particularly for the rural landless, (ii) to create productive and durable assets for strengthening rural infrastructure which will lead to rapid growth of rural economy and steady rise in the employment opportunities for the rural poor, and (iii) to improve the overall quality of life in rural areas.

(4) Training of Rural Youth for Self-Employment (TRYSEM)

TRYSEM was launched as a centrally sponsored scheme on August 15, 1979 with the sole aim of generating employment opportunities for the unemployed educated rural youth. The main thrust of this scheme is on equipping rural young in the age group of 18-35 years with necessary skills and technology to take up vocations of self-employment in the broad fields of agriculture and allied activities industry, services and business. During 1990-91 the number of youth were trained of 2.6 lakhs of which 70 per cent got employment.

(5) Crash Scheme for Rural Development

The CSRD employment was started in 1971 for three years to generate additional employment opportunities for unemployed youth in rural areas with the fundamental principal objectives of: (i) direct generation of employment opportunities in rural areas through the execution of labour intensive project; and (ii) creation of durable assets for all round development of rural areas with local development plans.

(6) Village Development Programme

In accordance with the recommendations of National Commission on Agriculture, Whole Village Development programme was introduced in the Fifth Five Year Plan. The main thrust of this programme was to increase productive capabilities in the rural areas and promoting the welfare and prosperity through equitable distribution of the benefit of development. This scheme, first of all was started in four states namely, Bihar, Orissa, Tamil Nadu and Uttar Pradesh on pilot basis covering 38 villages in all. Gradually, this scheme was extended to other parts of the country.

(7) Antodaya Yojana

In simple words, Antodaya upliftment of the last man in the row. Thus it aims of economic upliftment of the poorest of the poor families. The Government of Rajasthan followed by Uttar Pradesh has announced the adoption of Antodaya programme for improving the lot of poor folks in the rural areas of the state.

(8) Integrated Rural Development Programme (IRDP)

The concept of an integrated programme of Rural Development based on the local needs, resources endowments and potentialities was initiated in 1976-77 in 20 selected districts. The IRDP has the following important objectives:

(a) The major objective of the IRDP programme is to raise the production and productivity in agriculture and allied sectors.
(b) It aims at setting up agro-industrial complexes so that presently unemployed or underemployed person may get jobs in activities other than agriculture.

(9) Other Measures

Besides the above mentioned measures, the government of India has taken some other measures to control poverty in India. These are:

(a) Jawahar Rozgar Yojana
(b) Prime Minister's Integrated Urban Poverty Eradication Programme (PMIUPEP)
(c) Development of Tribal Areas.
(d) Small Farmers Development Agency (SFDA)
(e) New Job-Creation Schemes (September, 1993), etc.

RECENT PROGRAMMES

The important recent programmes to control poverty in India are:

(1) Prime Minister's Rozgar Yojana

The Prime Minister Rozgar Yojana was launched on 2nd October 1993.

(2) Mahila Samridhi Yojana (MSY)

Mahila Samridhi Yojana (MSY) was also launched on 2nd October, 1993 for the benefit of rural adult women.

(3) National Social Assistance Programme (NSAP)

The National Social Assistance Programme (NSAP) was announced on 15th August 1995.

CONCLUSION

All the states in India are suffering from the problem of poverty. The problem of poverty has created a great problem in the economic development in all the states of India. The problem of poverty has reduced in India than before the various poverty alleviation programmes which are taken by the government of India. Although the government of India has taken many important measures to control fully poverty but still how the government is not able to control the problem of poverty in India.

REFERENCES

Agrawal, H.S. (1985), "Poverty in India", in *Simple Indian Economy,* Lakshmi Narain Agarwal, Education Publishers, Agra.

Economic and Political Weekly (Sept. 2002), Bhagat Singh Road, Mumbai.

Economic and Political Weekly (Jan. 2003), Bhagat Singh Road, Mumbai.

Economic and Political Weekly (Feb. 2003), Bhagat Singh Road, Mumbai.

Lekhi, R.K. (1999), "Inequality of Income poverty and alleviation programmes," in *The Economics of Development and Planning*, Kalyani Publishers, Rajinder Nagar, Ludhiana.

Misra, S.K., Puri, V.K. (1999), *"Poverty in India" in Problems of Indian Economy,* Himalaya Publishing House, Mumbai.

Planning Commission (2002-07), Five Year Plan, Volume III, Government of India, New Delhi.

Rao, M. Govinda (2002), "Poverty in India—Trends, Macro Policies and Direct Programmes", in *Development, Poverty and Fiscal Policy* (Decentralization of Institutions), Oxford University Press, New Delhi.

Poverty, Old Age and Lack of Family Support

RAHUL S. MHOPARE

(1) In this paper an attempt is made to present some case studies of individuals who are senior citizens without family support. This is a very preliminary collection of information regarding the nature and causes of poverty verging almost on destitution. The objective of this data collection was to ascertain the reality of poverty those who either have no family or have some family members who do not consider it necessary to support such seniors.

(2) The study is restricted to one village from each taluka of one district only from each taluka of one district, i.e. Sangli. One senior female isolated from their families were selected by a process of actual visit to a village, meeting the officials as also the local people present at the time of visit. The sample profile is indicated as under:

One Male + One Female from each Village

Taluka	*Village*
Kadegaon	Hanmant Vadiye
Khanapur	Devikhindi
Palus	Tupari
Waiwa	Borgaon
Shirala	Khed

* The researcher is highly grateful to Prof. (Dr.) J.F. Patil, United Western Bank's Late Shri R.N Godbole, Chair in Financial Management and Banking Research, for his guidance and assistance.

Taluka	*Village*
Tasgaon	Shirgaon
Miraj	Kawalapur
Atpadi	Nelkaranji
Kawathe Mahankal	Ghatnandre
Jat	Kumbhari*

*No senior, isolated male citizen was identified.

It is therefore clear that the number of elements in the sample is nine males and ten females. We discuss below the sex-wise attributes of these poor old men and women.

II. THE MALES

1. We have information for nine males in the age group ranging between 66 to 80 years. The average age of the old people is 70-66 years. All those old persons are at present isolated from their families although they could have access to some kind of family support through one or combination of following relatives.

2. Wife, sons, daughters, brothers and sisters. However it is reported that none of these relatives are supporting these old people for a complex of reasons like—

(i) Separation from the wife either by divorce or by desertation;
(ii) Marriages of the daughters;
(iii) The death of the wife;
(iv) Desertation by sons after their marriages; and
(v) Alcoholism of the sons.

Food

There are three types of these old men if we consider the manner in which they feed themselves.

(A) *Casual work*: Four old men under study try to earn some money by doing some casual work locally available, e.g. marketing help, water supply, cattle herding, messenger work. One of them works as assistant in a cycle shop where he is paid only Rs. 5 for a difficult task which amounts to severe exploitation.

(B) The others earn their food by begging. However in most of these villages some of the local families dole out some food as per convenience to these people

(C) One of the old men reported that once in a while his married daughter sends him some eatables of a durable nature. He uses such eatables sparingly to satisfy his hunger. However, the general impression that the researcher got indicates that these old men at least in respect of their food requirements are virtual beggars.

(4) Housing

Of the 9 old men one is totally shelterless, finding out place to sleep during night in public places. One of these old men who was in his earlier days a ballad singer and had been abroad is provided with a room constructed out of state assistance, it is however a make, shift arrangement. Rest of the old men live in one of the dilapidated rooms in their ancestral houses. None of these old men has access to sanitary facilities of any nature.

(5) Work

The researcher tried to find out whether these old persons earned their maintenance through work. It was found that most of these old persons wanted to work but could not work because of physical inability. Some of them did work for brief spells of time where the work did not involve physical ability. However, it was seen that they were not given work because of their inability to do the work properly.

(6) Health Problems

Each one of these old men has some health problems from the routine problems like body ache, pains in the joints respiratory problems, problems of digestion, paralysis, tremors and in one case leprosy which, fortunately is a fully cured case. In case of temporary sickness they neglect and wait patiently for the sickness to subside in a natural way. Even when the sickness assumes serious dimensions they just languish.

(7) State Assistance

The researcher asked these old men whether they received State assistance under "Sanjay Gandhi Niradhar Yojana". Out of 9 old men only 3 reported receiving assistance under the above scheme. In the case of remaining 6 old persons assistance under the above scheme was not extended because they had some close relatives of the type of immediate family. It is however reported that some of them do not get the assistance because they don't no know how to submit the application although they know about the scheme. One of the old men admitted that he obtained the assistance of the scheme by reporting that he did not have any relatives. There is only one case where assistance under "Sanjay Gandhi Niradhar Yojana" is not received inspite of the fact that an application was submitted. Those who had applied and found eligible for the assistance, complained that they did not receive the help regularly every month. There are some complaints about the amount being less than what the scheme provided for.

(8) Ration Card

Although all these old men are included in ration cards only three of them possess their own ration cards. In the case of others the benefits of ration card are appropriated by their relatives or the ration shop owner by selling the food grains to others at higher prices.

(9) Savings

Except for three old men under study, none has savings of any kind any where. In the case of others the savings range between Rs.120, Rs. 500 to Rs. 4000. However, these are savings made during their working life and stand accumulated.

(10) Addiction

Each one of these old men is addicted to tobacco either in the form of beedi smoking or tobacco chewing. The ballad singer reported that in his earlier days he was an alcoholic as also a womaniser. At present tobacco and alcohol are his weaknesses.

(11) Other Dimensions

These old men under study very rarely move out of their place although some of them get 50% S.T. concession. Some of them visit temples and religious places preferably on foot. On holidays and festivals, surrounding neighbors give them sweets and occasionally clothes also. The one general expectation of these people is that they should get assistance through "Sanjay Gandhi Niradhar Yojana," their individual ration card and a proper place to live in. The general theme of the old age is waiting eagerly for a painless and peaceful death.

III. THE FEMALES

(1) We have information in respect of 10 senior women who live without family support of any kind. All these women belong to the age group 65 years to 86 years. The average age of these unfortunate women is 74.5 years. All these old women are at present isolated from their families although they should have received some kind of family support through one or combination of following relatives.

Husband, sons, daughters, brothers and sisters. However, in this case also none of these relatives are willing to support these old women for a complex of reasons like—

(i) Except for one they are widows, in the case of the exception the husband has absconded some 25 years back and no body knows where he is.

(ii) These old women are deserted by their sons particularly after marriages.

(iii) In the case of daughters although they strongly feel that they should support their mother, they are helpless in this respect because they cannot take independent decisions in the house of their husband. Moreover, these daughters themselves are married in such poor families where supporting or absorbing any additional non-working female member is not at all possible

(iv) In some cases sons who are married and alcoholic the neglect of the mother is total. However in one case the son tries to help his mother without the knowledge of his wife.

(2) Food

In the case of these old women although it can not be described as open begging, they have to depend on doles from neighbors and distant relatives in the same village. It is also reported that these women eat only once in a day and they go to bed on empty stomach with prayers. Most of these women are willing to cook their own food if they get the necessary inputs.

(3) Housing

Of the 10 women 3 live in rented rooms, 1 woman owns a house in fairly good conditions whereas 4 women live in dilapidated parts of the old house. 2 of these old women live under shades made out from torn pieces of gunny bags, taurpulin and heavy clothing along side the back of some houses. Such places just can not be described as rooms or houses.

(4) Work

Of the 10 old women three do not work at all because of their advanced age and sheer physical inability. The others undertake work as vegetable vendors, casual unskilled farm work and household work (washing clothes, cleaning utensils, etc.) one of these women moves around as a beggar.

(5) Health Problem

Except for one old woman (86 years) the rest suffer from some minor physical problems mainly arising from old age, lack of food and proper sanitation. These women suffer from audio and visual difficulties and none of them has received assistance in the form of hearing aids and glasses. In case of need these women approach public health centers and they are not able to afford private medical service. In fact most of the women suffer their plight without protest and without medical attention with the poignant hope that the adversity will automatically ease out. One old woman surprisingly reported that she uses as tooth powder, cow dung ashes which she stores from festival fire lit on 'Holi' which is one of the nationally observed holidays in India. This can be considered as one realistic measure of extreme poverty. One other woman under study, collects a local variety of oil seed known as Karanja by the side of brooks and sells the same for money to the local shopkeeper. This is her "Supplementary income".

(6) State Assistance

Of these 10 old women 6 are covered under "Sanjay Gandhi Niradhar Yojana" but the general complaint is that they do not receive the assistance every month and in the same amount. The remaining four old women could not avail of the scheme because they have sons but they do not support them.

(7) Ration Cards

Of the 10 old women 3 do not have the ration cards either because they do not know about it or because their relatives have deceived them. In the case of three old women they regularly use the ration-card for buying essential goods like food grains and kerosene. In the case of food grains these old women get additional subsidies because their ration cards belong to the B.P.L. category.

(8) Savings

Three of these old women reported accumulated savings of Rs. 5000, Rs. 2000 and Rs. 1000 respectively. Remaining women under study reported zero saving. From the discussion with the women who reported savings it appears that the savings are either secretly maintained or maintained in the face of frequent pressures from sons and daughters to withdraw the same.

(9) Addiction

These old women do not have any serious addictions except for brushing teeth with tobacco ash or using scented tobacco powder that is sneezing powder or snuff. It is to be noted that expenses involved are minimal and easily affordable.

(10) Other Dimensions

These old women under study very rarely move out of their place although some of them get 50% S.T. concession. Some of them visit temples and religious places preferably on foot. On holidays and festivals surrounding neighbors give them sweets and occasionally clothes also. One old woman although helpless herself, supports a grand daughter whose mother, her daughter-in-law eloped with some body. The one general expectation of these women is that they should get assistance through "Sanjay Gandhi Niradhar Yojana", their individual ration card and a proper place to live in. The general theme of the old age is waiting eagerly for a painless and peaceful death.

IV

The researcher is fully aware of the lack of sophisticated methods of data collection and subsequent application of fancy statistical techniques. It is strongly believed that the emotional impact that the interaction with these old deserted men and women left in the mind of the researcher describes their real poverty. Included here is a set of photographs, which amply prove what the researcher says. It is clearly revealed through such interactions that poverty of deserted people gets compounded in a socially painful manner, in the age group to which these men and women belong. It is not the adequacy of food

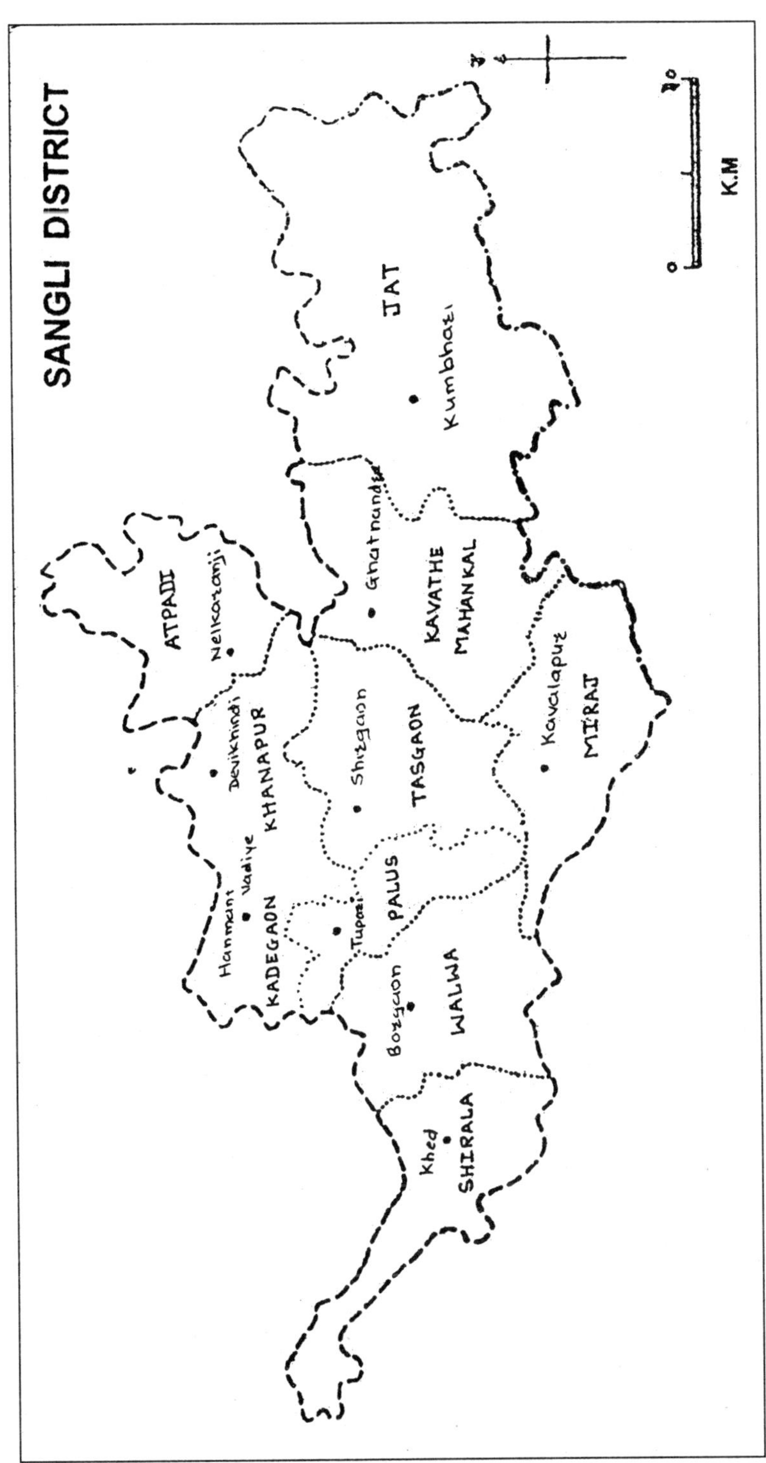
SANGLI DISTRICT
JAT
Kumbhari
KAVATHE MAHANKAL
ATPADI
Nelkaranji
KHANAPUR
Devikhindi
Vadiye
TASGAON
Shirgaon
MIRAJ
Kavalapur
PALUS
Tupari
KADEGAON
WALWA
Borgaon
SHIRALA
Khed
K.M
0
10

but the appropriateness of food which should be an indicator of poverty, in a negative way. For such men and women, poverty lies in the absence of sanitation facility rather than in the indecency and the quality of clothes, for such men and women it is not the quantity of medicines which matter but the affection and care of any person who listens to them, who talks with them and cares for them.

The intensity of poverty for such men and women is measured in terms of their tears, their loneliness, their isolation, their sense of deprivation and their torturing, slow and painful waiting for "emancipation". As a bridge between this reality and emancipation, it is necessary to strengthen the traditional social security of a well knit family to be supplemented by publicly financed old age houses with reasonable housing, food, medical and cultural components. Otherwise, death is preferable to lonely old age.

15

Poverty, Inequality and Sustainable Development in India

SWAMI PRAKASH SRIVASTAVA

1. INTRODUCTION

Poverty can be defined as a social phenomenon in which a section of the society is unable to fulfil even its basic necessities of life. When a substantial segment of a society is deprived of the minimum level of living and continues at a bare subsistence level, that society is said to be plagued with mass poverty. 75 per cent of the world's poor (using the dollar a day criterion) live in rural areas and rural sector will continue to account for over 60 per cent of the poor in 2025, a frontal attack on rural poverty would seem essential. Asia accounted for two-third of the world's poor in 2001 albeit with wide variations. The most of the world's poor reside in South Asia where India's rank is the first Rural South Asia (with head-count ratios hovering around the 40 per cent mark) has the highest incidence of poverty after Sub-Saharan Africa. In East Asia and the Pacific poverty fell sharply then rose in the after month of the currency crisis and is now on its way down. According to Human Development Report, 2000, the population below income poverty in national poverty line is 35 per cent. It is 44.3 per cent on the basis of purchasing power parity of US Dollar one per day. Human poverty Index of India is 34.6 per cent whose rank becomes 58. Thus, we have the obvious mission that if we cannot ameliorate poverty through the planning objectives, the fruits of the development will be meaningless.

Within countries poverty is increasingly concentrated, e.g., in remote northwest, Bihar, Western Orissa and the tribal belts of India. It has been observed from data, the rural poverty is much more higher than urban poverty. Nearly 360 million people are still living under poverty line. Though country's agricultural food production has increased by 197 million tons by the year 2002-03, still poverty and unemployment is persisting in India. Poverty is on the decline in India. There has been a shortfall in the percentage of people living below the poverty line. A higher GDP growth rate and a low inflation rate have improved the economic conditions of the poor. Of course, the poverty line itself is a misnomer. Theoretically, people at the poverty line have just enough money to provide themselves with food that translates into 2200 calories, but nothing else (housing, clothing, security, minimal comfort, schooling, medicines, etc.)

The present paper will examine the nature of poverty in India by considering two-folds approach, i.e., poverty in society sense and poverty in economic sense, with special reference to performance of Indian economy since independence. The plan of the paper is as follows. In section II, we shall assess the methodology. Section III gives review of Literature. Section IV shall focus on India's economic reforms and poverty. Section V outlines the poverty line and causes of poverty in India. Section VI shall focus on Poverty ratio in India. Section VII gives the share of development expenditure in the aggregate budgeting. In Section VIII, we shall assess the poverty alleviation programme in India. Section IX shall summaries the concluding observations.

2. METHODOLOGY

Considerable discussion has taken place recently about the database for poverty measurement in India. Doubts have been raised whether the household expenditure survey data (HCE) generated by the 50-year-old National Sample Survey system currently being used for poverty measurement is fully reflection the growth in consumer expenditure and capturing the extent of change in the poverty ratio. The official estimates of poverty principally pertain to the head-count Ratio (HCR), the most commonly used measure of incidence of poverty. The estimates are prepared on the basis of the poverty line defined by the task force on Minimumness and Effective Demand (1979) as the per capita expenditure level in 1973-74 (28th round of the NSS consumer expenditure) which could meet out of the all. India consumption basket the caloric norms of 2400 and 2100 calories per capita per day in the rural and urban areas respectively. Till recently, the poverty line was updated for subsequent years by using the implicit prices from the pice at constant and current prices, and the NSS household data on distribution of population by level of consumption expenditure was scaled up by the ratio of pice of the estimate of total consumption expenditure from the NSS. However, the Expert Group (Lakdawala Committee) on the Proportion and Number of Poor (1993) disapproved the aforesaid procedures of adjustment and recommended (i) Computation of state-wise poverty estimates on the basis of state-specific consumer price index numbers for agricultural labourers (CPI-AL) for the rural sector and the state specific consumer price index numbers for industrial workers (CPI-IW) for the urban sector for updating the poverty line; and (ii) the use of the NSS distribution of population by expenditure levels without any adjustment for the discrepancy between the NAS and NSS estimates of private consumption. Presently, the official methodology is based on these recommendations of the Expert Group.

3. REVIEW OF LITERATURE

The empirical literature on poverty in India is vast, and has covered many dimensions and generated a lot of controversy. The major data base has been provided by the consumer expenditure surveys conducted by the National Sample Survey Organisation (NSSO), supplemented by other sources like the Central Statistical Organisation, Planning Commission and reports of various ministries of the central and state governments. The first major issue is the choice of the poverty line to demarcate the poor from the non-poor, the idea of a basic minimum caloric requirement and estimation of cost of the diet that satisfy these requirements was the subject of intense debate among researchers during 1960s and 1970s, while Bardhan (1970) and Minhas (1968). There are several important literatures on Indian poverty scenario such as S.D. Tendulkar (1998), S.P. Gupta (1998), S. Mahendra Dev and Ajit Ranade (1999-2000), Montek Singh Ahluwalia (2000), and many others.

4. INDIA'S ECONOMICS REFORMS AND POVERTY

Faster growth through economic reforms in not always accompanied by a faster rate of poverty reduction. Poverty can be reduced if growth increases employment potential (quantity and quality). Similarly, the extent to which the working poor are able to integrate into the economic process also determines the impact of growth on poverty. For example, if there is a mismatch between the opportunities available due to economic reforms and skills of the workers, the poor will not be able to take advantage of such opportunities and gain from the reforms.

There are several important literatures on Indian poverty scenario and India's Economic Reforms such as S.D. Tendulkar (1998), S.P. Gupta (1998), S. Mahendra Dev and Ajit Ranade (1999-2000). Montek Singh Ahluwalia (2000), and many others. All concluded that the poverty ratio decreased in the post-reform period the poverty ratio increased as against previous years. He explained that increase in rural poverty was due to weather related forces, constricted maneuverability of government action, certain political economy factors which influenced by reform policies like depreciation and disprotection of agriculture. But, in mid-1991 was due to better management of government intervention in food economy. The decline in urban poverty was for slower pace of reform in industrial and public sectors and relaxation of fiscal correction and pick up in growth rate. Above all, the economic policy reforms are indirectly responsible for movement of poverty indicators in the post-reform period. Mr. Ravallion (2000) was also on the same opinion that despite of growth since reform began, there was a sign of slow down in India's rate of poverty. His findings were based on the facts that the poverty impact of aggregate economic growth depends on its sector's and geographic composition. Higher agricultural productivity is a Key factor in rural poverty reduction. Also higher agricultural growth reduces rural poverty directly. Since, it fosters the conditions for pro-poor growth in the non-farm sectors.

Recent study by the Planning Commission estimated that the revised estimates of rural poverty were 22.8 per cent in 1994-95, 19.1 per cent in 1995-96, 20.7 per cent in 1997 and 23.6 per cent in 1998 but the revised estimates of urban poverty were 18.3 per cent, 15.2 per cent, 17.8 per cent and 20.0 per cent respectively in the same period. This study also stressed that both the rural and urban poverty increased in 1998. This was due to change over of power in the center. From the studies of S.D. Tendulkar (1998) and Gaurav Dutta (2000), it was clear that the India's inequality became worse-off in the post-reform period.

5. POVERTY LINE AND CAUSES OF POVERTY IN INDIA

The population below poverty line in rural areas declined from 56.4 per cent in 1973-74 to 27.1 per cent in 1999-2000, registering a decline of 29.3 per cent. However, in absolute terms, the number of rural poor was about 261 million in 1973-74, which rose to 264 million in 1977-78, but thereafter the number of the rural poor declined from 252 million in 1983 to 193 million in 1999-2000. This was a healthy development. The population below the poverty line in urban areas was about 49 per cent in 1973-74, which declined to 40.8 per cent in 1983 and further fell to 23.6 per cent in 1999-2000. In order words, poverty percentage among the urban poor fell by about 15.4 per cent during the period 1973-74 to 1999-2000. The overall percentage of the poor fell from 54.9 per cent in 1973-74 to 26.1 per cent in 1999-2000. However, in absolute terms, their number decreased from 321 million in 1973-74 to 260 million in 1999-2000, a decline of about 28.8 per cent.

Jammu & Kashmir has the minimum number of people living below the poverty line and the overall percentage of poverty in the state was 3.48 in 1999-2000. The poverty ratio in Orissa was 47.15 per cent in 1999-2000. Delhi registered the lowest number of rural population living below the poverty line—0.4 per cent in 1999-2000. The ratio was 20.55 per cent in Tamil Nadu, 23.22 per cent in Maharashtra and 31.85 per cent in West Bengal for the same period. Delhi recorded a decline in the number of urban living below the poverty line from 52.23 per cent in 1973-74 to 9.42 per cent in 1999-2000. There has been a gradual decrease in urban people living below the poverty line of the states like 9.99 per cent in Haryana, 7.47 per cent in Manipur in the year 1999-2000. These figure were same at 7.47 per cent for Nagaland, Arunachal Pradesh, Meghalaya, Tripura, Assam and Sikkim in 1999-2000. Obviously, poverty eradication programme and economic development resulted in poverty reduction in various states.

Widespread poverty in India is attributable to a host of factors, viz.

population explosion, lack of industrialization, failures of land reforms and failures of fiscal policy to narrow the gap between the rich and the poor. Industrial development of the country has neither been on desirable lines nor at expected rate. Undue emphasis on capital-intensive industries has failed to genetrate sufficient jobs for the labour force. Land reforms programme was started with great fanfare soon after the independence. However, it has failed to achieve the desired, the incidence of poverty in rural areas in mainly due to the failure of land reforms. Similarly, taxation and expenditure policies of the government have not been used effectively to ridge the gap between the rich and the poor.

Table 1 given projections of national poverty ratios for the next 15 years. The planners have assumed the overall rates of economic growth of 7 per cent per year in the 9th Plan (1997-2002), 7.5 per cent in the 10th Plan (2002-07), and 8 per cent in the 11th Plan (2007-12) accompanied by growth rates of per capita consumption of 4.3 per cent per year, and 5.3 per cent per year in the successive plan period. Given these assumptions, poverty is estimated to have declined from 29.2 per cent in 1996-97 to about 18 per cent in 2001-02. It will further decline to 9.5 per cent in 2006-07 and 4.4 per cent in 2011-12.

Table brings to sharp focus the state-wise projections of poverty ratios. The projection appears to be very ambitions for states like Bihar, Orissa, M.P. and U.P. that high poverty ratios. For instance, to bring down poverty in Bihar from 44.1 per cent in 1996-97 to 6.5 per cent in a period of 15 years appears to be highly improbable, if not impossible. In a state with a very high level of political instability, to assume 7 per cent rate of growth is totally unrealistic, In Orissa, poverty ratio is sought to be reduced from 40.2 per cent in 1996-97 has been worsened during past thirteen years due to the LPG Policy (Liberalization, Privatization and Globalization).

TABLE 1

Projections of National Poverty Ratios

(per cent)

Region	*1996-97*	*2001-02*	*2006-07*	*2011-12*
Rural	30.55	18.61	9.64	4.31
Urban	25.58	16.46	9.28	4.49
Total	29.18	17.98	9.53	4.37

Source: Planning Commission Report (1998), 9th Five Year Plan (1997-2002).

6. NEXUS OF UNEMPLOYMENT AND POVERTY

Poverty cannot be eliminated without continuous process of eliminating it through employment providing employment continuously and its position constant and increasing, development is essential continuously. But the must thrilling position is that the growth rate of employment has remained less than

1% decreasingly from more than 20% In one hand population is increasing tremendously and on the other hand the opportunity of employment is decreasing The Prime Minister is deceiving the nation saying that more than one crore employment is being created, counting the whole prospect of increasing all kinds of probable employment (including part-time, temporary and muster roll employment created in roads' projects etc.) in all the sectors (agriculture, industrial service, trade, infrastructure, etc.) under private, public or/and joint ownership. This is a very fraud method of cheating the nation *en bloc*. The employment ratio is decreasing in public sector. The public sector is not in a position to provide more employment due to many reasons (like continuous loss running tendency of the government for public sector retrenchment, compulsory retirement, avoiding new and fresh appointment policies of the government, etc). Once Rajiv Gandhi was being criticized for launching computer and thus decreasing the opportunities of employment. But now due to computers alone, crores of unemployed youths got opportunities of employment. After all what the computers can do alone? Crores of unemployed are on the roads without bread. According to the previous economic survey, 2,24,000 industrial units are sick in the country. 473 out of 700 licensed sugar mills are in running position any how. 143 out of 271 sugar mills are closed in private sector and remaining is in loss. The cotton mills provided maximum number of employment previously and earned more and more foreign exchange. But almost all big cotton mills are in closed position till decade. 313 cotton mills had become closed up to 31 March, 1999. In the phase of liberalization unemployment took its acute form in developed countries on the record level. This level of unemployment became the largest thereafter 1994. This number became more than 90 lakh there. Now as the record of U.S.A. the rate of unemployment had decreased there. But it is not due to increase in the number of opportunities of employment: it is due to the fall in the number of job seekers who left the job market out of despair, job was available to them. In June 2002 the rate of unemployment there was 6.4% which became 6.2% now (July 2003). It became due to the fall in number of unemployed persons in the employment exchanges who could not get employment and became out of job market record. Such number of unemployed persons (not being recorded as unemployed) is more than 5.5 lakh there. Such persons are unemployed, but they are not treated unemployed as they became out of register. Besides this in the US economy many persons became prey of retrenchment due to depress such type of retrenched persons (really became unemployed but not recorded as unemployed) were more than 72 thousand in June, 2003 and again more than 44 thousand in July 2003. Maximum retrenchment took place in the construction companies there. Such retrenchment was more than 71 thousand.

50% of population of world spends their lives on the income less than $2 per day. Out of them about 70% are living in the rural areas of Asian and African countries, 23% overall are West Bengal (14.6 per cent), H.P. (14.7 per cent), J&K (15.0 per cent) and Manipur (17.8 per cent). Delhi achieved CAGR of 30.6 per cent during the period 1993-94 to 1999-2000. Table highlights the share of development expenditure in the aggregate budgeting expenditure of the 26 major Indian States, which declined by 5 per cent from 61.5 per cent in 1993-94 to 56.5 per cent in 1999-2000. At the individual level, many of the states have done even worse. Maharashtra, the most indusrialised state, for example, witnessed a sharp decline in the share of development expenditure from 66.6 per cent in 1993-94 to 52.6 per cent in 1999-2000. The share of development expenditure in the state's aggregate expenditure fell from 64.7 per cent to 57.7 per cent in A.P., from 66.1 per cent in Karnataka from 71.61 per cent to 58.71 per cent in Goa from 62.94 per cent to 55.65 in Rajasthan and from 66.4 per cent to 55 per cent in Tamil Nadu during the same period, i.e. 1993-94 to 1999-2000.

7. POVERTY ALLEVIATION PROGRAMMES IN INDIA

Poverty alleviation depends on both macro-economic policies and poverty alleviation programmes. The economic reforms open up opportunities for some groups and adversely affect some others. The key strategy for reducing poverty lies in creating productive employment for the poor through a labour intensive pattern of growth and better implementation of poverty alleviation programmes. Poverty eradication may either be left to the automatic mechanism of growth process and/or to programmes aimed at direct assault on poverty. The initial thinking of the Government relied on the automatic benefits of growth coupled with a progressive taxation policy. However, this strategy did not work on desired lines. As the English Five Year Plan (1992-97) observed, "The equity objective was sought to be pursued through redistribution of assets of assets but land reforms could not be implemented effectively. The problem of poverty could not be tackled through growth, which itself was slow over long period of time. Hence, direct intervention through poverty alleviation programmes became necessary." Lately, the Government has increasingly resorted to direct attack on poverty through rural development and rural employment schemes. Some major anti-poverty programmes of the Government of India are the following:

1. Integrated Rural Development Programme (IRDP) was launched in 1978-79 as a programme of total rural development.
2. The National Rural Employment Programme (NREP) was started as a part of the Sixth Five Year Plan to help those depended largely on wage employment in the agricultural sector.
3. Rural Landless Employment Guarantee Programme (RLEGP) was launched in August 25, 1983 with a view to expanding the employment opportunities for the rural landless. In February 1989, Government announced a new scheme called Jawahar Lal Nehru Rojgar Yojna for employment creation in 120 backward districts of the country. On April 1, 1989, the three employment schemes, viz. NREP, RLEGP and Jawahar Lal Nehru Rozgar Yojna were merged

into a single rural employment programme named Jawahar Rozgar Yojna.

TABLE 2

Projections of Poverty Alleviation Programme Mandays of Employment Generated

(in million)

	1999-2000	*2000-01*	*2001-02*
Programmes in Rural Areas			
Jawahar Gram Samridhi Yojna	268.30	268.3	97.70*
Swarnjayanti Gram Swarozgar Yojna	278.60	217.4	93.70*
Programmes in Urban Area			
Pradhan Mantri Rojgar Yojna	0.21	0.60	—
Urban Wage Employment Programme	10.14	15.87	3.63**

*Up to December 2001; **Up to January 2002.

In Table 2, the performance of poverty alleviation programme in India has been evaluated under two categories, namely rural areas and urban areas. The employment generation under the programmes in rural areas, viz. Jawahar Gram Samridhi Yojna shows a decline from 268.30 million in 1999-2000 to 97.70 million in December 2001. Another rural programme is Swarnjayanti Gram Swarojgar Yojna, which shows a decline from 278.60 million in 1999-2000 to 93.70 million in December 2001. The programmes in urban areas and Pradhan Mantri Rojgar Yojna and Urban Wage Employment programme. The Pradhan Mantri Rojgar indicates a marginal rise from 0.21 million in 1999-2000 to 0.60 million in 2000-01. The employment generated by Urban Wage Employment Programme increased from 10.14 million in 1999-2000 to 15.87 million in 2000-01. But there was a decrease to 3.63 million in Jan. 2002. Two new initiatives have been announced in the recent budget. One is expansion of the Antyodaya Anna Yojna. An additional allocation of Rs. 507 crore has been provided in 2003-04. It is doubtful whether 25 per cent of the population below poverty line would be covered in the next fiscal with this amount. The second initiatives are the group health insurance scheme, with the government promising to subsidize premium payment of the poor. One has to see whether the public sector corporation is enthusiastic about the scheme.

8. CONCLUSION

We have reviewed critically the major lessons that have emerged from the numerous studies on the estimates of poverty and the effectiveness of poverty alleviation schemes in India during the past five decades after her independence. The success we have achieved must be viewed in the context of the enormity of the problem that still remain. Deprivations in social and economic indicators spread across different regions and states, infrastructural bottlenecks and other growth constraints, distributional inequities compounded by ill targeting and wrong incentive signals, inefficiency of management and associated corruption and the challenges to grow and survive in a world of globalisation and market integration yet to make people live a better life, have all eluded our early efforts during fifty years of the Indian economic development.

The number of people living the poverty line is still substantially high. The government itself admits that about 260 million people lived below the poverty line in 1999-2000, of which 193 million were in the rural areas and 68 million in the urban areas. That the incidence of poverty is disproportionately higher in rural India is not surprising, the 2001 census has once again conformed the desperate dependence do the rural workforce on agriculture. Nearly three-fourth of all rural workers are employed by the agricultural sector. In many states, dependence on the agricultural sector for employment increased in the post-reform years. The continuous assured supply to the rural sectors clearly has a depressive impact on the daily wages of agricultural and other rural workers.

The fundamental task of new political economy of poverty in our country is to provide a long waited breakthrough in all these are as mentioned above. Besides, our industrial growth experiences do not suggest to be friendly to poverty alleviation so far—if we want to make them so, perhaps a major structural change in its growth patterns need to be initiated in the immediate future. This paper outlines these tasks ahead in the light of what we have learned about poverty in India during the first fifty-five years of her political independence. The independence of poverty may have declined, but its severity as well as the number of the poor people and the tasks of alleviating their poverty in multiple dimensions in a changed environment and liberalization remain a serious one. This is a challenge for our researchers as well as for the policy-makers of develop new strategies and solutions to the multitude of problems associated with poverty alleviation and growth for better life in the coming years. Providing productive employment in agriculture and rural non-farm sector is important for reduction in poverty. Access to land (as owners or tenants) and credit are important for the poor in agriculture. In order to develop the rural non-farm sector, there is need to look at issues such as rural-urban linkages, infrastructure markets, technology and training in skills.

References

Tendulkar, S. and Jain, L.R. (1995), Economic Reforms and Poverty, *Economic and Political Weekly*, June.

Kakwani, N. and Subbarao, K. (1990), Rural Poverty and its alleviation in India, *Economic and Political Weekly*, March.

Sinha, K.K. (1977), The Poverty Concept, *Indian Economic Journal*, Vol. II, Conference, Issue, IEA, Bombay, p. 51.

Dandekar, V.M. and Rath, W. (1992), Bharat Mein Garibi, Orient Logman, New Delhi, pp. 128-30.

Gupta, S.P. (1995), Economic Reforms and Its Impact on the Poor, *Economic and Political Weekly*, June.

World Bank (1990): World Development Report, 1990.

Vailerie Kozel and Barbara Parker (2003), A Profile and Diagnostic of 2Poverty in Uttar Pradesh, *Economic and Political Weekly*, Jan. 25, pp. 385-91.

Facts For You, March 2003, pp. 35-39.

Todarao, P. and Smith, C. (2002), Economic Development, p. 196.

Goyal, R.L., Economics of Growth and Planning, 1991, pp. 6 and 7.

Economic and Political Weekly, 22nd to 29th March 2003, p. 1138.

Indian Economic Survey (2002-03), March 2003, pp. 212-13.

16

Poverty Alleviation in India for a Sustainable Future

ASIM K. KARMAKAR

Poverty is commonly seen as broadly the antithesis of growth and development. They are not exact opposites, since poverty is a condition while growth/development as a process or a set of processes, but there is an inter-relationship between the two: growth has been associated with substantial reduction in poverty. In recent empirical literature, decline in poverty measure has often been found to be closely associated with high substantial reduction in poverty. In recent empirical literature, decline in poverty measure has often been found to be closely associated with high economic growth: a 2 per cent annual trade of growth in consumption per person will typically result in a decline in the poverty gap Index of 3 to 8 per cent, using local poverty like lines and assuming growth to be distributed neutral. Further, it is also noticed that in a country like India with high and persistent inequality. The trickle-down effects of even fairly high rates of growth have been so slow that without remedial pro-poor policy actions it will take an unnecessary long time before a sizeable dent is made in the backlog of poverty.

In the above backdrop, the present paper, after noting some aspects concerning the concepts and measurement of poverty, focuses some of the issues like poverty studies in India, recent reforms in India's anti-poverty programmes and eventually comes to the conclusion that growth as well as poverty eradication programmes in India both are necessary for a sustainable future.

I. CONCEPTS OF POVERTY

The term poverty is akin to a shortage of income. But the development literature stresses the multi-dimensionality of poverty. Health, education, social life, environmental quality, spiritual and political freedom, in addition to material consumption, is attached with the concept of poverty. When poverty is defined solely in terms of money, then it can be argued that economic growth is found to be the most effective way to reduce poverty. But basic needs such as health and education, etc. are valued then the development strategy is likely to put more emphasis on social policy. Two further conceptual issues are absolute *versus* relative poverty; and temporary *versus* permanent poverty.

Absolute poverty is measured against some benchmark such as the cost of getting enough food to eat or being able to write one's own name for literacy. Relative poverty is measured against social standards.

The distinction between the temporarily and the permanently poor is linked to the notion of vulnerability. The vulnerable are those at risk of falling into poverty. If there are poverty traps, then there is a good case for anti-poverty interventions to prevent this happening.

II. POVERTY MEASUREMENT

A country's GNP per capita is not a good measure of poverty for it takes no account of distribution and ignores other dimensions of poverty.

The most common income poverty measures is the head-count, i.e. the percentage of the population falling below the poverty line.

This measure takes, in fact, no account of how far people are below the poverty line so that a rise in the income of the poor which leaves them in poverty appears to have no effect. Hence another measure, the poverty gap, is often used which can be interpreted as the product of head-count and the average distance of the poor below the poverty line (expressed as the percentage of the poverty line) and the benefit of targeting.

The poverty severity index is a similar measure which puts together weights on those furthest below the poverty line. These three measures—then head-count, the poverty gap and the poverty severity index—are known collectively as the Foster—Greer—Thorbecke poverty measure. For a non-negative living standard indicator (say, consumption) y is distributed with density f (y) and with a poverty line z, the poverty measure P is given by.

$$P = \int_{0}^{z} \left(\frac{z - y}{z} \right)^{\alpha} f(y)\, dy, \alpha > O$$

When a is O, P is the same as the head-count measure, and when a is 1, P is known as the poverty gap index. As a increases, P becomes increasingly sensitive to the living standard indicator of the poorest people. Thus this measure is sensitive to differences in the depth of poverty or to inequality among the poor.

Over the years a number of composite measures of development have been proposed. A previous measure, the Physical Quality of Life Index (PQLI) has been superseded in recent years by the UNDP's Human Development Index (HDI); the latter being a composite of GDP per capita, life expectancy and measure of educational attainment. It is noteworthy that it is the UNDP which has done the most to address poverty in all its dimensions not least within the annual 'Human Development Report'. For example, one calculation made by UNDP is that the cost of eradicating poverty across the world is relatively small compared to global income—not more than 0.3% of world GDP—and that political commitment, not financial resources, is the real obstacle to poverty eradication.

Just as income per capita takes no account of distribution neither does the HDI. However, UNDP has also proposed a Human Poverty Index (HPI) which focuses on deprivation—specially the deprivation in living standards. This HPI is based on three main indices: the percentage of the population not expected to survive beyond the age of 40, the adult literacy rate, and a deprivation index based on an average of three variables—the per cent age of the population without access to safe water, the percentage of population without access to health services, and the percentage of children under the age of 5 years who are underweight through malnourishment.

Though HDI is widely used, there are several criticisms labelled against it, such as which variables are to put in the index, the arbitrary choice of weight in constructing the average and that information lost by combining three or four pieces of data into a single number. The technical appendix to the 1996 Human Development Report already has highlighted this. Thus it may be preferable to report a small range of social indicators rather than attempting to combine these to an overall poverty index.

III. POVERTY STUDIES: A LONG VIEW FROM THE EARLY 1950S TO THE MILLENNIUM

A major significant development for India's economic policy was Indira Gandhji's extension of Nehruvian socialism to poverty eradication in terms of affirmative actions for empowering the poor. For the first time, in the middle of 1960s, attempts were made to estimate poverty in terms of expenditures on a basket of consumer goods, thus arriving at some minimum requirements for a basic standard of living. And the Indian poor have been studied in more repetitive detail than the poor of any other developing country even though their number and situation may not have changed very much in recent years. As Sen put it: "The Indian Poor may not be accustomed to receiving much help, but he is beginning to get used to being counted". Several of the studies of poverty in India defined it in terms of food requirements as well as needs like housing, clothing, fuel, etc. Dandekar and Rath (1971) used their poverty line the amount of money that was necessary to purchase a low cost diet that provided 2250 calories per day. They found that 40% of the rural and 50% of the urban population lived below the poverty line in 1960-61.They also found wide regional variations in the extent of poverty. Bardhan (1974) found that in 1968-69, about 54% of the rural population and 41% of the urban population were in poverty, thus reversing the rural/urban position. The Planning Commission for figures for poverty, for 1977-78. suggested the incidence of poverty to be higher (48%) in rural areas than in urban areas (41%). National Sample Survey (NSS) of India suggested that about 46% of the total population of the total population was in poverty in 1973-74. Taking a longer period, 1956-74, and using his poverty line the amount of income necessary to purchase a low cost diet providing 2250 calories per person per day. Ahluwalia found no consistent upward or downward trend in the extent of poverty in rural India. The percentage in poverty declines initially, from over 50% in the mid-fifties to around 40% in 1960-61, rising sharply through the mid-sixties, reaching a peak in 1967-78, and then declines again (Ahluwalia, 1978). This finding was confirmed by Rao, who concentrated on starvation poverty in rural India for the same period (Bhanoji Rao, 1981). In what follows is the fact that over the 1960s and the early 1970 there was little or no change in the proportion of the Indian population in absolute poverty and the main beneficiaries have been the better-off groups due to the steady industrial and agricultural growth in this period. In fact, unregulated capitalist economic growth did not benefit of the poor.

India has reduced poverty substantially since the mid-1970s, as growth rose and human development indicators improved.

India has reduced the percentage of population living in poverty since the 1970s, but the progress has been uneven over time and across status and the number of poor has continued to rise. From the early 1950s and the mid-1970s, poverty rates fluctuated. (Ravallion and Datt, 1996). Then from 1973-74 to the mid-1980s, poverty incidence declined from 54% in 1973-73 to 38% to 1986-87. Poverty reduction slowed in the 1980s. Poverty incidence dropped sharply in 1990. In 1991-92, a transitory worsening of poverty incidence occurred with the 1991 BoP crisis and decline in growth and stabilisation measure.

Studies made by Tendulkar (1998), Batt and Ravillion (1998), Dubey and Gangopadhyay (1998) show that during the early 1990s the increased poverty incidence was associated with factor like poor harvests, limited agricultural imports and high food prices as well as statistical questions related to the small samples in those years and the price indices used to deflate the expenditure data. By 1993-94, the incidence of poverty had fallen to 35%—well below the 53% of the early 1970s, slightly below the 38% achieved in 1987-88.

India reduced the depth and severity of poverty even faster than the head-count ratio. Thus the decline of poverty was the process through which poverty was being reduced improving the consumption of those far below the poverty line. Despite these successes, over 310 million people were living in poverty in 1993-94.

The Planning Commission has been estimating the incidence of poverty at the national and state level using the methodology contained in the Lakdawala Committee Report and applying it to consumption expenditure data from the large sample surveys (55th round) on consumer expenditure conducted by the NSSO. In the late 1990s, the decline in poverty happened sharply, in rural areas, according to the data of NSSO. An estimates 27.1% of the population was below the poverty line in the poverty ratio from 54.9% in 1973-74 to 36% in 1993-94 and 26.1% in 1999-2000. The poverty ratio declined by nearly 10 percentage point between 1993-94 to reach 26.1% in 1999-2000. The proportion of poor in both the rural and urban areas declined sharply between 1973-74 to 1999-2000. In absolute terms, the number of poor also declined to 260 million in 1999-2000. This indicates that India has reduced poverty substantially but poverty rates has declined marginally.

IV. REFORMS IN INDIA'S ANTI-POVERTY PROGRAMMES

There is no denying the fact that the on-going reforms process will increase the rate of per capita growth. The controversy crops up over the question whether reform will promote a type of growth which is anti-poor. The nineties and the early millennium have seen variations in overall growth rates and changes in the incidence of poverty across different states in India—between rural and urban areas as also in the rates of decline in poverty. For example, Orissa, Bihar, West Bengal and Tamil Nadu had more than 50% of their population below the poverty line in 1983. By 1999-2000, while Tamil Nadu and West Bengal has reduced their poverty ratio by nearly half, Orissa and Bihar continued to be two poorest states with poverty ratio of 47% and 43% respectively (*Economic Survey* 2002-03). This definitely implies that a detailed analysis of the interstate variations in poverty and growth parameters is revealing. But we find no evidence that high-growth states have been seen a worsening distribution of income so much so that the benefits of higher per capita income have been wiped away by greater degree of inequality. Of poverty does not mean that there is no space for specific anti-poverty programmes. Specific anti-poverty programmes should go hand in hand with the rise of the growth rate of the economy.

Central Government's recent launch of three types of anti-poverty programmes as rural works, self-employment and food subsidy-programme are very welcome as they are made of with better designs and rationalization. IRDP has been scrapped, along with five other small self-employment programmes, all of which were replaced in 1999 by a single programme—the Swarnajayanti Gram Swarozgar Yojana (SGSY). Among rural works programmes, the two main schemes—the EAS and the JGSY have been renamed the Sampoorna Grammen, Rozgar Yojana (SGRY) to provide additional wage employment, food security, creation of durable commodity, social and economic assets and infrastructure development. While these reforms are very welcome, so far the rationalization and better targeting are concerned, there is still many miles to go in so far as the institutional and governance problems remain virtually unresolved. It is an irony that only one per cent of GDP is spent over these programmes.

V. CONCLUDING OBSERVATIONS

We can readily infer from the above discussion that growth as well as poverty eradication programmes are means by which the extent of poverty can be minimised to a sizeable amount. The most important way for economic growth to help the poor is by expanding their opportunities for productive and gainful employment. Just as growth can enhance redistribution, there are many redistributive projects which, by relieving the severe impediments faced by the poor and improving their lot, can help the economic growth in the process. The Government's measure should take into account the fact that the real dimension in terms of how exactly poor they are. Finally, institutional and governance structure should be better suited in poverty eradication devices, in the process if we rely more on local self-governing institutions and community involvement to improve the material conditions and the autonomy of the poor.

REFERENCES

Datt, G. and M. Ravallion (1997): Macroeconomic Crises and Poverty Monitoring: A Case Study for India, *Review of Development Economics*, Vol. I, No. 2, pp. 135-52.

Dubey, A. and S. Gangopadhyay (1998): Counting the poor, *Sarvekshna Analytical Report*, No. 1, Dept. of Statistics, Ministry for Planning.

Foster, J., Green, J. and Thorbecke, E. (1984): 'A' Class of Decomposable Poverty Measures', *Econometrica*, 52

Tendulkar, S.D. (1998): Indian Economic Policy Reforms and Poverty: An Assessment in I. Ahluwalia and I.M.D. Little, India's Economic Reforms and Development, OUP.

SECTION V

POVERTY AND ECONOMIC REFORMS

17

Plan Strategy, Economic Reforms and Eradication of Poverty

ARUN PRABHA CHOWDHURY

This paper endeavours to study the concept and extent of poverty, planned strategy for poverty eradication and impact of economic reforms on poverty. This paper brings out that since 52 years of planning and 12 years of economic reforms, the situation of poverty especially rural poverty is till grim in the country. So there is a need to formulate the pro-poor policies so that poor could get the actual benefits. The paper has been divided into five parts. Part I discusses the concept of poverty, Part II deals with efforts made under five year plans for poverty eradication, Part III discusses estimates of poverty by planning commission, Part IV deals with the impact of economic reforms on poverty and suggests some measures for poverty eradication, and Part V gives concluding remarks.

I. CONCEPT OF POVERTY

Poverty is a social phenomena in which a section of the society is unable to fulfil even its basic necessities of life. This inability is generally expressed in terms of a level of expenditure that is considered necessary to satisfy those minimum needs: those who are not able to attain that level of income or expenditure are counted as poor while others are regarded as non-poor. When a substantial segment of a society is deprived of the minimum level of living and continues at a bare subsistence level, that society is said to be plagued with mass poverty.

Poverty has been defined on the basis of minimum or good life obtained in the society. All the definitions of poverty approach to the average level of living in a society and reflect the existence of inequalities in a society. In India, the definition of poverty emphasise minimum level of living, rather than a reasonable level of living.

It means that for some decades it would not be possible to provide the masses even a minimum quantum of basic needs and therefore, to talk about a reasonable level of living or good life may appear to be wishful thinking at the present stage. Political considerations also enter the definitions of poverty because programmes of alleviating poverty may become prohibitive as the vision of a good life widens. The upshot of the entire argument is that the absolute standard of poverty expressed in terms of minimum requirements of cereals, pulses, milk, vegetables, butter, clothing or calorie intake is conditioned by the relative levels of living prevalent in the country. The deprivation of a significant section of the society of minimum basic needs in the face of a luxurious life for the elite class, makes poverty more glaring. Dandekar and Rath (1971) have defined poverty as "an inadequate level of employment . . . in terms of its capacity to provide minimum living to the population."

There are two broad concepts of poverty: The absolute and the relative. In the absolute concept, minimum physical quantities of cereals, pulses, milk, butter, etc. are determined for a subsistence level and then the price quotations convert physical quantities into monetary terms. Aggregating all the quantities, a figure expressing per capita consumer expenditure is determined. The population, where level of income-(expenditure) is below the figure, is considered to be below the poverty line. On the other hand, relative poverty is measured in terms of inequality in the distribution of income. In other words, relative poverly arises entirety as a consequence of an unequal distribution of income irrespective of what the income level or the corresponding state of deprivation of the people at the bottom end of the income scale might be. Absolute poverty expresses a collective view on deprivation in its somewhat physical manifestations. Thus any measure of relative poverty is, therefore, inextricably embedded in the measure of inequality, whereas a measure of absolute poverty primarily depends on an exogenously determined standard or poverty line, which represents a socially acceptable minimum level of living.

II. POVERTY ERADICATION UNDER PLANS

First Five Year Plan 1951-60 began with the objective to initiate a process of all round balanced development which would ensure a rising national income and a steady improvement in living standard over a period. By the end of the plan period, per capita income recorded an increase of 10.5 per cent and the per capita consumption level had increased by 8 per cent.

The objective of the Second Five Year Plan (1956-61) was to achieve 'Socialist Pattern of Society.[1] This means that the basic criterion for determining the lines of advance must not be private profit but social gain. During the Third Five Year Plan, the basic objective was to provide, the masses, equal opportunities for gainful employment. The major focus of the Fourth Plan (1969-1974) was on the attainment of economic self-reliance with adequate growth rate and the acceleration of the progress towards a socialist society. The plan aimed at ensuring better standard of living for the people by enlarging the income, supplies of food articles, agricultural raw materials, agriculture production, reducing the growth rate of population and the development of human resources by providing substantial additional facilities in the social service sector, specially for rural areas.

The principle objectives of Fifth Five Year Plan (1974-79) was the development of different small scale industries, to facilitate the attainment of some of the major tasks for the removal of poverty and inequality, in consumption standards of the people concentrated in rural and backward areas through the creation of large scale opportunities for productive employment and improvement of their skills to increase their level of earnings.

There were two Sixth Plans. First was Janta Party Plan (1978-83) which openly said that Nehru Model of growth is responsible of growing unemployment, in equalities in income and wealth and concentration of Economic power in few hands. The focus of Janta Sixth Plan was enlargement of employment potential in agriculture and allied activities, encouragement to household and small industries, producing consumer goods for mass consumption to raise the income of the lowest income classes through a minimum needs programme. When the new Sixth Plan (1980-85) was introduced by the Congress, the planners rejected the Janta approach and brought back Nehru Model of Growth by aiming at a direct attack on the problem of poverty by creating conditions of an expanding economy.

The Seventh Plan (1985-90) sought to emphasise policies and programmes which could accelerate the growth in food grains production, increase employment opportunities and raise productivity.

During the Eighth Plan (1992-97), there were a series of changes and reforms which were reflected in the polices adopted to accelerate economic growth and improve the quality of life of the common man.

The Ninth Plan (1997-2002) laid special emphasis on seven basic minimum services viz. safe drinking water, universal primary education, nutrition to school and preschool children, shelter for poor, road connectivity for all villages and habitations and the public distribution system. The Ninth Plan covered four important dimensions of the state policy viz. quality of life, generation of productive employment, regional balance and self-reliance. The focus of the Ninth Plan was on 'Growth with Social Justice and Equality'.

Approach paper to the Tenth Five Year Plan (2002-07), suggested that during the 10th plan—

- SGSY should be transferred into a micro-finance programme to be run by the banks and other financial institutions with no subsidy.
- Funds to gram sabhas should be extended only when the people

contribute, either in cash or in kind, 15% in normal blocks and 5% in tribal poor blocks.

- There should be a single wage employment programme to be run only in areas of distress. The focus should be on undertaking productive works and their maintenance, such as rural roads, watershed development, rejuvenation of tank, afforestation, irrigation and drainage. The payment of wages should be mainly in the form of food grains with some cash component.
- Grassroots women's groups should be empowered and encouraged to implement selected poverty alleviation schemes, particularly food for work scheme in areas affected by natural disasters.
- Special efforts should be made to strengthen the economy of marginal and small farmers, forest produce gatherers, artisans, unskilled workers, etc. The poor should not merely benefit from growth generated elsewhere, they should also contribute to growth.
- Special efforts must be made to encourage development of tiny and village industries suited to rural areas to provide non-form employment.

III. ESTIMATES OF POVERTY IN INDIA BY PLANNING COMMISSION

Poverty has been an important issue in India since independence. The Planning Commission has been estimating the incidence of poverty at the national and the state level using the methodology contained in the report of Expert Groups on Estimation of Proportion and Number of Poor (Lakdawala Committee) and applying it to consumption data from the large sample surveys on consumer expenditure conducted by the National Sample Survey Organisation (NSSO) at an interval of approximately Five Years.

The latest large sample survey data on consumer expenditure are for the 55th Round covering the period of July 1999-June 2000. In the early surveys, the NSSO estimated monthly consumption expenditure on the basis of responses using a 30 days recall period for all food and non-food items. In the 55th round, consumption expenditure on clothing, footwear, medical, education and durable goods were collected using a 365 days recall period. For non-food items the 30 days recall period was used and the data on food consumption expenditure were collected using two reference periods of last 30 days and last 7 days from the same households. Poverty at the national level is estimated as the weighted average of state-wise poverty levels. Table 1 shows the poverty ratios estimated for the period of 30 days recall period for 1973-74 to 1999-2000 along with the poverty projection for 2007.

Table 1 shows that the combined poverty ratio has declined from 54.9 per cent in 1973-74 to 36.0 per cent in 1993-94. The poverty ratio declined by nearly 10 percentage points in the 5 years period between 1993-94 to reach 26.1 per cent in 1999-00. While the proportion of poor in the rural areas declined from 56.4 per cent in 1973-74 to 27.1 per cent in 1999-00, the decline in urban areas

TABLE 1

Estimates of Incidence of Poverty

Year	*Poverty Ratio (%)*			*Number of Poor (million)*		
	Rural	*Urban*	*Combined*	*Rural*	*Urban*	*Combined*
1973-74	56.4	49.0	59.9	261.3	60.0	321.3
1977-78	53.1	45.2	51.3	264-3	64.6	338.9
1983	45.7	40.8	44.5	252.0	70.9	322.9
1987-88	39.1	38.2	38.9	231.9	75.2	307.1
1993-94	37.3	32.4	36.0	244.0	76.3	320.3
1999-00	27.1	23.6	26.1	193.2	67.1	260.3
2007 (Projections)	21.1	15.1	19.3	170.5	49.6	220.1

Source: Tenth Five Year Plan, Vol. 1, Planning Commission.

Estimates of Incidence of Poverty

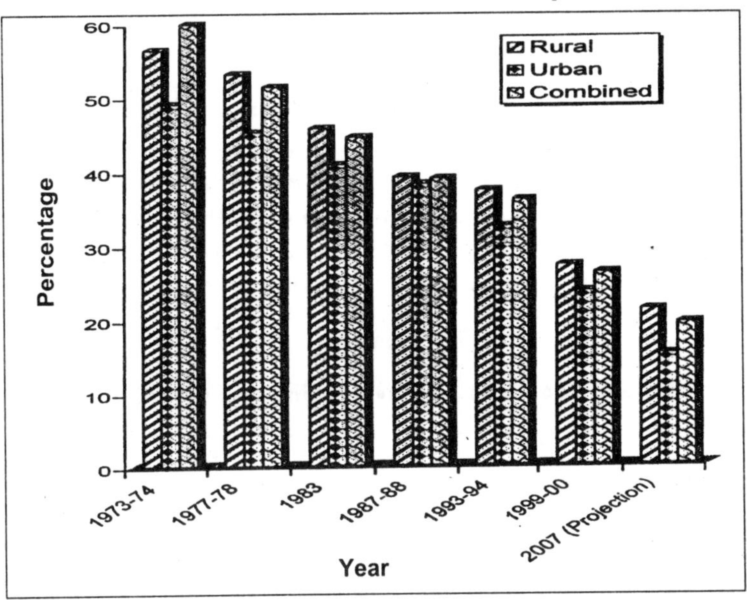

has been from 49 per cent to 23.6 per cent during this period. In absolute terms, the number of poor declined to 260 million in 1999-00 with about 75 per cent of these being in the rural areas. The poverty reduction target set by the Planning Commission for the Tenth Five Year Plan aims at achieving a poverty ratio of 19.3 per cent for the country as a whole by 2007, 21.1 per cent for the rural and 15.1 per cent for the urban areas.

Although various studies have been conducted for poverty estimation, the present paper has taken the poverty estimation by Planning Commission.

IV. ECONOMIC REFORMS AND POVERTY

Initially Economic Reforms were introduced by Mr. Rajiv Gandhi in 1985 with the aim of improvement in productivity, Absorption of modern technology and full utilization of capacity. In this regime private sector has to play grater roll. Since then the reform process continues. In 1991, a number of stabilization measures were adopted. Now the phase of second generation reforms has also been started. Elaborating on the philosophy of Second Generation Reforms, the then Finanee Minister Mr. Yashwant Sinha in his budget speech 2000-01 stated, "Growth is not just an end in itself. It is the critical vehicle for increasing employment and raising the living standards of our people, especially of the poorest. Sustained broad-based growth, combined with all our programmes for accelerating rural development, building roads, promoting housing, boosting knowledge-based industries and enhancing the quality of human resources, will impart a strong impetus to employment expansion. There can be no better cure for poverty than this in our country."

In this section of the paper, efforts have been made to analyse the impact of economic reforms on poverty on the basis of GDP growth, employment growth and reduction of population living below poverty line.

GDP Growth and Reduction of Poverty during Reform

Planners assumed that a fast rate of growth of national income will by itself create more employment and produce higher income for the poor. But the theory of trickle down effect did not work and the benefits of high GDP growth could not reach to the poor. The Table 2 gives a glance of GDP growth and population below poverty line from 1983 to 1997.

TABLE 2

Percentage of People Below Poverty Line and GDP Growth Rate

Year	*NSS Round*	*GDP Growth rate at Factor cost (1993-94 Prices)*	*Percentage*			*Absolute Numbers (million)*
			Rural	*Urban*	*Combined*	
1983-84	(38th) LS	7.5	45.65	40.79	44.48	322.8
1987-88	(48th) LS	3.4	39.09	38.20	38.86	304.9
1989-90	(45th) TS	10.7	33.70	36.00	34.28	276.0
1990-91	(46th) TS	5.2	35.04	35.29	35.11	291.0
1992-93	(48th) TS	4.5	41.70	37.80	40.70	348.0
1993-94	(50th) LS	6.0	37.27	32.36	35.07	320.5
1994-95	(51st) TS	7.0	38.03	34.24	36.48	328.0
1995-96	(52nd) TS	7.3	38.29	30.05	36.08	328.0
1996-97	(53rd) TS	7.2	38.46	33.97	37.23	348.8

LS = Large sample, TS = Thin Sample.

Source: Compiled from Household Consumption Survey, NSSO, GOI and *Economic Survey*, 2001-02.

Percentage of People Below Poverty Line and GDP Growth Rate

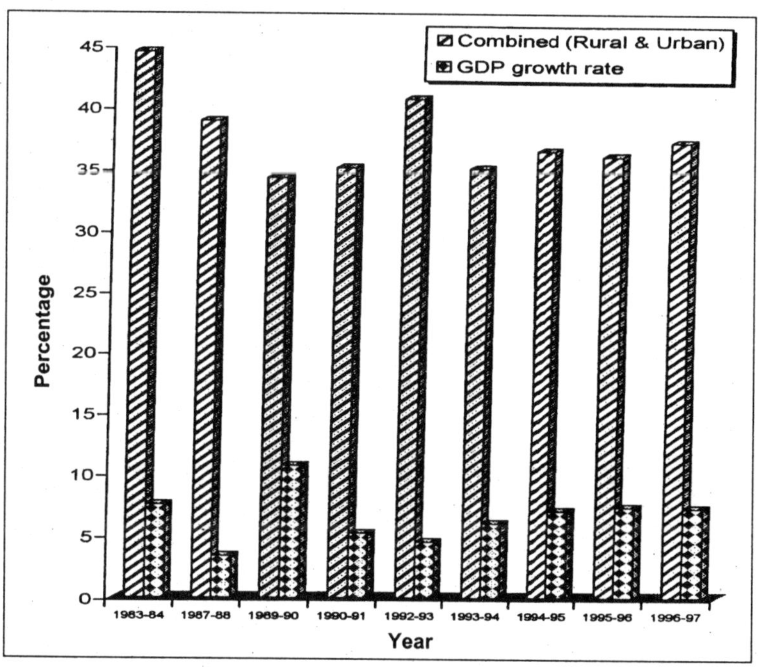

Table 2 shows that economic reforms have been able to promote relatively higher growth during 1993-94 to 1996-97, i.e. growth rate averaged to more than 7 per cent per annum. During the same period the poverty percentage increased from 35.07 per cent to 37.23 per cent in aggregate. In this period, GDP growth rate increased to around 6.9 per cent per annum, the highest ever witnessed consecutively for four years in India. Thus during 1993-94 to 1996-97, inverse relationship has been observed between poverty reduction and GDP growth.

Dr. S.P. Gupta, member Planning Commission, in his lecture on "Trickle-down Theory Revisited: The Role of Employment and Poverty" brought out the fact that "In India the poverty reduction over 1983 to 1990-91 was around 3.1 per cent per annum, but it reversed to 1 per cent in the 1990s, i.e. between 1990-91 to 1997. In contrast to this, the GDP growth in India between 1983 to 1990-91 was around 5.6 per cent and between 1990-91 and 1997, this is expected to go beyond 5.7 per cent".

Dr. Gaurav Datt, of World Bank, has compared the decline in head-count index, poverty gap index and squared poverty gap index for rural and urban India in the pre-reform and post-reform period. In his study entitled "Has Poverty Declined Since Economic Reforms." Dr. Gaurav Datt has identified stagnation in rural growth as a basic cause of showdown in poverty reduction. Table 3 gives poverty profile of India from 1973-97 workout by Gaurav Dutt.

TABLE 3

Poverty in India, 1973-97

NSS Round	*Survey Period*	*Head-count Index*		*Poverty Gap Index*		*Squared Poverty-Gap Index*	
		Rural	*Urban*	*Rural*	*Urban*	*Rural*	*Urban*
Pre-reform							
28	Oct. 73–June 74	52.72	47.96	17.175	13.602	7.128	5.219
32	July 77–June 78	50.60	40.50	15.025	11.687	6.057	4.526
38	June 83–Dec. 83	45.31	35.65	12.649	9.517	4.841	3.557
42	July 86–June 87	38.81	34.29	10.013	9.100	3.700	3.395
43	July 87–June 88	39.23	36.20	9.275	9.121	2.982	3;056
44	July 88–June 89	39.06	36.60	9.504	9.537	3.291	3.293
45	July 89–June 90	34.30	33.40	7.799	8.505	2.575	3.038
46	July 90–June 91	36.43	32.76	8.644	8.509	2.926	3.121
	July 89–June 91	35.37	33.08	8.222	8.507	2.751	3.080
Post-reform							
47	July 91–Dec. 91	37.42	33.23	8.288	8.244	2.680	2.902
48	Jan. 92–Dec. 92	43.47	33.73	10.881	8.824	3.810	3.191
50	July 93–June 94	36.66	30.51	8.387	7.405	2.792	2.417
51	July 94–June 95	41.02	33.50	9.285	8.382	2.995	2.799
52	July 95–June 96	37.15	28.04	8.098	6.781	2.527	2.222
53	Jan. 97–Dec. 97	35.78	29.99	8.321	7.762	2.757	2.725
	July 95–Dec. 97	36.47	29.02	8.205	7.273	2.642	2.474

Source: Gaurav Datt, Has Poverty Declined since Economic Reforms?, *Economic and Political Weekly*, December, 11-17, 1999.

Table 3 shows that there was a marked decline in both rural and urban poverty between 1973-74 and 1986-87. For the rural sector, for the period 1973-74 and 1990-91, head-count index of poverty declined at the annual rate of 2.7 per cent, but the rate of decline in post-reform period is not significantly different from zero. For the urban sector, the annual rate of decline in head-count ratio of poverty remained 2.2 per cent in pre and post-reform period. There is continuous reduction in poverty in urban areas in the process of growth but rural poverty reduction was choked-off by lack of rural growth.

GDP Growth, Employment Growth and Reduction in Poverty during Reforms

Poverty is directly liked with unemployment or underemployment so impact of economic reforms on employment has also been observed to know its linkage with poverty. Table 4 gives employment trends.

TABLE 4

Trends of Employment, 1983-97

Year	*Organised sector*	*Unorganised sector*	*Total*
1983	240.1	2,785.9	3,026.0
1990-91	270.6	3,297.0	3,567.6
1997-98	282.5	3,546.0	3,828.5
	Annual Growth of Employment (%)		
1983 to 1990-91	1.73	2.41	2.39
1990-91 to 1997-98	0.6	1.1	1.0

Source: Computed from NSSO data.

Table 4 reveals that total employment increased from 3026 lakhs in 1983 to about 3568 lakhs in 1990-91 and then improved to about 3829 lakhs in 1997-98. The rate of growth of employment was 2.39 per cent per annum during 1983 and 1990-91 which was just equal to the rate of growth of labour force during this period. But the reform period (1990/91 to 1997/98) reveals that the overall growth rate of employment was only 1.0 per cent. The growth rate of employment in organised sector also decelerated to 0.60 per cent during 1990-91 to 1997-98 as against 1.73 per cent per annum in pre-reform period of 1983 to 1990-91. There was also a substantial slow down in the employment growth rate of the unorganised sector to merely 1.1 per cent during 1990-91 to 1997-98 as against employment growth rate of 2.41 per cent during 1983 to 1990-91. This shows that the tricle down effects of the growth process did not benefit the poor. Obviously, the pattern of growth followed after 1991 has reduced employment growth rate and increased the proportion of people below the poverty line. World Development Report (2000-01) has quantified that in India, in 1997 (using $ (dollar) 1 per day as the measure of International poverty line), 44.2 per cent of population was living below the poverty line. The World Development Report has estimated that 1199 million people were living in poverty in the world in 1997, the share of India in the world's total poor worked out to be 34.95 per cent.

The basic factor responsible for the slowdown in poverty reduction is the slow and fluctuating growth rate of agriculture (3%) inspite of around 7 per cent growth in industry and 6 per cent growth of GDP in 1990s. This low growth in agriculture sector has stagnated household consumption expenditure by reducing job opportunities.

Following measures can help in removal of poverty:

- Asset base of rural poor should be increased.
- Capabilities of the poor should be enhanced by investing in their health and education. Social infrastructure should be developed for educating and keeping poor healthy and disease free.
- Measures should be taken to accelerate growth in agriculture and

non-farm activities, increase employment opportunities in rural areas by building up rural infrastructure.

- Inflation must be checked for removal of poverty as it accentuates inequalities and wipeout the incomes of the poor classes.
- Poverty eradication programmes should be administered more efficiently and transparency should be maintained.
- To encourage the production of items of mass consumption, especially wage goods, in small scale and cottage industries so the employment potential of the economy is enlarged.

V. CONCLUSION

It may be concluded that Nine Five Year Plans and around 12 years of economic reforms failed to eliminate poverty inspite of high growth of GDP because the philosophy of automatic transmission of the benefits arising from an increase in production, to the bulk of small farmers, landless labourers or factory workers was a failure. Martin Ravillion, making a survey of growth process after reforms, concludes: "The indications that the pace of poverty reduction in India has not picked up in the 1990s make it even more compelling that efforts be made now to assure that conditions are in place for more pro-poor growth in future".

So removal of poverty requires concentration on agriculture, agro-based industries, small scale and rural industries, building up of rural infrastructure, health and education of the poor and public distribution system. This will increase efficiency and skill of the poor along with the job potentials and enable them to cross poverty line.

REFERENCES

1. Dandekar, V.M. and Nilkantha Rath: "Poverty in India", Indian School of Political Economy, Bombay, 1971.
2. Gupta, S.P. (1999), "Trickle-down Theory Revisited: The Role of Employment and Poverty", V.B. Singh Memorial Lecture at the 41st Annual Conference of Indian Society of Labour Economics, Nov. 18-20, 1999.
3. Datt, Gaurav (1999), "Has Poverty Declined Since Economic Reforms?", *EPW*, Dec. 11-17, 1999.
4. Ravillion Martin (2000), "What is Needed for a Pro-poor Growth Process in India?" *EPW*, March 25-31, 2002.
5. Planning Commission (1998), Ninth Five Year Plan (1997-2002), Vols. I, II.
6. *Economic Survey*, 2003, GOI.
7. Datt, Ruddar (2000), "Economic Reforms in India—An Appraisal and Policy Directions for Second Generation Reforms."
8. World Development Report (2000-01).
9. Datt, Ruddar: "New Economic Reforms: Need for some Rethinking", *The Indian Economic Journal*, Vol. 42, No. 3, Jan.-March 1999.
10. Ahluwalia, Montek: "Rural Poverty and Agricultural Performance in India", *The Journal of Development Studies* (1977).
11. Planning Commission: "Mid-Term Appraisal of Ninth Five Year Plan (1997-2002).
12. Planning Commission: "Approach Paper to the Tenth Five Year Plan, Sept. 2001.

18

Poverty, Unemployment and Economic Reforms

R. ARUNACHALAM

Poverty and unemployment continue to be major zero sum factors *inter alia* which perpetuate underdevelopment in India. There is a paradigm shift from Macro-level Planning coupled with greater interventionist policy of the Government to that of Liberalization, Structural Adjustment Programmes (SAP), Globalization and Marketization. The Strategy of Import-substitution-led industrialization is rather replaced by structural adjustment programmes.

The paradigm shift is not merely at the level of policy instruments, but probably at the basic economic ideology that is, from less of mixed economy coupled with egalitarian socialistic pattern of society to that of rather capitalist dictated Bretton Woods system in the name of privatization, marketization and globalization. Notwithstanding the shift in policy instruments, the goal remains the same namely, eradication of poverty and bringing down inequalities of income and wealth. A decade of economic reform measures is complete and the second generation of economic reform measures continue. It is at this back drop, this paper attempts to marvel the efficacy of the new economic policy in reducing poverty and unemployment and the issues connected to the same.

CONCEPT OF POVERTY

Poverty of an individual or household is a situation where the economic unit in question is unable to meet the minimum needs of survival. It can be understood as absolute or relative poverty. In the U.S. for instance, the poverty line was derived by ascertaining the amount of money needed to purchase a nutritionally adequate consistent with the food preferences of the poorest groups in the population and multiplying the same by a factor three, since the poor spend nearly one-third on their food. (Garys, Fields, 1983).[1] In India, the Planning Commission prescribed Rs. 20 per capita p.m. (1960-61 = 100) as the nutritionally minimum food standard. As on 1993-94 the same is enhanced to Rs. 211.30 per capita p.m. in rural areas and Rs. 274.88 per capita p.m. in urban India. As on 1999-2000, it is further revised to Rs. 335.46 in rural India and Rs. 451.19 in urban India.[2] (NSS 50th and Round of 1993-94 and 99-2000 respectively). Since the early 1960s upto 2001-02, India has abundant estimates on poverty, though there are differences in such estimates, which happen to be the outcome of empirical studies by individual researchers and those of Government estimates.

Though poverty is a widespread phenomenon of LDCs as well as developed nations, its nature and magnitude are not the same. For instance, by U.S. standards, virtually the entire population of some of the nations would be classified as poor. By Indian Standards virtually no one in the U.S. would qualify as absolutely poor.[3] This apart, there is lot of differences within absolute poverty measures estimated interms of per capita income, per capita expenditure and calorie requirements. The non-income measures evaluated interms of Capability Poverty Measure (CPM) take into account three factors.[4] They are: (a) the percentage of children under five who are under weight, (b) the percentage of births unattended by trained health personnel, and (c) the percentage of women with 15 years and above age who are illiterate.

Sociologists like Jackson treat poverty as a social phenomenon.

PROFILE OF POVERTY IN INDIA[5]

(a) Poor are mostly found in rural areas and urban slums.
(b) Skewness is land distribution account for major cause for rural poverty.
(c) There is greater correlation between age (prime age) and incidence of poverty.
(d) Incidence of Poverty is greater among rural women.
(e) There is also correlation between employment status and poverty, i.e. self-employment category and poverty.
(f) Larger the family size, greater the level of poverty.

METHODS ADOPTED TO REDUCE POVERTY

The earlier policy measures since the time period of Fifth Five Year Plan basically aimed at reduction of poverty by direct action. They are IRDP, RLEGP, TRYSEM, NREP, Jawahar Rozgar Yojana and a host of both urban and rural self-employment schemes. The new policy measures in the name of SAP focus on accelerated economic growth. Herein, the crucial question is what is the correlation between growth rate and poverty?

The study of Ahluwalia (1979)[6] considers income shares of poorest 20%, 40% and 60% (alternatively as dependent variable) and logarithmic GNP, share of urban to rural population, literacy ratio, secondary school enrolment rate, population growth rate and the system of socialist-non-socialist (as dummy variable) as independent variables. The second test of Ahluwalia considers actual income shares of the poorest units. By both tests he found that total income of the poor is positively related to the level of economic development.

The empirical work of Galenson (1977)[7] will reference to selected nations found that there exists negative correlation between growth and rural poverty. This study employed indicators namely per capita food consumption, health and medical care and education and concluded that there is positive correlation between growth rate and living standards of people.

On the other hand, the contemporary work of Griffin[8] (1977) found persistence of poverty, irrespective of growth rate. Thus one finds a contradictory result with regard to the relationship between growth rate and poverty in the contribution of Galenson and Griffin. Another interesting work on these lines by Ahluwalia and Chenery (1974) in the name of Ahluwalia-Chenery Index examined the relationship between growth and distribution. It has brought out the relationship between growth and distribution of 13 LDCs with varying results. Economic growth, as measured, has at best a weak relationship with poverty, as measured (Deaton)[10].

MECHANISM OF REDUCTION OF POVERTY BY SAP

(a) They aim at sustained high growth rate with trickle-down effect.

(b) The Bretton Wood system hopes to reduce the debt burden of LDCs.

(c) The SAP also strives to achieve domestic balance as well as external balance, by finding solution to Bop crises.

(d) In the domestic economy, aggregate demand for goods and services should be increased through market prices, attain stability and ultimately alleviate poverty. On the other hand, greater export promotion measures in the long run should find solutions to deficit in Bop.

(e) By focusing on remoulding of development process the IBRD and IMF expect the market to play a greater role in economic activities than the Government. This would enhance competitiveness and productivity.

IMPLICATION FOR GROWTH AND POVERTY

(i) If the programmes of IMF, IBRD are not followed by India, it has to find its own solution to problem of debt.

(ii) There is apprehension in some quarts that these policies are followed vigorously, they may lead to reinforced private ownership in both capital and leading to growth inequality.

(iii) To make the SAP more effective, good governance of the state is a prerequisite.

(iv) The UBDP focuses on development of Human capital by promoting education, health and food-security.

(v) The benefits of SAP are found to go to export crop growers at the expense of food crops.

POVERTY TREND IN INDIA DURING REFORM PERIOD

As per the 55th Round of NSS on Employment and Unemployment, the direction of change in poverty is mixed.[11] The main findings are:

(1) At the National level, in 8 out of 15 states poverty pre valence ratio has declined over 1990s.

(2) In respect of rural areas, in 6 states namely Assam, M.P., Karnataka, Orissa, Tamil Nadu and West Bengal, Poverty Prevalence Ratio is higher in 1999-2000 than in 1993-94.

(3) In another 7 states (including Bihar, Haryana, Punjab and U.P.) PPR remained constant. While in UP the PPR increased by 6 per cent during 1990s in Assam and Kerala, it has increased by 13 per cent.

TRENDS IN UNEMPLOYMENT: IMPACT OF NEW POLICIES[12]

(1) The labour market is characterzed by dualism—a market for educated, skilled and trained labour and for those with less skills, less qualification and not trained. These new policies have greater adverse effect on women and self-employment.

(2) Foreign imports have kicked-off growth of small scale units and medium units. A number units in Mumbai, M.P. and other states are closed and rendered lakhs of labour as jobless.

(3) The task force on job opportunities shows absolute decline in the number of employed in agriculture sector between 1993-94 and 1999-2000 at the national level.

(4) Studies also point out the possibility of deleterious effect of competition arising out of these SAP and closure of non-farm enterprises in rural areas.

ASPECTS OF DISTRIBUTION OF WORK FORCE[13]

(a) Between 1961 to 1999-2000, in the total work force, there is 16 per cent decline in the share of agriculture and allied sectors, i.e. shift of labour from rural to urban areas.

(b) Of the 16% decline in labour force of the agriculture sector, 3% has gone to manufacturing sector and another 3% to construction sector. As much as 10% is gone to service sector, where trade, hotels and restaurants account for major share of the new addition of labour force.

(c) However, the decline in female workforce in the agricultural sector is during the above period is much less.

(d) With the clubbing of repair services with the manufacturing sector in line with the current practice in National Accounts, the share of workforce in manufacturing sector has gone up.

(e) The textile sector which is a sub-sector of manufacturing sector has suffered loss of work force in absolute terms during this period.

(f) The addition of work force to construction industry highlight another aspect namely; the elasticity which is a positive development as it is considered as a low productivity sector.

Occupational distribution of workforce between 1993-94 and 1999-2000 reveals that India remains a land of farmers, fishermen, hunters and loggers (73%). Professional, technical workers and administrative staff account for 7 per cent of workforce and the remaining workforce of around 20% is accounted by production and production process workers.

At the National level, employment-friendly claims of the 1991-92 economic reforms are no-where in the sight. It is undoubtedly a period of sufferings of the common people.

The state-wise situation of employment growth ratio is a mixture of upswings and downswings. Non-farm sector employment has also declined. Informal sector employment expands during 1990s. Overall growth rate of employment has declined to 1.02 per cent during post-reform period from 2.06 per cent per annum during the pre-reform period.

CHALLENGES AHEAD

(1) Major problems of implementation of poverty and employment programmes are deficiencies in identification of beneficiaries and leakage of benefits. This is due to lack of political will, administrative ineptitude and indifference of beneficiaries themselves.

(2) How will the policy-makers combine the State with market forces to stimulate economic growth?

(3) The composition of growth is important as the growth rate in agriculture and allied sectors should be sustained to reduce poverty and unemployment in rural areas.

(4) How will the new policy strengthen the linkages between agriculture and industry and in turn to service sector for sustained higher growth rate?

(5) How will we manage the formation of a class of 'new poor', emanating from the implementation of liberalization and globalization?

NOTES AND REFERENCES

1. Fields, Garry, S. (1983), Poverty, Inequality and Development, Cambridge University Press, London, p. 138.
2. NSS 50th Round and WSS 55th Round as quoted in Sundaram, K., Employment and Poverty in 1990s (2001), *Economic and Political Weekly,* Vol. No. XXXVI, 32, Aug. 11-17, p. 3047.
3. Fields, Garry, S. *op. cit.,* p. 138.
4. UNDP Human Development Report (1996), NCAER (1996) as cited in Kirit S. Parikh, India's Development Report (1997), Oxford University, Pron, p. 71.
5. Fields, Garry, S. *op. cit.,* p. 160. Based on empirical data poverty profiles of six less-developed countries have been presented.
6. Ahluwalia, Montek Singh (1976 b: table 6) as cited fields, Garry, S., *op. cit.,* 165.
7. Galenson, N. (1977), Economic Growth, Income and Employment, paper presented at the conference on Poverty and Development in Latin America, Yale University.
8. Griffin, K. (1977), Increasing Poverty and Changing Ideas about Developing Strategies, paper presented at the Conference on Distribution, Poverty and Development, Bogota.
9. Ahluwalia, Montek and Holis Chenery (1974), The Economic Frame work, in Holis B. Chenery *et. al.* (ed.), Redistribution with Growth, Chap. 2, Oxford University, New York.
10. Angus Deaton (2001), The World Bank Research Observer, Oxford University Press, p. 125.
11. NSS 55th Round, Sundaram, K. *op. cit.,* p. 3048.
12. *Ibid.,* pp. 3046-47.
13. *Ibid.,* pp. 3042-46. Also refer to Chaha, G.K. and Sahu, P.P., Post-Reform Setbacks in Rural Employment, *Economic and Political Weekly,* Vol. XXXVII, No. 21. May 25-31, 2002, pp. 1998-2035.

19

Impact of Globalization on Poverty

PUSPA TARAFDAR

The focus of this paper is on the impact of globalization on developing countries and especially on the poor people. About one-fifth of the world's population live on less than $ 1 per day, and that is unacceptable in a world of such plenty. Whether economic globalization reduces poverty and how it can be achieved more effectively, these are the main issues examined in the paper.

Globalization in its economic aspect refers to the increasing integration of economies around the world, particularly through trade and financial flows. The term sometimes also refer to the movement of people (labour) and knowledge (technology) across international borders.

SECTION 1

Globalization generally reduces poverty because more integrated economies tend to grow faster and this growth is usually widely defused. For the first time, the low-income countries have been able to harness the potential of their abundant labour to break into global markets for manufactured goods and services. Manufactures rose from less than a quarter of developing country exports in 1980 to more than 80 per cent by 1998. Countries, that strongly increased their participation in global trade and investment include China, Brazil, Hungary, India and Mexico. Some 24 developing countries with 3 billion people have doubled their ratio of trade to income over the past two decades. The more globalized countries have increased their per capita growth rate from 3 per cent in 1970s to 4 per cent in 1980s and 5 per cent in 1990s. Their growth rate now substantially exceed those of the rich countries. While new globalizers are beginning to catch up, much of the rest of the developing world with about 2 billion people is becoming marginalized. Their aggregate growth rate was actually negative in the 1990s.

FIGURE 1

Divergent Paths of Developing Countries in the 1990s GDP per capita Growth Rate (per cent)

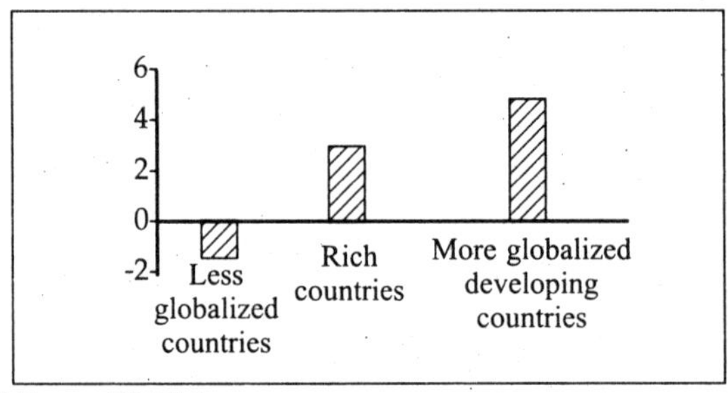

Source: Dollar and Kraay (2001b).

The potential for global integration to reduce poverty is well illustrated by the cases of India, Uganda and Vietnam. As Vietnam has integrated it has had a large increase in per capita income and no significant change in inequality. Thus, the income of the poor has risen dramatically and the level of absolute poverty has been cut in 10 years.

The potential for global integration to reduce poverty is well illustrated by the cases of India, Uganda and Vietnam. As Vietnam has integrated it has had a large increase in per capita income and no significant change in

FIGURE 2

Poverty Reduction in Uganda, India, Vietnam, and China Closely Related to Growth

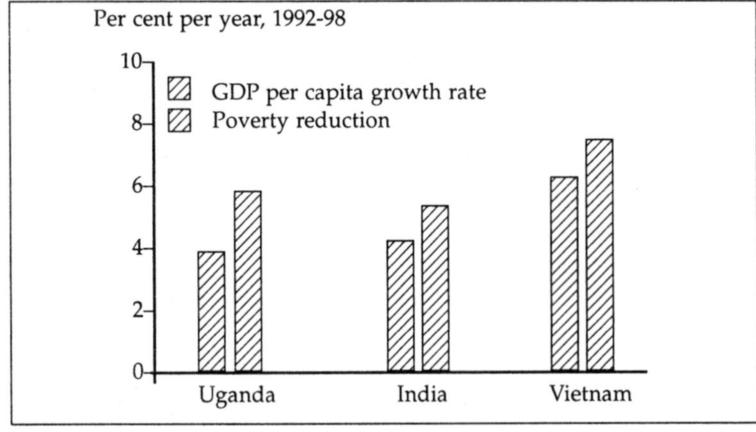

Note: India poverty reduction figure is for 1993-99.
Source: World Bank (2001 d): Dollar (2001).

inequality. Thus, the income of the poor has risen dramatically and the level of absolute poverty has been cut in 10 years.

India and Uganda also had absolute poverty reduction as they integrated with the global economy. While some aspects of the data are controversial, the evidence for substantial reduction in poverty in India in the 1990s is strong. In Uganda poverty fell by about 40 per cent during the 1990s and school enrolments doubled. Globalization clearly can be a powerful force for poverty reduction.

Since 1980 the overall number of the poor people has fallen by an estimated 200 billion. It is falling rapidly in the new globalizers and rising in the rest of the developing world. Non-income dimension of poverty are also diverging. Life expectancy and schooling are rising in the new globalizers. They are falling in parts of Africa and Former Soviet Union.

In a new book Imagine there's no country, Surjit Bhalla claims that by 2000 we have already met the Millennium Development goal set out by World Bank of having the 1990 incidence of poverty 15 years ahead of time. By Bhalla's assessment economic growth has been far more pro-poor than the number given by the World Bank. Imagine concludes that poverty in the world has fallen dramatically over the last 20 years due in large part to economic growth.

FIGURE 3

World Poverty, 1820-1998
People Living on less than $1 per day (million)

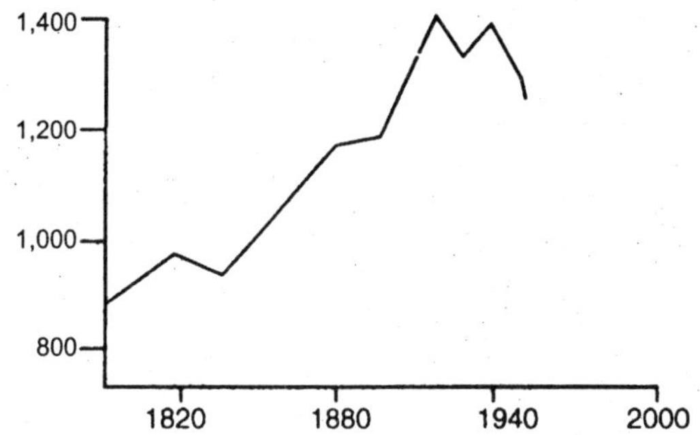

Source: Bourguignon and Morrisson (2001): Chen and Ravallion (2001).

Imagine reports that poverty rate has virtually halved over the decade, implying that Millennium Development Goal of having the 1990 '$ 1 day' poverty rate by 2015 has already been achieved. By contrast, the World Bank's estimates indicate a far more modest drop in poverty incidence.

The most striking difference in the regional composition is for south Asia which Imagine reports to have a poverty rate well below the average while World Bank finds a above average poverty. Another notable difference is for Sub-Saharan Africa (SSA). Imagine's poverty count is substantially higher than the Bank's for this region. Imagine reports a small drop in the poverty rate for Sub-Saharan Africa, while Bank estimates a rise over this period. Imagine reports a 80 per cent drop in the poverty rate for east Asia, as compared to a drop of almost 50 per cent reported by the Bank.

TABLE 1

Alternative Estimates of Poverty Incidence by Region

	Imagine		*World Bank*	
	1990	*2000*	*1987*	*1998*
East Asia	31.3	6.0	26.6	14.7
South Asia	18.5	7.8	44.9	40.0
Sub-Saharan Africa	55.3	54.8	46.6	48.1
Middle East and North Africa	5.2	7.8	4.3	2.1
Latin America	5.3	5.2	15.3	12.1
East Europe	0.0	0.0	0.2	3.8
Developing World	25.4	13.1	28.3	23.5

Note : PPP $ 1.80 per day for Imagine; 1.08 for World Bank.
Sources: Bhalla (2002), Chen and Ravallion (2001) as represented in Martin Ravallion, *Economic and Political Weekly*, November 16, 2003.

Almost all those who know the literature will not disagree with Bhalla's conclusion that economic growth reduced absolute poverty. Indeed, we have been pretty confident of this for the last 10 years based on available empirical evidence.

CROSS COUNTRY VARIATIONS IN INCOME INEQUALITY

Recent studies of the World Bank Development Report (1999-2000) contains by for the best data on the extent of income inequality (Gini ratios) covering around 50 economies. This paper touches on the trend of income inequality in Asia.

For few countries in South Asia have data on income distribution. The consumption expenditure Ginis in Table 2 does not provide are indication of high levels of inequality, but with poverty levels (that is percentage of people in poverty) in the high 30s or more in most countries, the low expenditure Ginis are merely a reflection of shared poverty. It is also of note that the expenditure Ginis show the considerable income inequality prevailing in these countries.

None of the south Asian economies have had the pervasive land reforms of the type implemented in China or Taiwan. In the South Asian economies in general and India in particular. There are a wide variety of subsidies on fertilizers, food, electricity, road and rail transport and education and health. In addition, trade unions are powerful in the organised sector. Despite subsidies and unionism, the overall impact is negligible and hence inequality must be relatively high and it is unlikely that income inequality will decline significantly in the near future in the absence of rapid economic growth and institutional changes specifically aimed at lowering inequality.

TABLE 2

Gini Ratios for per Capita Expenditure

Bangladesh	1992	28.0
India	1994	29.4
Sri Lanka	1990	30.1
Pakistan	1995	31.2
Nepal	1995-96	36.7

Source: World Development Indicators, 1999.

TABLE 3

Normal Gini Ratios for Five East Asian Economies (Based on per Household Income)

Economy	*Normal Oline*
Hongkong	0.45
Korea	0.40
Malaysia	0.40
Taiwan	0.30
Thailand	0.50

Source: Rao, 2001 as represented in Bhanoji Rao (2003) in *Economic and Political Weekly*, April 26, 2003.

A summary picture of income Ginis in East Asian economies is presented in Table 3. These Ginis have a significant limitation since they are based on income per household and not on per capita household income. Notwithstanding the limitation, it is possible to note that each economy has a "normal" Gini ratio that characterises the income disparities typical of its economic and social structure and institutions (Rao, 2001).

While many developing countries including relatively poor ones in Southern Africa have seen significant increase in the share of manufactures in their export, a large proportion of the population in developing countries is still closely tied to the rural sector and in agriculture. This sector is where the bulk of the poverty is concentrated and can therefore not be ignored if significant inroads are to be made in reducing poverty.

II. POVERTY AND INEQUALITY IN INDIA

Poverty trends in India has been a matter of intense controversy and confusion still remains about the extent to which poverty has declined during the period. The evidence of inequality is discussed in this section when we focus mainly on the period between 1993-94 and 1999-2000. Based on further analysis on National Sample Survey data and related sources, we argue that there has been marked increase in inequality in the nineties in several forms. First, there has been strong divergence of per capita expenditure across states, with the already better-off states (Southern and Western regions) growing more rapidly than the poorer states. Second rural-urban discrepancies of per capita expenditure have risen. Third, inequality has increased within urban areas in most states. The combined effects of these different forms of rising inequality is quite large. In rural areas of some of the poorest states, there has been virtually no increase in per capita expenditure between 1993-94 and 1999-2000. Meanwhile, the urban population of most of the better-off states have enjoyed increases of per capita expenditure of 20 to 30 per cent, with even larger increases for high income groups within these population.

We begin with an examination of household per capita consumption expenditure and the most commonly-used poverty indicator Head-Count Ration (HCR) i.e., the proportion of the population below poverty line.

The latest year for which relatively uncontroversial HCR estimates are available is 1993-94, corresponding to the 50th Round of National Sample Survey, a "Quinquennial round". In contrast to this official counts for the latest quinquennial round (55th round, 1999-2000) suggest considerable poverty decline between 1993-94 and 1999-2000. According to official estimates All India HCR declined from 36 per cent to 26 per cent in this short period.

Table 4 presents official and adjusted estimates of all India Head-count Ratio. The fully adjusted estimates in the last row of each panel show what lower rural poverty estimates and much lower urban poverty estimates for 1999-2000 than even the official estimates. The rural-urban gap based on adjusted estimates is much larger than that based on official estimates.

TABLE 4

All India Head-count Ratio

(per cent)

	1987-88	*1993-94*	*1999-2000*
Rural			
Official estimates	39.4	37.1	26.8
Adjusted estimates			
Step 1: Adjusting for changes in questionnaire design	39.4	37.1	30.0
Step 2: Revising the poverty lines	39.4	33.0	26.3
Urban			
Official estimates	39.1	32.9	24.1
Adjusted estimates			
Step 1: Adjusting for changes in questionnaire design	39.1	32.9	24.7
Step 2: Revising poverty lines	22.5	17.8	12.0

Source: Planning Commission Press Releases (March 4, 1997, Feb. 22, 2001)

State specific 'Head-count' ratios are presented in Table 5. The latter suggest that basic pattern of sustained poverty decline between 1987-88 and 1999-2000 at the all India level applies at the level of individual states. The main exception is Assam where poverty has stagnated in both rural and urban areas. In Orissa, there has been very little poverty decline in the second sub-period with the result that Orissa has the highest level of rural poverty among all Indian states, according to the adjusted 1999-2000 estimates.

The Head-Count Ratio (HCR) has a straight forward interpretation and is very easy to understand. In that sense it has much 'communication' Value. Yet the HCR has serious limitations as poverty index. It ignores the extent to which different households fall short of poverty line. An income transfer from a very poor person to some one who is closer to the poverty line may lead is a decline in the head-count ratio if it lifts the recipient above the poverty line. Similarly, if some poor households get poorer this has no effect on the head-count ratio.

TABLE 5

State Specific Head-Count Ratios

(Per cent)

	Official Mythology			*Adjusted Estimates*		
	1987-88	*1993-94*	*1999-2000*	*1987-88*	*1993-94*	*1999-2000*
1	*2*	*3*	*4*	*5*	*6*	*7*
Rural						
Andhra Pradesh	21.0	15.9	10.5	35.0	29.2	26.2
Assam	39.4	45.2	40.3	36.1	35.4	35.5
Bihar	53.9	58.0	44.0	54.6	48.6	41.1
Gujarat	28.6	22.0	12.4	39.4	32.5	20.0
Haryana	15.4	28.3	7.4	13.6	17.0	5.7
Himachal Pradesh	16.7	30.4	7.5	13.3	17.1	9.8
Jammu & Kashmir	25.9	30.4	4.7	15.3	10.1	6.1
Karnataka	32.6	30.1	16.8	40.8	37.9	30.7
Kerala	29.6	25.4	9.4	23.8	19.5	10.0
Madhya Pradesh	42.0	40.7	37.2	47.7	36.6	31.3
Maharashtra	41.0	37.9	23.2	44.0	42.9	31.9
Orissa	58.7	49.8	47.8	50.0	43.5	43.0
Punjab	12.8	11.7	6.0	6.6	6.2	2.4
Rajasthan	33.3	26.4	13.5	35.3	23.0	17.5
Tamil Nadu	46.3	35.9	20.0	49.0	38.5	24.3
Uttar Pradesh	41.9	42.3	31.1	34.9	28.6	21.5
West Bengal	48.8	41.2	31.7	34.9	28.6	21.9
All India Rural	39.4	37.1	26.8	39.0	33.0	26.3

(Contd.)

1	2	3	4	5	6	7
Urban						
Andhra Pradesh	41.1	38.8	27.2	23.4	17.8	10.8
Assam	11.3	7.9	7.5	13.6	13.0	11.8
Bihar	51.9	34.8	33.5	38.1	26.7	24.7
Gujarat	38.5	28.3	14.8	16.4	14.7	6.4
Haryana	18.4	16.5	10.0	11.8	10.5	4.6
Himachal Pradesh	7.2	9.3	4.6	1.7	3.6	1.2
Jammu & Kashmir	15.0	9.3	2.0	3.8	3.1	1.3
Karnataka	49.2	39.9	24.6	26.0	21.4	10.8
Kerala	39.8	24.3	19.8	21.0	13.9	9.6
Madhya Pradesh	47.3	48.1	38.5	20.7	18.5	13.9
Maharastra	40.3	35.1	26.7	21.2	18.2	12.0
Orissa	42.6	40.6	43.5	20.8	15.2	15.6
Punjab	13.7	10.9	5.5	6.6	7.8	3.4
Rajasthan	37.9	31.0	19.4	19.8	18.3	10.8
Tamil Nadu	40.2	39.9	22.5	26.2	20.0	11.3
Uttar Pradesh	44.9	35.1	30.8	29.3	21.7	17.3
West Bengal	33.7	22.9	14.7	22.3	15.5	11.3
Delhi	15.1	16.1	9.2	4.7	8.8	2.4
All India Urban	39.1	32.9	24.1	22.5	17.8	12.0

Source: Calculations based on NSS unit record data from 23rd, 50th and 55th Rounds.

A related issue is that changes in HCR can be highly sensitive to the number of poor households near the poverty line. If poor households are heavily 'bunched' near the poverty line, a small increase in average per capita income could lead to a misleadingly large decline in the head-count ratio.

In interpreting and comparing poverty declines overtime, it is useful to supplement the poverty index with the information on the growth rate of a average per capita consumption expenditure (APCE).

State specific estimates of APCE growth between 1993-94 and 1999-2000 are shown in the Table 6, where states are ranked in ascending order to APCE growth for rural and urban areas combined. Here a striking regional pattern emerges except for Jammu and Kashmir. The low-growth states form one contiguous region made up of the Eastern states (Assam, Orissa and West Bengal) the so-called BIMARU states (Bihar, Madhya Pradesh, Rajasthan, U.P. and Andhra Pradesh).The high-growth states consist of the Southern States (except Andhra Pradesh), the western States (Gujarat, Maharashtra) and North-western region (Punjab, Haryana, Himachal Pradesh). It is interesting to note that this pattern is reasonably consistent with independent data on growth rate of per capita 'State domestic product' (SDP); these are shown in the last column of the Table 6. All the states in the low APCE growth set had comparatively low rates of per capita SDP between 1993-94 and 1999-2000 (say below 4 per cent), and conversely, all the states in the 'high APCE growth' set had comparatively high annual growth rates of per capita SDP.

TABLE 6

Growth Rates APCE and Per Capita SDP: 1993-94 to 1999-2000

	Six Year Growth of APCE (Adjusted) 1993-94 to 1999-2000			
	Rural	*Urban*	*Combined*	*Annual Growth Rated Per capita SDP 1993-94 to 1999-2000*
Assam	0.9	8.8	1.7	0.58
Orissa	1.4	-0.0	3.3	2.34
West Bengal	2.1	11.5	3.3	5.48
Jammu & Kashmir	5.4	8.0	5.3	2.49
Bihar	6.9	4.8	7.1	2.10
Madhya Pradesh	6.6	14.1	7.8	2.78
Andhra Pradesh	2.8	18.6	8.3	3.57
Rajasthan	7.0	15.4	8.6	4.60
Uttar Pradesh	8.3	10.1	9.0	2.99
Karnataka	9.5	26.5	14.1	5.82
Maharashtra	14.1	16.7	15.9	3.53
Gujarat	15.1	20.9	16.8	4.88
Himachal Pradesh	16.2	28.5	17.6	5.06
Tamil Nadu	15.7	25.1	18.9	5.39
Kerala	19.6	18.2	19.6	4.01
Punjab	20.2	17.9	19.9	2.74
Haryana	31.0	23.0	29.2	3.05
Delhi		30.7	.30.7	5.69

States are arranged in ascending order of the growth rate of APCE for rural and urban areas combined.

Calculations based on data for the 55th rounds of NSS. For SDP calculations based as data supplied by Planning Commission (as presented in *EPW*, Sept. 7, 2002).

The correlation coefficient between Rural APCE Growth and growth rate of per capita SDP = 0.224798. The correlation coefficient between urban APCE, Growth and growth rate of per capita SDP = 0.722811.

The correlation coefficient between combined rural and urban APCE Growth and growth rate of per capita SDP has been calculated. It shows a medium correlation coefficient between the two series (0.45).

Calculation of Correlation Coefficient between Combined Rural and Urban APCE Growth and Growth Rate of per capita SDP

	Six-year growth of Rural and Urban Combined APCE (adjusted) 1993-94 to 1999-2000 (x)	Annual growth rate of per-capita SDP, 1993-94 to 1999-2000 (y)	$(x-x_m)$	$(y-y_m)$	$(x-x_m)^2$	$(y-y_m)^2$	$(x-x_m)(y-y_m)$
1	2	3	4	5	6	7	8
Assam	1.7	0.58	–11.468	–3.1478	131.508	9.9086	36.09803
Orissa	3.3	2.34	–9.8677	–1.3878	97.3715	1.926	13.69439
West Bengal	3.3	5.48	–9.8677	1.7522	97.3715	3.0702	–17.29018
Jammu & Kashmir	5.3	2.49	–7.8677	–1.2378	61.9007	1.5321	9.738639
Bihar	7.1	2.1	–6.0677	–1.6278	36.817	2.6497	9.877002
Madhya Pradesh	7.8	2.78	–5.3677	–0.9478	28.8122	0.8983	5.087506
Andhra Pradesh	8.3	3.57	–4.8677	–0.1578	23.6945	0.0249	0.768123
Rajasthan	8.6	4.6	–4.5677	0.8722	20.8639	0.7607	–3.983948
Uttar Pradesh	9	2.99	–4.1677	–0.7378	17.3697	0.5443	3.074929
Karnataka	14	5.82	0.8323	2.0922	0.69272	4.3773	1.741338
Maharashtra	15.9	3.53	2.7323	–0.1978	7.46546	0.0391	–0.540449
Gujarat	16.8	4.88	3.6323	1.1522	13.1936	1.3276	4.185136
Himachal Pradesh	17.6	5.06	4.4323	1.3322	19.6453	1.7748	5.90471
Tamil Nadu	18.9	5.39	5.7323	1.6622	32.8593	2.7629	9.528229
Kerala	19.6	4.01	6.4323	0.2822	41.3745	0.0796	1.815195

(Contd.)

1	2	3	4	5	6	7	8
Punjab	19.9	2.74	6.7323	–0.9878	45.3239	0.9757	–6.650166
Haryana	29.2	3.05	16.0323	–0.6778	257.035	0.4594	–10.86669
Delhi	30.7	5.69	17.5323	1.9622	307.382	3.8502	34.40188
SUM	237	67.1	–0.0186	–0.0004	1240.68	36.962	96.58367

Number of records n = 18

Mean of x = Σ x/n = 237/18=13.1677

Mean of y = ym = Σ y/n = 61.41/18 = 3.7278

Correlation Coefficient between x and y = $\Sigma (x/y_m)(y-y_m)/\sqrt{\Sigma(x-x_m)^2}\sqrt{\Sigma(y-y_m)^2}$
= 0.45

FIGURE 4

Combined Rural and Urban APCE

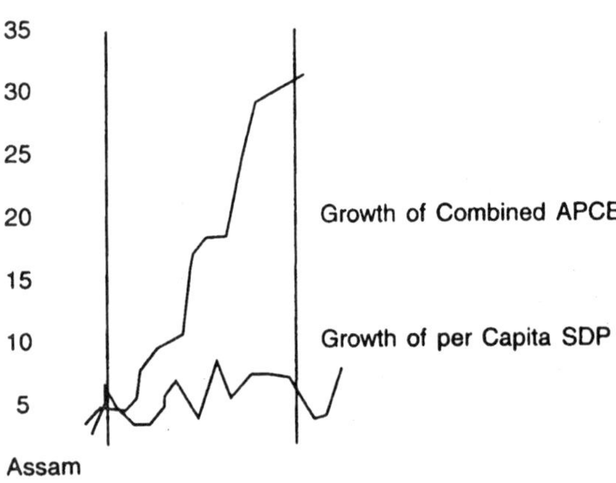

Notes: Value of Correlation Coefficient ranges between 0 and 1
0 means low correlation, 1 means high correlation
Correlation Coefficient for Rural is VERY LOW (=0.224798)
Correlation Coefficient for Urban is HIGH (=0.722811)
Correlation Coefficient for Combined is MEDIUM (=0-45)

Agricultural wages provide an important source of future information on poverty. Real wages are highly correlated with standard poverty indexes such as head-count ratio where poverty is higher wages tend to be lower, and *vice versa*, It is also possible to think about real wages as a round poverty indicator.

According to recent estimates-based on agricultural wages in India (AWI) data, real agriculture wages were growing at about 5 per cent per year in the eighties and 2.5 per cent per year in the nineties. But even the reduced growth rate of agricultural wages in the nineties at 2.5 per cent per year points to significant growth of per capita expenditure among the poorer section as found earlier.

The data on real wages also provide some independent corroboration of state-specific patterns of poverty decline. This is illustrated in Fig. 4 where we plot state specific estimates of the growth of real agricultural wages in the nineties against the estimated proportionate decline in the head-count ratio. Here two main outliers are Punjab and Haryana, where the head-count ratio has declined sharply without a correspondingly sharp increase in real wages. Learning out these two outliers, the association between two series is remarkably close (with a correlation coefficient of 0.88).

At interesting sidelight emerging from Fig. 5 is that a healthy growth of real agricultural wages appear to be a sufficient condition for substantial poverty decline.

Eradication poverty remains a major challenge for planned economic

FIGURE 5

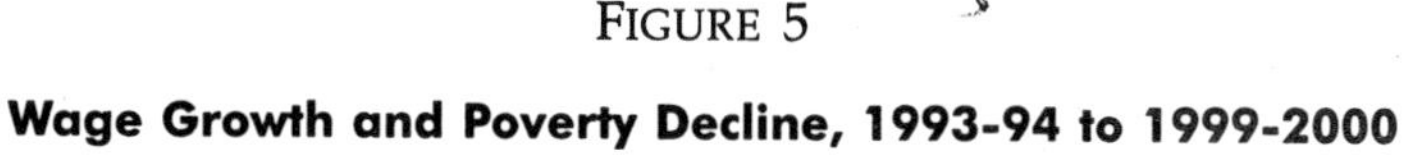

Wage Growth and Poverty Decline, 1993-94 to 1999-2000

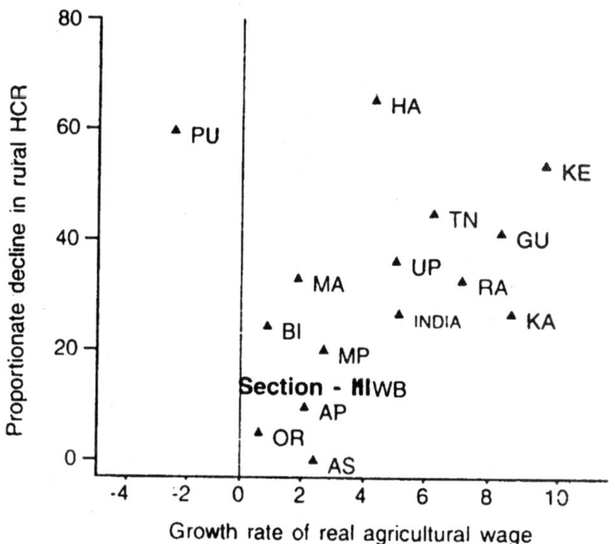

development, Experience of different states with economic growth and poverty reduction have been so varied that it is difficult to offer any general policy prescription. There are states that followed the path of high agricultural growth and succeeded in reducing poverty (Punjab and Haryana) and states that focussed on human resource development and reduced poverty (Kerala). There have been states that implemented land reforms with vigour, empowered panchayats and implemented poverty alleviation programmes effectively. (West Bengal).

Poverty had declined substantially in 1980s. However, recent estimates suggest that projections on reduction of proportion and number of people living below poverty line made in the Ninth Plan have not been realised. The possible factors that contributed to this were the following:

(i) fiscal crisis followed by the state governments resulting in lower spending on sectors,
(ii) slowing down of and less dispersed agricultural growth, especially food grains,
(iii) decline in employment intensity in the agricultural sector with a small increase in real wages,
(iv) failure of Targeted Public Distribution System (TPDS) to reach the poorest in the Northern and Eastern states, and
(v) negligible expansion in the farm sector and indifferent functioning of the poverty alleviation schemes.

Given the enormity and complexity of the task, the Ninth Five Year Plan envisaged a multi-pronged approach. Besides, recognising the role of high economic growth in tackling poverty, the strategy comprised creation of entitlements (through self-employment and wage employment schemes, food security and social security) and building up of capabilities (through basic minimum services like education, health and housing). We shall examine the effectiveness of programmes of the Ministry of Rural Development in alleviating poverty.

Integrated Rural Development Programme (IRDP) was started in 1980-81 in all blocks of the country and continued as a major self-employment scheme till April 1999. Then it was restructured as the Swarnajayanti Gram Swarojgar Yojna (SGSY) which aimed at self-employment of the rural poor. The objective will be achieved through acquisition of productive assets or appropriate skills that would generate an additional income on a sustained basis to enable them to cross poverty lime. Rural poor families have remained constant in number in 55 million in the last 20 years despite high growth and high investment in IRDP and wage giving programmes. Since the inception of the programme till 1998-99, 53.50 million families have been covered under IRDP at an expenditure of Rs. 13,700 crore.

IRDP has been extensively evaluated by researchers, scholars, various national institutions and international organisations. They have all pointed out several conceptual and administrative problems. With it IRDP has several allied programmes like training of rural youth for self-employment, development of women and children in Rural Areas, Ganga Kalyan Yojna, Million Wells Scheme and supply of improved Toolkits to Rural Artisans. Together they presented a matrix of multiple programmes without desired linkage. They were implemented as separate programmes without keeping in mind the overall objective of generating sustainable incomes. Not only are there no linkage between different programmes, there has been lack of co-ordination with other departments as well.

Eradication of rural poverty from level of 55 per cent in 1973-94 to around 36 per cent in 1993-94 has been a major achievement of India's growth strategy that combined accelerated rural growth, both farm and non-farm and a direct attack on rural poverty through various programmes including investment in human development. Various states experienced reduction in poverty in varying degrees, the strategy also differed across states making it difficult to prescribe a single model of poverty reduction for the entire country. It is however, evident that without growth any substantial reduction in rural poverty is not possible.

The role of anti-poverty programmes to supplement the growth effort not only is valid in the post-reform period but becomes even greater to protect the rural poor against adverse consequences of economic reforms.

IV. ROLE OF WORLD BANK

Developing and developed countries have a shared interest in reducing global poverty and improving the lives of the million. Developing countries have an interest in becoming a part of the global economy and seeing a reduction in poverty and inequalities. The design of anti-poverty programs remains the primary responsibility of member-countries with assistance of the World Bank and other development agencies. The IMF and World Bank are co-operating closely and working with the governments in individual countries on a new approach that strengthens the link among poverty reduction, economic growth and debt relief.

The World Bank has taken initiative in easying the burden of debt of the poor countries. The Debt Initiative for Hearbily Indebted Poor Countries (HIPCs) provides debt relief to the world's poorest and most heavily indebted countries. Begun in 1996 by the World Bank and the IMF the initiative was enhanced in 1999 to provide deeper and faster debt relief with a stronger link between debt relief and poverty reduction.

Forty-two countries could qualify for HIPC assistance. At the end 2001, 24 countries were receiving relief to the amount of $36 billion. The total debt relief to all countries could reach $50 billion.

Under the enhanced HIPC initiative average debt service due in 2001-03 will be about 30 percent less than that paid before relief began in 1998-99. For the 24 countries now receiving debt relief, the average annual debt service to export ratio will fall from 17 percent to 8 percent less than half the average for developing countries.

V

Although trade liberalization is limited to more rapid growth, this does not necessarily imply that it is an effective instrument for reducing poverty. If a growth strategy based on trade openness leads to significant worsening of income inequality of the households at the bottom of the income strata. It may not make-any discernible Inrods in alleviating poverty.

Recent evidence indicates that inequality in India have been rising since the initiation of the economic liberalization since mid-1991. The reforms in India do not appear to have generated significant employment in the export-oriented labour-intensive manufacturing industries. This compares unfavourable to the experience of East Asian Economies in the 1980s and 1990s, which have emerged as important global players in labour-intensive manufacturing.

Poverty incidence in India has been falling at a trend rate of 1 percentage point per year since 1970. However, performance has been uneven between the states. Some states have been doing better than other states. Widening regional disparities and limited growth in lagging areas have made the overall growth process less pro-poor overtime. As a result, even when poverty is reported to have declined in the economy, the rural poverty ratio continues to be high in the states of Bihar, Orissa, Madhya Pradesh and North Eastern States.

It is also true that sustained high growth rates may not be sustainable if they are not accompanied by wide dispersion of purchasing power with higher levels of employment. Agricultural development and development of agro-industries must be viewed as a core element in this dimension since growth in this sector is likely to lead to the widest spread of benefits especially to the rural poor.

However, while growth may be a necessary condition to make dent in poverty levels, it is by no means sufficient. It is seen that growth-oriented strategy that is embeded in rural areas and focusses on creation of rural, social and economic infrastructure has much greater chance of success than an urban-oriented, industry-based growth strategy.

REFERENCES

Asian Development Bank (2002), Economic Research Department Working Paper No. 18.

Centre for Monitoring Indian Economy (1997), Approach to the Ninth Five Year Plan.

Deaton, A. and J. Dreze (2002), Poverty and Inequality in the 1990s, *Economic and Political Weekly*, Sept. 7

Harris John (2001), Globalization and World's Poor, Institutions, Inequality and Justice.

Planning Commission, Government of India Mid-Term Appraisal of the Ninth Five Year Plan, 1997-2000.

Ravallion, M. (2003), Have we already met the Millennium Development Goal for Poverty, *Economic and Political Weekly*, Nov. 16

Rajan, R. (2003), Trade liberalization and Poverty, Revisiting the Age Old Debate, *Economic and Political Weakly*, December 7 (2003).

Rao Bhanji, Explaining the Cross Country Carination in Income Inequality, *Economic and Political Weekly*, April 26.

Thamarajakshi, R. (2003), Growth and Poverty in India in the 1990s, *Economic and Political Weekly*, April 26.

World Bank (2002), Globalization, Growth and Poverty, Oxford University Press, New York.

World Bank, World Development Indicator, 1999-2000.

World Development Report, 1999-2000.

Changing International Scenario and the Poor in India

BASUDEB SAHOO

The International Scenario has undergone perceptible change since the collapse of the Soviet Union in early 80s. In a unipolar world, IMF, World Bank and WTO at the instance of USA and some developed countries are influencing the economic policies and conditions of the developing countries. The policy of globalization, liberalization and privatization imposed on the member-countries by the international organizations has affected adversely the economic conditions of the poor, the small marginal farmers and unorganized labour by undermining the protective and ameliorative role of the state. The paper analyses has how the rate of decline of poverty has come down in India in 90s due to the new economic policy and openness of the Indian economy. The paper pleads that unless the developing countries are alert about the menace of unchecked capitalism and take appropriate steps to strengthen the bases of their domestic economies and streamline their administration and reform social organizations and build up right type of motivations of the common people, mere openness and liberalizations of the economy will not bring in describable prosperity to alleviate poverty.

In the period when globalization and liberalization reign supreme in the international field, three international institutions namely—IMF, IBRD and WTO wield tremendous influence on the economies of the countries of the world. These three institutions constitute the 'trinity' of which WTO is the latest incarnation of GATT, which is assigned a vital sole in the international world.

Revolution in Information Technology (IT) and communication has accelerated openness to trade and investment. Openness affects productivity and efficiency by making available new and cheaper capital goods bringing in new ideas and imposing market discipline. Openness to trade affects income distribution by increasing the export of the internationally low skill-product from the developing countries to the developed countries and thereby raising the wage of the workers engaged in the concerned production compared to wages of other labour as in Mexico and Chile. It may affect income distribution by raising food prices and thereby hurting the poor landless labourers. Openness will weaken collective bargaining institutions as in reality capital mobility shifting from one product to another would be greater than labour mobility. Openness affects economic security; it makes some sectors gain while others lose. Schumpeter's creative destruction gets a booster. There is of course the possibility of reduction of agricultural price fluctuations due to extended trade. Openness coupled with technological revolutions has made the traded commodities more substitutable than before and therefore the competition is much more intense today. When competition is intense and openness is unavoidable in the context of the present day world economy and international policy, can the World Trade Organization mitigate the concomitant hardship to the member-countries, promote well-being at the grassroots level and ensure a bright future for the common people? This is the moot point in any discussion on WTO.

In the developing countries the grass root consists of the rural poor, small marginal farmers, agricultural labourers, village artisans, shopkeepers and non-agricultural workers. The rural poor depend crucially on local commons such as common environmental resources, forestry, fishery, irrigation water grazing lands. Extreme commercialization in the private hands and extreme nationalization alienate the common people from the community management of the rural, resources. Equity and efficiency here go together and redistributive reform, land distribution and involvement of forestry improve the resource use and is not seriously threatened by globalization. The new economic policy in the garb of reform has not touched these vital rural resources, which have bearing on the 70 per cent of people of our country and other developing countries. Their views on globalizations and free trade under the Regime of WTO matter much as their reaction has great impact on the governance of the country, which determines the state of things to come through effective implementation of reform. In the name of globalization or adherence to the WTO norms, loss of monetary and fiscal options for the nation state and subservience to rules sometimes made by the international trade and financial interests as in Argentina may spell disaster. Variability in tax-rates exists within states in USA among countries. The question is how intelligently you adjust to the rules of the game laid down by the international bodies of which whilhy nilly you are a member.

For the world as a whole and most essentially the poor-weak countries, the supreme goals of the common future are elimination of poverty, reassertion of sovereignty and world peace. It is often apprehended that submission to the conditions laid down by the world organization would jeopardize sovereignty of the poor countries aggravate poverty and in the name of greater integration of the countries may help flourish 19th century capitalism and pernicious neo imperialism.

Detailed discussion of the implications of the acceptance of the membership of the WTO would dispel the doubts of the people and enable the government to take necessary steps to mitigate the evil effects if any. A country of the size and importance of India which was primary member of GATE (now converted in to WTO). Since 1947 becoming a member of the WTO is quite natural and desirable. In this state of *fait accompli* "the best way to fight fear is to confront it, but at the same time to take prudent and cautions actions."[1]

II

WTO was born on 1st January 1995 out of GATT on the conclusion of the Uruguay Round of trade negotiation. GATT was a loose and provisional organization concerned with trade on only manufactured goods while WTO as based on a sound legal footing spreading its jurisdiction not only over the trade on manufactured goods but also over the trades on service, capital, agricultural products and intellectual prosperity rights. Obviously the ramification of its regulatory power over almost all important aspects of economic activities is likely to have immeasurable impact on the international economy and the individual economies of the member-countries WTO has replaced bilateral trade arrangement by multilateral trade agreement to realize the benefits of free trade in a greater degree and help build up a well-integrated world through unrestricted export-import along with the financial and development aid and co-operation promoted by IMF World Bank. WTO has also provided for a quick and legal method of dispute settlement among trading nations.

The impact on grass-root is best manifested by the impact on agriculture. The agreement on agriculture and trade reflected investment agriculture as related to a measures are very much important. The agreement has resulted in reduction of tariff, minimum import access. The least developed countries have been given certain benefits *vis-a-vis* agriculture. For example, they don't have to cut domestic support and export subsidies. In turn the developed countries have wrested some benefits. The so-called green box subsidies are allowed which will help economies like—the European Union to continue with a major chunk of the subsidization of agriculture. But certain measures included in the so-called amber were disbox lowed. These measures directly affect trade and production. Domestic support measures like subsidies, pest control assistance are controlled by the agreement. An aggregate meas use of support (AMS) has been calculated. The AMS will be reduced with economic development.

Some of the rules under WTO provide legitimacy to trade practices which border on criminality including Intellectual piracy's MNC derogation of plant breeders' rights by technology, life forms including plants, animals, microorganisms, genetic material and human life form Under the Trips Agreement the provision under GATS provides legitimacy to large scale financial speculative manipulations, privatizations of service economy and banking economy have dismantled welfare state of Europe and north America. Peasant economies have been devastated due to dumping of EU US grain production, genetically modified seeds. Produces by Cargill and Monsanto have been forced upon farmers often leading to mass poverty. 30 per cent of grain farmers in Western Canada went bankrupt in 1999-2000. China aware of the consequence said, "a nation can not develop and become strong without a sense of urgency and a sense of crisis[2]. This implies sacrifice of farmer's interest at the altar of the expanded trade. The unfettered freedom has given much scope to MNCS, which is feared to go a long way to liquidate national enterprises and would destroy people's lives. History does not conclusively prove that a 'free market system will bring about global prosperity'.

Longback Marx pointed out the propensity of capital to destroy itself. The trinity including WTO, which has paved the way for aggressive capitalism in the garb of openness may be disastrous in the long-run unless there are some countervailing force. Speaking of correlation between Keynesianism and viability of capitalism Galbr wrote, "The survival of modern market system was in large measure with our achievement. It would not have so survived had it not ban for the success efforts of the social left. Let us not be reticent; we are the custodians of a political tradition that saved classical capitalism from itself."[3] Similarly, Hobsbawn observes, "It is one of the ironies of this strange century that the most lasting results of the October Revolution, whose object was the global overthrow if capitalism was to save its antagonist both in war and in peace—by providing it with injunctive to reform itself after second world war and by establishing the popularity of economic planning furnishing it with some of its procedures for its reform"[4] capitalism by its very nature is a process of colonization not only of countries but of people. It breeds over-capacity and the problem of absorption. Same thing has appeared in the international economy at present. The problem of wage fall and reduction of social expenditure shows its ugly head. Neo-capitalism and neo liberalizing don't get rid of Marx's. Ghost.[5] The impending danger of unchecked neo-capitalism has to be borne in mind by the developing countries to take precautionary measures as far as possible within the saving clauses of the WTO and other institutions.

Lowering of tariff and dismantling of other restrictions would open up world market whose advantage may be taken of by the entrepreneurs. But they are to know quite well where in their comparative advantage lies. The developing countries have cost advantages in textiles and agriculture. The developed countries would benefit by opining up service sector and tightening of intellectual property rights.

In the service sector the developing countries too benefit by selling their services either as skilled labourer, high technician—computer engineers of India and China. Migrants from struggling countries in Latin America, South

East Asia and other regions are increasingly securing jobs at wages that while low by rich country standards are far higher than they could dream of back home. In 2001 workers from low to middle income countries sent home a staggering 84.3 billion—more than double the level of a decade earlier and $ 5 billion more than that years official foreign aid to these countries. Labour mobility is bound to be accelerated under WTO regime. Sometimes of course developed countries put restriction or migration.

There are certain clauses on labour conditions and wages, which stand on the way of, expanded trade of cheap products of the developing countries. They insist on 'fair wage' living wage payment in developing country, otherwise they label the product trade as "unfair trade". To deny trade on these grounds world be to push such a country farther into poverty. Same arguments are raised against the export of goods produces by child labour. Rigorous application of the norm laid down by ILO or WTO may worsen the living condition of the poor in developing countries. These issues are to be considered sympathetically by the developed countries. The developing countries being member of the international institutions should make honest attempt to gradually remove the practices in production trade that appear to contravene the rules of the game. For example, with trade liberalization food prices may group as a result of more exports. This may harm the interest of the poor consumer while benefiting the farmers. The solution of the problems is not to stop agricultural trade. The problem can be mitigated by targeted public distribution of 'food or by food for work' or public work programmes.

WTO has forced the member-countries to reduce tariff. While doing so it has given some concession to the developing countries. The average reduction of tariff rates offered by developed countries was 38% of existing level for imports from all sources taken together. Developing countries offered average tariff reductions of 24%.

Duty free and quota free accession to developed markets of the developed world for LDC will cause problem for India respect of garments where Bangladesh is competing. Quantitative restrictions have been abolished. Non-tariff barriers however continue to be used often arbitrarily against exports from developing countries. This issue has to be looked into. Rich nations continue with politics of protectionism, which prevents weaker nations from getting the full benefit of free trade. How to get at the level playing and induce the rich nations to be genuinely interested in making the world economy a free but just and growing one is the crux of the problem.

No one would dispute the fact that our common future is a happy stable and prosperous world in which all countries would play their due and get the legitimate share of benefit of free trade. All international institutions have been built with such lofty objectives. Powerful rich nations manouvre to make the institutions dance to their selfish depraved desire tunes. The entire humanity would be in peril. The slowing down of the world economy's progress and continuing poverty and marginalisation of the poor, growing unemployment in developed and developing countries despite product expansion bring to the fore the inherent weakness of the free capitalist economy without countervailing force.

In India rural poverty declined at an annual rate of 2.5 per cent during 1970-1980s and at 0.73 per cent during the 1990s. Poverty levels declined from 57%. In 1970s to 33% in 1989; on the other hand urban poverty declined at the rate of 2 per cent in 1970s to 1980s and at 3.05 per cent in 1990s. The acceleration in the decline of urban poverty is due to the high-income growth achieved during the period of liberalization. The widening rural-urban disparity in incomes is a matter of concern.

The pace of change did not accelerate during the post-reform period. Total unemployment growth rate declined from 1.57% per annum during 1977-87 to 1.45 per cent during 1987-99, rural non-agricultural employment growth rate declined from 4.32% to 2.06% while agricultural employment growth rate remained around one per cent in pre and post-reform periods (1977-87 and 1987-99)[7]. The underlying factors behind this phenomenon and its likely impact on rural economy have not been fully understood. Nonetheless it is obvious that liberalization, ushered in by new economic policy of WTO has not met the problem of rural or urban unemployment. Of course, the problem of unemployment has not been so much sharpened by liberalization in our country as in Latin American countries.

Every country tries to secure a condition wherein its export is promoted and imports restricted. This is not possible to achieve. Yet a country like India should determine wherein its commercial interest lies. Inspection of India's 30 export items in period 1995-99 indicates only one agricultural item. Rice, with a market shares of about 6.5% in 1999. The other items like tea, coffee; spices are hardly affected by agricultural protection in developed countries. The dominant export items are cotton textiles; carpets and leather apparel with market shares in range of 12 to 30 per cent. This defines our interest in both MFA and Social clause. We are to see what phasing of the MFA would do to Industrial tariffs. The other major export interest IT for India is export of IT services.[8] This intangible services should be exempt from trade restrictions. Public debate on such issues will enlighten and pressurize the Government to take appropriate steps to secure concessions from WTO.

In conclusion, it may be stated that India needs to expand its external trade, which forms only 0.64 per cent of the world trade. Trade is an engine of growth, which could act vigorously only when supplemented by strong domestic policies promoting infrastructure development, productivity efficiency of the export sector. To take advantage of the changing international environment a country has to have boldness clear perspective and determination to sacrifice some at present to gain. In future it pays to keep in mind what Herman Hesse said, "The values of a future order will be as great as the sacrifice we make today."[9]

Notes and References

1. Bardhan, Pranab: "Social Justice in the Global Economy," *Economic & Political Weekly*, Feb. 3-10, 2001.
2. Michel Chossudovsky "Seatle and Beyond: Disarming New World Order," *EPW*, Nov. 15, 2000.
3. John Kenneth Galbraith, Preface in New Political Economy. Vol. 2, No. 1, March 1997, p. 5.
4. Eric Hobsbawr, The Age of Extremes, The Short 20th Century 1914-51, London, pp. 7-8.
5. Jacques Hersh ELL en Brun, "Ylabialisation and the Communist Manifesto," *EPW*, Jan. 15th 2000, p. 105.
6. Scou Walsten, "Spreading Prosperity," *Economic Times*, June 25, 2003.
7. R. Radha Krishan, "Agricultural Growth, Employment and Poverty: A Policy Perspective," *EPW*, Jan. 19, 2002, pp. 243 and 250.
8. Manoj Pant, WTO Negotiation—Identity Interises not Positions, *Economic Times*, 31st Aug. 2001.
9. Herman Hesse, Reflections, New York 1971.

Index